ST. PETER'S COLLEGE

SALTLEY

1944~1978

GW00675356

R.D.H.SEAMAN, M.A.(Oxon.),

Vice~Principal 1953 ~ 1976

Commissioned by the Governors,

St. Peter's College, Saltley,

Birmingham

FOREWORD

It was a privilege to be invited by the Governors to write this book and I have been grateful to all those who have contributed in one way or another towards it. Charles Buckmaster has given me every help and encouragement and my old colleagues, Jack Cornwell and John Taylor, have made critical and invaluable appraisals at every stage of its writing. A number of members of Staff and Old Students have written to me about aspects of the history of which they are especially well-informed and their full contributions will be handed over for preservation with the College archives. I have been most grateful to those who have read and corrected the proofs and to members of the College Office staff who have assisted me by finding items in the College files and particularly to Gena Penlington who has typed my original untidy drafts into orderly and coherent form for the critics and printers to get to work upon.

I have tried, as far as was realistic, to withhold my own opinions and have relied whenever possible on such written and printed evidence as was available to me. But where judgments are made, then they are my own alone and they follow no prescribed party line. I was most grateful to be given free run of the College records and files and I have spared no one in the use I have made of them. I found the annual "Salt" magazines (1948-1970) an incomplete but useful account of events and an interesting reflection of attitudes ; the more informal "Saltette" was by contrast of little literary or historical worth. The Minute Books are of varied merit ; some like the Delegacy Minutes and the Academic Board Minutes are little more than formal statements of business transacted, unenlivened by cut and thrust of discussion ; the Governors' Minutes contained far more detail during the final ten years and include a full and lively account of the closure debates ; there is extant no complete record of Staff meetings, but there is one delightful book of Minutes from 1959 to 1966 compiled by J. K. G. Taylor. I was grateful to the Secretary of the University Faculty of Education for lending me four of the Institute Minute Books and to the Chairman of the Governors for lending me his copy of the Church Synod debate in which he made his fine speech to save the College.

I hope that readers will not be too much put off by the manner in which I have tackled this operation; inevitably there are overlaps between one Section and another and the boundaries are blurred. I realise that I have sacrificed some fluency in favour of rationalisation and it may be that I have omitted to mention events and persons that deserve a place within the record. Certainly there would be scope for a much longer work, although I think it might be too specialist a subject to command a wider public. I would hope that at some time a full and critical study might be undertaken of the work of the Church colleges during this period and that Saltley Training College would occupy its rightful place in that history.

R. D. H. Seaman.
January, 1978.

CONTENTS

Photographs — College Principals :-

1 TOWARDS A NEW BEGINNING (1945-1950)

Chapter 1

The fact that Saltley Training College was able to face a new future in 1945 was due in no small measure to the achievements of Principal F. T. Cooper, who succeeded Canon Blofield in 1923 and did not retire until 1947, by which time that future was assured. An account of his Principalship appears in the "Saltley College Centenary" which was published in 1950 and is well worth close study.

The Principal of an "independent" College like Saltley, although he was supported by a Governing Body, bore (and still bears) a quite unusual personal responsibility for the formulation of strategy and a total responsibility for its detailed implementation. He could be at one and the same time Chief Executive, Treasurer, Secretary, Architect; all communication with the Central Government and with the Church Central Board of Education was conducted through him ; only in academic affairs, where he shared his responsibility with the College academic staff and where he worked on equal terms with other Principals, was his scope to exercise his own initiative limited. The post-war College was therefore unduly indebted to Principal Cooper ; it would be difficult to imagine what character the all-male College would have acquired without the sports ground at Stechford which was purchased in 1927 or how the College could have coped during the years of expansion without the South Block, which was commenced in 1928 ; it brought together 60 study bedrooms and a College Library and it was to become during the Sixties and Seventies the central part of the Student Union daily life. But more than this, Principal Cooper guided the College through the economic crisis of the Thirties when some Church colleges were closed, due to the necessity of making cuts in public expenditure and by reducing the number of teachers.

During the Second World War, almost unaided, Principal Cooper kept the College in being ; at first it was easy, since teaching was a "reserved occupation" ; the College was full, and was even able to offer succour to St. Paul's, Cheltenham, and King Alfred's, Winchester. But when the "Blitz" got under way and life in Saltley with its factories and marshalling yards became dangerous and unconducive to study and the College sustained war damage itself, it could have been so easy for Principal Cooper to throw in the sponge. The small number of students left could have been farmed off to other Church colleges and the College might never have revived. Instead, he moved himself with a small number of students and two staff and a small "office" to Exeter, where with the assistance of the staff of St. Luke's, the College remained alive until May 1942 when the enemy found out about this move of Britain's strategic resources and delivered a heavy load of bombs on St. Luke's. The Principal and the "First Year" then moved to St. John's, York, and despite further bombardment remained in existence there.

1

Sometime during 1944, the Principal returned to Saltley, the College now being in the hands of the Home Guard and of the British Restaurant ; with V1's and V2's not reaching as far as Birmingham, he determined to get the College moving again ; he acquired 22 students in September and in January 1945 brought back 40 students from York ; with the open co-operation of Birmingham University, Saltley Training College was in action once again. He had been rejoined by Jimmy Chance, the V.P., and Billy Burrow who had been teaching in Caerleon, Wales, and a staff cadre was reconstituted. The College was ready to take its share in post-war planning ; it could easily have been otherwise if Principal Cooper had been more cautious and less determined. It was a real personal achievement.

A small file of letters has survived in the College office from this war-time period. Mostly they reflect the problems that faced Principal Cooper during the summer months of 1945 and there are a number of letters from Headmasters anxious to obtain places at the College for senior pupils ; only those who would still be 17 at the beginning of October were eligible, since others would become subject to call-up and thus not available. A copy of a letter exists from the Principal to the Ministry of Education which indicates that the 22 students admitted in September 1945 were all in this category of 'under 18' ; and reveals that the whole arrangement had been an opportunist one :

" .... I was informed verbally by Mr. Arnold, H.M.I. that the Ministry would allow me to accept them at Saltley (8 candidates who could not be accommodated at York) and at the same time it was suggested that I might increase the number in view of the need for teachers. I approached the University concerning the number they could accommodate for instruction with the result that I admitted 22 men. I did not receive any documentary authority from the Ministry in this connection and I therefore assumed that the Ministry would prefer that I should not mention it unnecessarily .... "

The College architect wrote to the Principal in July 1945 :

" .... the main drain in the old part of the College has become choked, and sewage has been found in the foundation space under the entrance, so much so, that it has to be pumped out. I find the drain connection is very unsatisfactory, very old and inadequate, and the manhole actually in the Basement. This must be removed and a new manhole constructed ... in the Quadrangle ... It will not be possible to open the College in September unless this work is put in hand at once."

British Restaurant who were still installed in the kitchen and dining hall (and continued to be until 1946) had to be informed at the same time that the water supply would be off for a week while the main supply was repaired in two places. On 23rd August, the Principal cancelled a visit to Rugby in October on the plea that :

"Unfortunately, the whole position regarding the reopening of the College is in a state of confusion owing to our not being able to get

2

the renovations and re-decorations done within the time expected. In consequence of this, I am prevented from making any outside engagements as I am required daily on the premises to deal with the problems that are arising."

But the rubble was cleared from the field, the bomb craters were filled in, the rooms and dormitories were cleaned and prepared for occupation, and the foreman of Messrs. Sapcote and Sons written to demanding that he avoid using College desks to put planks on.

At least the College was under way again in Saltley, but only just ! By September there were seven full-time members of staff and nine part-time recruited mostly from the University. There was a lively demand for student places, mostly from ex-service men, wishing either to complete courses begun before their call-up or to commence a two-year teaching course from the beginning. They were splendid recruits for the teaching profession.

One document still extant is the programme of teaching practice for the Session 1945/46 ; the Schools to be used included names which were to become most familiar to generations of post-war students : Nansen Road, Alston Road, Thornton Road, Sladefield Road, Golden Hillock and many others. A happy little group of letters follows this programme :

"If this School can help your students at any time or in any way, I shall be delighted." (D. E. Brock of Alum Rock, later to become Shaw Hill School).

"We were very happy to have the students with us and the happiness of the students while with us and the enthusiasm they showed for the work were sufficient reward for any support given by my staff and myself." (H. H. L. Smith, Marlbro' Road Secondary Modern).

"I congratulate you on securing so many really keen men. They were some of the most industrious I have met for many years." (J. .W Smith, Ingleton Road Junior).

"We are very glad indeed to see the College functioning again and shall be delighted to help you in any way." (Harry Wise, Bierton Junior).

Unfortunately, the College archives have no letters remaining from 1946 or the early months of 1947. The autumn term 1946 began with 234 students, some 50 more than the average numbers before the War, and of these 186 were "resident" and "recognised" — presumably offering a full two-year course ; there were also some 27 students, dubbed rather oddly as "private", who were taking the Further Education and Training Scheme.

The Statement of Account for 1946/7 leaves little indication of the Herculean tasks still to be tackled ; £890 was spent on replacement of furniture, apparatus and equipment, and a further £177 on capital expenditure in respect of furniture ; maybe it just wasn't possible in that year of bitter winter and public austerity to obtain the materials that

3

were needed out of a total income of £36,000. £4,600 remained unspent and a further £700 was paid on the loan charge for the building of the South Block in the 1930's.

The Ministry of Education Inspectors' Report (published 1950) had this to say :

"In July 1947 the Principal retired after many years' service. .... the Inspectors desire to express their appreciation of the great devotion and effort of the Principal and the nucleus of staff who got the College going again in the very different conditions which operated after the re-opening ; there is no doubt that those who have since joined the College, whether as members of staff or as students, owe them a very great debt."

Despite these achievements, it seems probable that Principal Cooper had little personal joy from them. He was a man whose moods changed rapidly and few people were at ease in his company, though he had much charm and was an excellent talker. Students, for the most part, were frightened of him and the power that he was able to exercise over their lives. To be fair, none of this emerges from any study of surviving correspondence :

"Dear Mr. Cooper," wrote one Old Salt in 1943. "Remember me, Sir? I'm one of those bad pennies who keep turning up at awkward moments .... I suppose I could wander all round the Wrekin before coming to the point of this letter, but I will not. You see, I've applied, or rather I am in the process of applying for a post in Liverpool (after the war, of course) and require a testimonial — a dreadful moment in a man's life ! ....

My respects to the College, all the staff and to all Old Salts, wherever they may be.

Yours most sincerely and respectfully, Sir,
      W.

P.S. Do you remember the first letter I addressed to you, Sir ? I typed it — a painful effort — and then, posted it without appending my signature !"

Principal Cooper found it particularly difficult to adjust himself and his office to the post-war situation. Many of the students had held high responsibility in the Forces and were aware of the qualities involved in leadership. They reacted badly to the distinctly suspicious and perhaps restrictive atmosphere that they now encountered. The Principal's own reaction seems to have been withdrawal ; he excused himself from appointments which he had made under the plea that he was overworked ; certainly for a time he handled all letters as well as accounts ; but it would be difficult in the interests of the College to justify his absence from a most important meeting of the Council of Church Colleges in the summer of 1945 when matters of fundamental concern for the future of the colleges were to be debated.

Most serious was the alienation which had developed between the Principal and the Governing Body and the Foundation. Before the War, the Quarterly Meeting of Governors had grown ever smaller ; in October 1938 and February 1939 only five Governors attended ; at the latter meeting, the last before the war, one Governor "raised the question of the work of the Governing Body and the reason for the lack of interest as indicated by the poor attendance at Meetings". The question was remitted for discussion to the next Annual Meeting of Friends and Subscribers to the College — which has never been held. There is no record in the Minute Book of any meeting of Governors between February 1939 and July 3rd, 1945, although the Archdeacon of Birmingham, the Acting Chairman, had signed the minutes of the 1939 Meeting in March 1940. There is evidence that a War Emergency Committee had been formed, although by whom it was formed and who attended its meetings is not known ; no known evidence of minutes is preserved at the College.

A letter from Principal Cooper to Lord Cobham, President of the College, reads :

"My Lord, 6th June, 1945.
After your departure from the meeting of the War Emergency Committee yesterday morning, it was decided to hold a meeting of the full Committee of Governors in order to place before them for their consideration, the proposed scheme for the re-constitution of the Governing Body of the College. The date suggested for the meeting is Tuesday, July 3rd at 11.30 a.m."

This Special Meeting was duly held and a short hand-written minute exists. 35 members were present, although their names are not listed ; it would be interesting to know who attended that meeting and what they said to each other. The only business recorded was a consideration of the suggested scheme of government which had emerged "after consultations in London between representatives of the College, the Council of Church Training Colleges and the Central Board of Finance".

No further meeting has been recorded until March 1947. Only five governors were then in attendance, three from the Birmingham Diocese, one from Coventry and one from Worcester. The Birmingham representatives included the Diocesan Bishop, Bishop Barnes, who had not hitherto attended any official meeting during the Rev. Cooper's entire Principalship. Another newcomer was the Archdeacon of Aston, Michael Parker, who was to play so important a role in the coming years. Michael Parker was made Chairman for the meeting and he signed the minutes of the meeting on July 3rd, 1945. The meeting considered the proposed constitution, during which it formally discharged the War Emergency Committee with deep appreciation for all the work that Committee had done ; its honourable discharge is the only official evidence that that committee ever existed. At the end of the meeting this note was added :

"It was resolved that the recommendation of the Selection Committee that Rev. T. G. Platten be appointed Principal of the College from 1st September, 1947 be accepted."

5

That is all. There was no note that Principal Cooper had resigned his office, nor were the names of the Selection Committee appended. By the next meeting in October, the new Principal was in residence and the four Governors who attended wrote a letter of appreciation of Principal Cooper and instructed that it should be recorded in the Minutes. Principal Cooper returned to Saltley for the Centenary celebration and his official photograph was taken but he played no further part in the post-war story. He had evidently been aware of the situation ; in November 1945 he had hoped to appoint a Secretary, but instead wrote to the lady concerned :

"Since I wrote to you the whole question of the administration of the College has been under review by the Governors and the amount of secretarial assistance has not yet been finally settled. Immediately I know the position I will inform you."

As early as January 1945, Principal Cooper had rejected an offer made to him of a country parish ; in doing so, he wrote a letter, a copy of which he placed in the College files. He said that he felt that the fact that he had not, unlike all his predecessors, been made a Canon of the Cathedral, indicated a lack of interest by the Diocese in the College and its task.

" .... the work of the training of teachers in a Church foundation within its area has not been regarded during recent years as a matter which concerns the Diocese. You will probably remember that Earl Grey when he visited the College spoke very strongly about the lack of interest which the Diocese in general had shewn in the College which he called a 'very compact parish'. I noticed the difference in this connection very much whilst I was temporarily in charge at St. Luke's College, Exeter. There we were made to realise that we were an important element in the life and work of the Diocese. . . . .

I do not seek personal honour. . . . I would wish, however, that the College to which I have devoted myself entirely during the best years of my life could have received recognition of a kind which would have made us feel more closely related to the Church in this area, and which would have given some prestige to the College in comparison with other Church Colleges such as Exeter, Cheltenham and Bede College, Durham."

Chapter 2

It is necessary at this point to consider the national scene. While the College was rising Phoenix-like from the ashes of 1942, much occurred to change the outlook for English education. Britain, with U.S.A. and U.S.S.R. for allies, having overcome the nastiest part of the war, was able to contemplate the possibility of the new Britain to be built for the next generation. All agreed with the words which opened the Government White Paper on Educational Reconstruction, 1943 :

"Upon the education of the people of this country the fate of this country depends".

A series of public enquiries and reports stimulated excitement for educational reform — the Norwood Report, 1943; the White Paper, 1943; the Fleming Report, 1944; the McNair Report, 1944; the Percy Report, 1945; the Barlow Report, 1946. The War-time National Government had decided that no harm could follow discussion about the arts of peace, provided no resources were diverted from the achievement of victory. For this reason Churchill had placed one of his most progressive and able young ministers at the Board of Education and thus R. A. Butler became the organising genius of the new structure of English education. The Labour Party was as firmly committed to educational reform and so well had Butler and his Labour counterpart, Chuter Ede, co-operated, that the new Labour Government in 1945 was able to build on Butler's foundations rather than start from the beginning again. Indeed this Government was determined that, although Britain was plunged into a post-war economic crisis, the education reforms must go ahead.

The Butler Education Act of 1944 may not have received the attention it deserves since argument about it has neglected much in the restructuring of education that rapidly came to be taken for granted. The first section of the Act replaced the Board of Education and its President by the Ministry of Education and a Minister. This was not designed merely to enhance honourable status, but it signified an enlargement of statutory power of the Minister and the civil servants under his authority. The Minister's duty was "to secure the effective execution . . . of the national policy . . . . in every area". National policy is in the final resort a matter for the Prime Minister and Cabinet; but, subject to the operation of Parliamentary control over their actions, the Minister and his secretaries were in a position, if they chose to use it, to exercise virtually dictatorial power. They could and did require local authorities to submit detailed development plans for schools and colleges in their areas, could call for their amendment if out of line with government policy and had the power to withhold public funds in the face of obstreperous opposition. The limits to a Minister's power and that of those who served him were political and not professional, although machinery was created to allow for some professional advice or criticism to be available. It is well to remember that this imposing edifice was built by an eminent and liberal-minded member of the Conservative Party and that few since 1944 have challenged its value to the community.

Secondly the Act aimed to concentrate power in the hands of the County and County Borough Education authorities and their appointed adjutants, the Chief Education Officers with their staffs. This was achieved in several ways. Notably the old (1902 Act) Part III authorities (urban and rural district committees) surrendered their control to the counties, except in a few special cases. Powers, which the counties possessed before permissively, now became compulsory; all authorities had to submit detailed plans for a universal system of free secondary education with a school-leaving age at first of 15, but, as soon as nationally feasible, 16. The local authorities received important new responsibilities in Further and Higher Education; they were again required to submit detailed development programmes for full-time and part-time education for those past school-leaving age ; by the Act they acquired powers, capable of wide interpretation, which allowed them to give grant aid to university institutions, to conduct their own educational research or to organise conferences. One section of the Act stated that the Minister "may give to any L.E.A. such directions as he thinks necessary requiring them to establish, maintain or assist any training college". As a result, during the next thirty years the scope of interest by Local Education Authorities in both Further and Higher Education became hugely increased ; Colleges of Advanced Technology, Polytechnics, County Colleges, Colleges of Education, Colleges of Further Education were created and flourished like green bay trees. Authorities became justly proud of their achievements and their importance in the educational structure was much enhanced by reason of these new responsibilities. The way in which the voluntary colleges could be fitted into the structure was still to be worked out.

Meanwhile the McNair Committee had been engaged in studying the principles which ought to influence government in the urgent matter of the recruitment and training of teachers, and they published their report in 1944. Their committee had been established in March, 1942, long before Stalingrad and El Alamein, as a sign of confidence in Britain's future in which the teachers would be in the front of public progress. The report when it was published revealed a conflict of opinion which may at that time have seemed to be academic, but which thirty years later was at the centre of the troubles in which colleges were to find themselves. Who ought to have the overall control of teacher education ? The Committee divided itself neatly 5/5 in its advocacy of two possible schemes ; one group, anxious lest "education" and "training" might be thought to be two separate things, advocated that the Universities should become responsible by means of Schools of Education ; the other group preferred the establishment of regional bodies, which while they contained university representation, would contain other interests as well, including H.M. Inspectorate, to watch over the standards of the teaching profession. Other recommendations were less controversial, although they were to exercise a significant influence upon future developments ; one was that the aim should be to create a unified teaching profession, in particular that the long established differences should be broken down between those who taught children before or after the age of eleven. In a way this was rendered more urgent by the school reorganisation. Before the War there had been Grammar School teachers and Elementary School teachers with their associated "Senior" Schools. Now there were to be Secondary Schools and Primary Schools and a high proportion of all teachers would be educated in Training Colleges. It seemed important to make sure that there should be no essential differences between them, and Colleges themselves became most anxious to prevent the creation of what might be thought to be inferior institutions devoted to the training of Primary teachers alone. The McNair Committee recommended, in the same vein, that the normal course for training for all non-graduate teachers should be increased from two to three years ; more of this hereafter.

8

In the meantime, Government had to decide the major question of control over teacher education. In the light of the Butler Education Act's decision to build up the responsibilities of the County and County Borough Authorities, it was, perhaps, surprising that teacher education should have been placed so firmly in the hands of the Universities, by means of new Institutes of Education, each under Professorial direction and subject to the authority of Vice Chancellor and University Senate. Principal Platten arrived at Saltley in September 1947, just in time to attend the first meeting of the Delegacy of the Birmingham University Institute. The association with the Universities proved most popular among the staffs of the training colleges and certainly ought not to be judged unsuccessful, although Government was to reverse its decision within thirty years. The reasons for this change of heart should become apparent as this narrative develops, since the history of Saltley College during this period ran parallel to that of the institution to which it had become affiliated.

Government post-war reconstruction in education presented major problems. During the war enemy action had destroyed or severely damaged more than 5,000 schools and the greater proportion of the remainder needed attention from the builder. There was a grave shortage of materials for construction, which needed special government licence. It was true that there were many teachers happily released from the Forces able to return to the classroom, but the wastage had been heavy and the replenishment light. It was known that during the next few years a steep rise in the birth-rate might increase the school population by more than a million pupils ; the plans for universal secondary education coupled with the long-anticipated raising of the school age to 15 would further increase the total by more than 350,000. But if education was the basic essential for social progress — and we believed it was — then classes must be so reduced in size that teachers would be able to give that degree of personal attention which alone could ensure satisfactory results. We need to remind ourselves that similar reconstruction was necessary in many other areas of public life and that the nation passed through a period of intense economic gloom and shortage.

The immediate response to this challenge was the Emergency Training Scheme whereby mature members of the Forces were to be specially selected and offered a year's intensive training and education before admission to the teaching profession. The scheme was limited in time and was put in the hands of the local education authorities, who used the hutted camps which were to be found all over Britain to house the new students. The scheme was most successful and some yawning gaps were capably filled. Saltley appears to have had a few — very few — local students under Further Education regulations, but was like other voluntary colleges more concerned with the longer-term arrangements for teacher provision. Involvement in the Emergency Training project gave many L.E.A's. which had hitherto had no part in teacher education a strong taste for the enterprise ; and emergency, hutted establishments with their staff cadres grew inevitably into permanent, brick-built Colleges as soon as the 'emergency' was over. In the West Midlands, the Colleges at Coventry, Worcester,

9

Kidderminster, Birmingham, Madeley (Nelson Hall), all had their origins in this manner.

The implementation of the McNair proposals required, however, long term plans which would involve the Church Colleges. This predominant group of voluntary foundations, 26 of which were Anglican, was a legacy from the 19th century to the community. They were autonomous in their government, but possessed few endowments and depended for their continued existence upon generous subscribers and fee income from their students. When it had been necessary to find capital for expansion as for the South Block at Saltley, the practice had been to borrow the money on an extended mortgage and to repay the loan and service its interest out of fee income ; this was the main reason why the regime in such colleges had been so spartan, as Saltley students in the Thirties knew to their cost. In 1945, all these colleges were shabby as a result of the long war years when it had not been possible to maintain their fabric effectively, even when they had been — unlike Saltley — continually used. Before they could take expanded numbers, they would require much redevelopment at large financial cost.

In the national circumstances of the time it would have been unthinkable for the Government to have ignored the existence of these colleges in its plans for providing teachers. There is no evidence whether the State seriously considered the proposition that it might buy out these foundations, lock, stock and barrel, and present them to the local education authorities to manage. As things turned out, this might have been the most sensible policy ; but there would have been legal complications from the Charity Commissioners and no one could have guessed the political consequences. It is interesting to speculate how the Church Assembly and the Dioceses would have reacted in 1945 had they received a generous offer from the State.

Instead, the Minister of Education, still R. A. Butler, made an interesting but different offer. The voluntary training colleges would be brought fully into the future planning and encouraged to develop ; they would retain their autonomous status, but under entirely new financial arrangements. The system of colleges working out their own fees and charging the students was to be scrapped ; instead, the D.E.S. would pay the fee income directly to the colleges, each of which would calculate its own annual maintenance costs and submit its budget for approval to the Ministry. But what seemed to matter most urgently was the intention to forbid for the future the pre-war system of mortgaged loans, serviced out of fee income. Instead, the Government agreed to pay 50% of all capital expenditure, provided that the foundation could provide evidence that it could furnish the other 50% from its own resources.

R. A. Butler would appear to have made this offer early in 1945. The voluntary college Principals were agitated and distressed ; on 23rd April, Miss Stewart, Principal of Lincoln Training College, wrote to Principal Cooper :

Rev. F. T. Cooper (1923–1947)

Rev. T. G. Platten (1947–1968)

Rev. C. Buckmaster (1968–1978)

College Principals

"Several of the Principals of the Church Colleges held an informal meeting in the train last Thursday on the way down to Canterbury to discuss the new regulation . . . that loan charges cannot in future be paid out of students' fees or grants. We were very much distressed by this regulation for if it is implemented it will make our extension schemes impossible to carry out ; few or none of the Colleges have endowments or other sources of income on which to draw, and it is obvious that the Church cannot possibly provide the necessary funds.

"We feel that in this matter the whole future of the Church Colleges is at stake, for unless we are able to carry out the necessary improvements and extensions to meet modern requirements, the Colleges will sooner or later have to close.

"The question seemed to us to be of such urgent importance that we all agreed to write to Canon Cockin (Secretary of the Council of Church Training Colleges and shortly to become Bishop of Bristol) asking him to call an immediate meeting of the Principals . . . "

It is sad to know that Principal Cooper was not one of those gathered in the railway compartment, although there remains in the files the letter to Canon Cockin in which he added Saltley's protest. He was not present either at the meeting held in response to these pleas on May 17th, when the Chairman and Treasurer of the Church Central Board of Finance attended as well as a representative from the Ministry of Education. It was a momentous meeting. The Council agreed that if the Colleges were to survive, the Ministry's terms must be accepted and the Church must be asked to put down the money. During the following months the Church conducted an agonising appraisal of the situation ; eventually in its summer session in 1946 the Church Assembly passed this resolution :

"That the Assembly accepts in principle the responsibility of the Church for securing the future of the Church Training Colleges."

and at its following session it proceeded to authorise the Central Board of Finance to "formulate a policy of finance with regard to the equipment and extension of Training Colleges". The Central Board itself published a report for the Church Assembly in May 1957, in which it indicated that the Church's share of the cost of putting the Colleges in order had been estimated to be £1,611,950 and the report concluded with the following ominous paragraph :

" . . . there can be no finality to the development of the Training Colleges. The present is a period during which improvement and extension of the Colleges is proceeding rapidly ; but . . the work which is necessary exceeds the resources that are in sight. Even if further funds become available, so that the present phase of operations may be completed, it is certain that the Church will find it necessary to make fresh injections of capital from time to time for the improvement of the Teacher Training Colleges so long as they continue to exist."

It is notoriously unfair to pass judgment on the decisions of our predecessors in the light of subsequent events; one can easily gloss over the significance of the decision of the Church leaders in 1946; R. A. Butler was asking the Anglican Church (and other providing bodies) to make a capital levy towards teacher education. Although at the time the terms of this levy may have appeared to be generous, thirty years later, when St. Peter's, Saltley and other church colleges were being discarded in a further wholesale reorganisation, parishioners were still paying through their diocesan contributions for the burden of debt incurred for the 1947 reorganisation.

The decision of the Church to rally to the support of its colleges owed much to the advocacy of the Bishop of Bristol and to the new Church Colleges Moderator, Robert Stopford, soon to become Bishop of London. It sprang clearly from the genuine conviction that through its Training Colleges the Church was best able to inspire and consolidate Christian education throughout the country. But the opposition from many clergy and laity was keen and it grew over the years as the full extent of the commitment became apparent. What was the value of the colleges to the Church? Many of the new Local Authority colleges were staffed by fine Christian men and women; how did the Church Colleges differ from them? We shall see hereafter how Saltley Training College tried to resolve these implied criticisms and to answer the challenge made by its benefactors. The need to operate a Church and Christian College in an increasingly secular background was foremost in Principal Platten's mind as he commenced his Principalship in September 1947.

Before leaving the subject of the future of the Church Training Colleges in the immediate post-war period, we should pause briefly to consider a letter from R. A. Butler written in February 1945:

"Dear Canon Cockin,

.... Now that our Regulations have been published covering grants towards the capital expenditure of existing voluntary Training Colleges on improvements, extensions or replacements, I should like if I may to let the Council for the Church Training Colleges know what is in my mind as to the way in which the Anglican Training Colleges could perhaps most effectively deal with their problems.

.... I need hardly say that it is not in my mind that we here should elaborate a plan for the future lay-out of Church Training College provision, and then proceed to impose it upon the Colleges. I do, however, suggest that the several Governing Bodies should look at the Church's provision as a whole and consider together how the whole plant available ... can be used and developed to the greatest advantage.

I appreciate, of course, that the Governing Bodies are severally masters in their own houses, but I should hope that in the Council they would find a medium through which they could combine to survey the field as one, and present a plan for the future of the Church Training Colleges as a whole ....

If the Council can do anything to get this approach sympathetically considered and accepted, I shall be very grateful, as I believe that it is the right approach to dealing with the matter.

Yours sincerely,

R. A. Butler."

The Minister was surely aware that the coherent plan he called for would have been most difficult to achieve. A crisis at the end of World War I had led to the establishment of a "Federation of Church Training Colleges" with an elected "Board of Supervision", but the Resolutions whereby it was formed did not trespass against the autonomy of the separate Colleges. The Board of Supervision had played some part in the further crisis of the 1930's and had set up a common fund in 1934 whereby the stronger colleges could assist the weaker ones. World War II swept it away as it did so much else, and no body existed in 1945 comparable to the Roman Catholic Council of Education, with the authority to undertake strategic planning for the Church colleges as a whole which Butler requested. This is not to undervalue the Council of Church Training Colleges or the regular meetings of Church Principals or the work done by Moderators and Secretaries. The truth of the matter is that it might have been wise in 1945 for the Church to have planned its forward policy more intensively on a narrower front, having first decided the criteria on which that policy would be based, despite the fact that some of its Colleges would have to be jettisoned in the process ; this was, after all, what had to be done in a hurry and piece-meal between 1975 and 1977. On the contrary, the Church advanced on a wide front with no strategic plan or control.

Chapter 3

In September 1947 the new Principal applied himself to his task. It was both formidable and varied, but he was well equipped to meet it. His "double first" in Physics and Anthropology at Cambridge was evidence of high intellectual ability and of his capacity to cope with administrative problems in depth ; his experience as a teacher of physics and of religious knowledge, and on the staff of St. Mark and St. John's College, Chelsea, as tutor and chaplain, enabled him to bring to his task an understanding of the traditions and values, spiritual and professional, of Church Training Colleges, so that Old Salts bred in the same traditions were able to recognise how quickly their College recovered its best features. During the War he had been Warden and Professor of Physics at Madras Christian College and his long association with the Church of South India and with Indian students gave him evangelical strength and much sympathy and skill in his dealings with students. Further he brought to his task tireless energy, a fine sense of humour and a quite indomitable will, qualities immediately recognised and respected by his colleagues and students.

The problems awaiting solution tumbled one upon the other and mostly needed immediate attention ; in this narrative it is easier to follow a different logic.

A. The Governing Body.

It will be apparent from Chapter 1 that Principal Cooper had already produced a new scheme, but the Ministry of Education, having reorganised the financial arrangements, now required such a scheme to be submitted to their legal branch. Principal Platten submitted a new draft to the interim committee of Governors in May 1948, the Scheme received final approval in April 1949 and the new Governors first met in May 1949. Of necessity this involved significant changes. Before the War, the Annual Meeting of the Friends and Subscribers of the College elected a committee of Governors which met quarterly ; this was constituted from clergy and laymen of the five dioceses contributing to the College. Now, the Diocesan Bishops were to be permanent members and each Diocesan Education Committee submitted the names of one clergyman and one layman to serve for three years as Representative Governors ; in addition eight co-optative governors were named under the scheme, including Viscount Cobham who had presided over the College since before the First World War. Lord Cobham was once more elected Chairman, but he died before he was able to assume his office. Michael Parker, Archdeacon of Aston, was elected Chairman and he presided over the College most wisely and keenly until he left the area on his appointment as Bishop of Bradford. One important change which he instituted at once was that Governors' Meetings should be held at Saltley instead of at Queen's Chambers in Paradise Street. All subsequent meetings have been held at College, usually in the Conference Room, and they have made it possible for staff and sometimes students to meet the Governors socially.

It is difficult to assess the importance of the contribution which the Governors have been able to make to College events. Since 1947 academic and professional matters have been under the Boards of Study of the University School of Education and the detailed financial maintenance of the College the concern of the Ministry of Education. It must, therefore, have been frustrating for able and busy men and women to attend meetings at which they could often do little more than comment upon and accept the highly competent reports of the Principal and rubber stamp the latest policy statements from the Ministry. Some Governors were able to give invaluable assistance in interviewing and appointing staff, but even here visiting Governors probably found it difficult to assert their own views strongly in the face of their lack of knowledge of the detailed running of the College. The far-flung character of the dioceses and the increasing perils of the city roads doubtless added to the unattractiveness of being a Governor of Saltley. Occasionally it was practicable to invite Governors to events in College, but for the reasons stated it was rarely possible to welcome any large gathering. In general, the co-optative Governors, mainly members of the education profession, were often able to express informed views with some independence of mind and it was a mistake when, during the Sixties, their numbers were reduced to three. With these reservations, one would still wish to pay tribute to some particularly distinguished public men and women, clerical and lay, who served the College well during some part of its last thirty years ; these included its three Chairmen, Sir Geoffrey Templeman (now Vice Chancellor of the University of Kent), Sir Wilfred Martineau, Professor Jeffreys and Sir Lionel Russell, (Birmingham's eminent Chief Education Officer). Many meetings were held on Saturday mornings in order to facilitate Sir Lionel's presence.

B. Development of Buildings and Grounds.

The first letters that Principal Platten wrote to the Ministry of Education, revealed the urgency of College needs :

2nd October, 1947.

"On taking over the Principalship of this College I find that there are a number of serious deficiencies in its furniture and equipment. The College was evacuated during the War, after damage by enemy action, and much loss of material so caused has apparently never been made good.

In particular, it is urgently necessary to remedy an acute shortage of chairs for use in class rooms, and for assembly etc. . . . A minimum quantity of 200 such chairs is required . . . I beg, therefore to apply for a certificate enabling me to place an order for this quantity.

I find also that there is no stock whatever of bed linen (sheets and pillow cases) for use in the College sick bay, or of towels for sick bay or kitchen. . . . "

The reply from the College's Territorial Officer at the Ministry (received within 15 days !) to this cry from the heart was most helpful :

". . . . as you have only recently come to the College, you may be interested to see the enclosed copy of a circular letter on furniture and equipment which we sent out last March, and which is still a reasonably up-to-date account of what we can and cannot do in these difficult times to help Colleges obtain what they need."

In the matter of the specific requests, that if the chairs were not obtainable he would send a certificate to allow the College to purchase the wood to make them ; a certificate for the linen would be forthcoming if the Principal would fill in Form 552G. Would that all difficulties had been so quickly resolved ! This small exchange set the seal on a long and detailed history of communication between the College and its appropriate Officer in the Civil Service. Although such Officers changed their posts frequently, the relationship established often proved most helpful for the College. To be properly sustained it called for tact and, sometimes, a quite long-suffering patience. If months of letter writing achieved no result, just occasionally the Principal was able to invite his opposite number to the College to see for himself and this usually seems to have done the trick. For example, an exchange occurred which lasted several months regarding the College request for Ministry of Education support

16

to the College demand to be allowed to build two staff houses at Stechford ; in the end the Officer visited Stechford and the support was immediately forthcoming.

However, it took the best part of ten years from 1945 before the immediate post-war problems had all been dealt with. The Principal needed first to identify the various projects requiring attention, and these had to be costed ; it was then necessary to gain the approval of the Secretary of the Church Council (then R. W. Stopford) and the Treasurer of the Central Board of Finance ; finally, fortified by the knowledge that the Governor's 50% would be forthcoming, the proposals had to be placed before the Ministry. It was tedious and wearisome. Both the Church and the Ministry had their own priority lists ; if you were late in making your bid, you might find yourself one or two years delayed before your emergency requests were considered. In any case priority lists were reviewed afresh each year. The first real blow was that the Ministry determined to give high priority to providing for Primary education ; this, coupled with a lack of effective liaison between the Church and College during the period 1945/47 meant that, when in May 1949 the Central Board of Finance published the distribution figures of Priority I Capital Commitments to Church Colleges, out of a total of £440,000, Saltley had been allocated only £471 ! By the time Priority IA and Priority II were considered, the State itself had become much less generous.

A number of factors improved the situation somewhat. One was that the Ministry, pressed hard by the Church Council, agreed to allow colleges still faced with pre-war debts to pay them off out of maintenance costs ; in this way the long standing debt to the Central Board of Finance for South Block was finally liquidated. The Ministry also generously allowed some costly and necessary items of expenditure to be adjudged maintenance and not capital, so that with careful housekeeping in one direction one might make improvements in another ; the ground at Stechford was levelled and reseeded in this way. Finally, the Ministry was much more liberal in its approval of minor projects (under £5,000) and the Principal astutely divided the Major project (Gymnasium and New Block) into a series of at least four minor works.

At this point we should pay tribute to the contribution made by H. W. Hobbiss. Head of a well-known Birmingham firm of architects, Hobbiss was the son of a former Vice Principal and had been born in the College ; he had become its devoted servant and played a full part in all College plans, almost till the day of his death. He and the Principal produced the first Development Scheme by December 1947, obtained the approval of the Church Council and despatched it to the Ministry.

Priority I

				Estimated Cost
Renewal of hot water system	....	....	....	£3,000
Renewal of electric wiring	....	....	....	£500
Modernisation of plumbing	....	....	....	£300
Improvement of Sick Bay	....	....	....	£1,500

17

Priority I—*continued*   *Estimated Cost*

Improvement of lavatory accommodation, conversion of disused rooms (8) into study
bedrooms £3,250
Improvement of kitchens £1,000

£9,550

Priority II

Conversion of cubicles into study-bedrooms £4,000
Building a new hostel for 60 students £40,000

£44,000

Priority III

Building new gymnasium £10,000
Conversion of present gym into Assembly Hall £1,000

£11,000

Further item to Priority I, but not submitted to Council of Church Training Colleges — reconditioning of College Playing Fields and relaying hard tennis courts at a total estimated cost of £1,600.

The scheme had many points of interest. Highly urgent was the abolition of the corrugated tin cubicles which remained in the North and West corridors ; (the East cubicles had disappeared in 1946 under war damage repair) ; but an even higher priority was to find somewhere, other than classrooms, for students who slept in cubicles to sit and work — hence the conversion of the disused rooms. There were powerful precedents to support other priorities ; in February 1937 the Governors had approved a request to the Church Board of Supervision for "improved quarters for the sick, a new Gymnasium (or Assembly Hall), reconstruction of the Chemistry laboratory and a Sports Pavilion", and approval had been received for improvements up to £5,500 for these items just before the War.

The reply to the scheme was quick and dampening :

"I am sorry it has not been possible for us to hold out more immediate hope of your carrying out the rather large works envisaged at the College, but in fact the Ministry's building programme for 1948 was drawn up a considerable time ago and the shortage of labour and materials now makes it virtually impossible to add to it further if we are to be realistic ; it is only fair for me to add also that that share of the building programme which can be allotted to the improvement of facilities for the training of teachers must necessarily at present and for some time to come, be devoted mainly to the expansion of the provision for training women teachers, as that is where the need is greatest."

In the outcome, the College was allowed to undertake the sports ground and tennis court improvements under "maintenance". The conversion of the disused rooms was pressed hard and eventually agreed and this accounts for the £471 of Church capital under Priority I ; it was money well spent. Presumably the plumbing and wiring items were also squeezed into maintenance accounts, since the files show no further reference to them. Soon the Principal adopted a fresh approach ; if it was not yet possible to have the new gymnasium, perhaps the Ministry would agree to a stage to be built on to the back of the existing gymnasium ; this would cost £1,500 and would help towards the ultimate conversion into an Assembly Hall. The Ministry, anxious to be helpful, dithered ; the Principal perserved, persuasively :

"The College at present possesses no Assembly Hall, and it is impossible to gather the whole student body together except in the Gymnasium, which naturally presents many practical disadvantages. For dramatic entertainments etc. at present the Gymnasium has to be used, with the erection of a temporary stage which occupies floor space and prevents the use of the Gymnasium for its proper purpose. It would greatly add to the amenities of the College to carry out the proposed conversion into a Hall and to build a new Gymnasium.

"A sum of £5,000 as a "Permissible amount" has been agreed by the War Damage Commission in respect of the Practising School, which would be available towards the cost. It is understood that this agreement is valid for two years. For this, among other reasons, we are anxious that work on the new gymnasium should be taken in hand . . . but I also desire to submit that the existence of the present ruined school buildings in the College precincts is a source of potential danger . . . "

The Ministry approved the Stage immediately ! But the other parts of the scheme were put off from year to year. In December the College was informed :

" . . . . it is just within the bounds of possibility that we may be able to include a substantial building project for the College in 1951-2 building programme. I will let you know what the prospects are as soon as possible, but I think you might be wiser to proceed if you can by way of instalments costing less than £5,000 as you suggest . . ."

Sketch plans were in the post before the end of the year and approval was given for the construction of the first staircase of Adderley Block in February, 1951 ; in fact this building cost £6,800. In August 1952, permission was given for the remainder of Adderley Block, but not the Gymnasium, and the Principal took the opportunity to remind the Ministry that the conversions of the cubicles into study bedrooms had not yet been put into effect. He was allowed to start on this and to complete the conversion in another series of minor projects. Not until November 1956 was the news received that "provided you can continue to use your present changing rooms and showers for a few more years, we

19

shall be able to approve the erection of a gymnasium in light construction as a minor works project costing under £10,000". The scheme of modernisation put forward by Principal Platten at the end of his first term in 1947 was on the point of realisation. Excluding the gymnasium, the Central Board of Finance of the Church of England paid out nearly £27,000 for these Saltley post-war projects out of a sum of £1½ million made available to its colleges as a whole. Much of the detailed planning for this work was done by the Principal personally in company with the architect. Arguments on financial points abounded and were conducted by the Principal firmly and patiently ; he never appeared to lose heart ; on the contrary, the evidence is that he enjoyed every moment of it.

There were from the beginning other problems, some long standing, where he needed to give battle. The sports ground at Stechford was a constant source of anxiety. Before the war the Governors had been perplexed about security at the ground and the absence of pavilion facilities. During the War the Territorial Army had used the site and had erected a number of Army huts and by 1945 the ground was in poor condition. The T.A. were slow in returning the field to the College and anxieties concerning Stechford became a regular feature of discussion at Governors' Meetings. There was a distinct possibility at one time that the land, designated as "public playing field area" under the 1947 Town and Country Planning Act, might be compulsorily purchased by the Local Education Authority ; the crisis never materialised but the Principal sought advice from the Ministry. In 1947 the ground retained its ridge and furrow surface from earlier times and permission was sought for it to be ploughed and resown. In 1952 an exchange of some of the land with the L.E.A. (which had to be approved by the Charity Commissioners) gave an opportunity for a relevelling, although costs did not permit the whole area to be treated. One of the old T.A. huts was bought and showers were added to it, but the erection of a permanent pavilion remained one of the Principal's objectives. Another most desirable aim was to build two houses in Flaxley Road to ensure that there would be some permanent residents from the College continually on the site. This encountered many problems, partly financial, and it was not until 1951 that a licence to build the houses was obtained from the City Public Works Department. By the summer of 1953 both houses were occupied by College staff and their families and it was becoming possible to visualise much more use of the Stechford ground.

C. Launching the Birmingham Institute of Education.

One of the letters awaiting the immediate attention of Principal Platten in September 1947 was an invitation from Professor M. V. C. Jeffreys, the Director of the newly-created University of Birmingham Institute of Education, to discuss with him the establishment of Boards of Studies and the educational policies to be adopted. From the first these two formed a splendid working relationship based on deep mutual respect and a common fund of idealism ; twenty years later Canon Platten requested that Professor Jeffreys should be invited to speak, as chief guest, at his farewell gathering at Saltley.

Birmingham University was one of the pioneers of the new Area Training Organisations. While some Universities showed reluctance to take on these new responsibilities, Birmingham's enthusiasm for its "Institute of Education" was well illustrated by the frequent attendance at Delegacy Meetings of the Vice Chancellor himself and by the rapid development of both educational research and teacher training within the University. Professor Jeffreys was a well known educationist of warmth and humanity and was anxious to launch the Institute with standards which were both sound and progressive. The constitution for the Institute was created with the minimum of bother along the lines which the Director proposed and was accepted by the University Senate and Faculties and Schools, who agreed to co-operate where appropriate, especially in the operation of the Boards of Studies which would have the task of forming and maintaining the academic and professional standards to be applied. The Governing Bodies, including the Saltley Governors, also accepted the proposals without demur, almost without discussion.

Various important academic decisions were made at the outset, in which Birmingham was blazing a trail, subsequently followed by most other universities. First, the colleges were to be granted a bold measure of academic freedom beneath the umbrella of some pretty wide regulations; each college had its own syllabuses, individually vetted by the Boards of Studies, and conducted its own examinations with some arrangements for inter-collegiate moderation; there was to be a Common Paper in Education, but this was constructed out of questions submitted by the colleges; there were to be visitations to the College by University-appointed external examiners, but it would have been difficult for them either to advance or withdraw the mark lists to any appreciable extent; they certainly never attempted to at Saltley. These arrangements, far removed from the 19th century examinations, have now become quite normal within the world of education and they have a similar basis to Mode III practised for the C.S.E. examinations in secondary schools. Twenty years later when B.Ed. Courses were being discussed, these liberal departures caused some University misgivings.

The second area of innovation concerned the examinations themselves; it now became possible for the students' final grades to be decided upon an accumulation of course work marks rather than upon final written examination papers; here again, colleges were free to make their own arrangements, provided these were clearly stated in the regulations. Probably no college cut out examinations completely, at least at first, except in areas of work like Art and Craft; and it was many years before the University agreed to the disappearance of the Common Education Paper. But the emphasis became increasingly upon continuous assessment throughout a student's course and, although in practice this involved many problems, the regime favoured the less literate students and offered to all (at least in theory) a stimulus for hard work and for initiative.

A third area for possible innovation was less successful — that of producing "larger Boards of Studies with wider terms of reference"

21

(Professor Jeffreys). In this the Sciences were notably more progressive than the Humanities; originally the Board of Social Studies contained history, geography and social studies courses; but a few years later the author of this book led the historians in a breakaway, which was accepted, provided they met on the same day so that it would be possible for them all to come together again; they never did!

In the first post-war edition of the "Salt", the annual college magazine, published in June 1948, the Principal had this to say about the new structures:

".... There is perhaps a good deal of vagueness about some of this, and if it is pressed too far the real discipline of mental effort and scholarship may be smothered under a featherbed of generalities. At the same time it does call attention to the danger of academic studies becoming separate little watertight departments of knowledge. It is essential that in our education we should produce a synthesis which can be the basis of a working philosophy of life. To the founders of this College that synthesis is provided by the Christian religion, and to that, through all changes of position and method, we continue to look for the real integration of education and life."

The constitution of the Institute provided for a Professional Board of University and College representatives to work out the details of professional and academic activities, including the approval of course results and following the recommendations of Boards of Studies. A formal committee of the Director and the Principals, known as the Assessment Committee, and an informal meeting of the same persons gave opportunity for frank policy discussion between the University and its colleges. But the body which determined overall strategy within the A.T.O. area was the Delegacy; it contained a strong component from the University Senate as well as from the Institute itself. At first the Vice Chancellor attended frequently and took the Chair. The College Principals and a small number of elected staff attended, in addition to a representative from each of the Governing Bodies of the Colleges; this meant that many of the Chief Education Officers of the Midland Local Education authorities were able to influence teacher education through this channel; the H.M.Is. who were concerned with this sphere of educational activities were present, but with traditional caution said little; one or two of the civil servants from the Ministry invariably travelled from London and the Delegacy listened intently for indications of government policy from their lips. In addition, the Headteacher and Teacher Unions were well represented by leading figures from their ranks and, if one throws in for good measure one or two well-known public figures who were co-opted, one can see that by the time the A.T.O. had fully developed during the 1960's the Delegacy had become a most imposing forum for regional debate. One of the Chief Education Officers once calculated the public cost of a meeting in terms of the salaries of the persons engaged. Whether the Delegacy was ever worthy of this cost may be open to doubt, but just now and again the curtain seemed to be lifted and a few of the tensions underlying teacher education during the period were thereby revealed.

The first meeting of the Delegacy was held on 30th October 1947 and Principal Platten represented Saltley. There were then only five other constituent colleges in the region, two of these, the City of Leicester and the Leicester Domestic Science College, were from the East Midlands and were expected to leave the Birmingham A.T.O. as soon as a Leicester University Institute was formed. The other three were St. Paul's at Rugby, a voluntary Roman Catholic foundation, and Hereford and Dudley Colleges, both pioneer local education authority foundations. It should not escape the notice of the reader that three of these four older West Midland foundations were to be destroyed during the first of the "dissolutions" of the 1970's, shortly after the A.T.O. itself.

At its first meeting the Delegacy gave full constituent membership to the Selly Oak Colleges and within a year Westhill College, a nonconformist foundation within the Selly Oak complex, had received permission for its Froebel courses to be certified by the University as well as by the National Froebel Foundation ; this opened the way for Westhill College to become the second voluntary college in Birmingham offering a full range of teacher education courses.

In the meantime, the important group of local authority colleges engaged on the Emergency Training Scheme received recognition by the University as associate members with some representation on the Delegacy. It was clear that the Ministry visualised that some or all of these might be developed into permanent institutions within the A.T.O. There were, however, significant unanswered questions about the size, character and siting of the new colleges and both Director Jeffreys and Principal Platten believed that these were issues to be debated, if not decided, by the Delegacy. To Professor Jeffreys it was a matter of the status of the Institute ; if policy decisions were to be made with regard to the distribution of teacher training places, then how far the Director's views were consulted would be indicative of the Ministry's real intention to share responsibility with its new A.T.O.'s ; Principal Platten wished to ensure that the contribution of existing institutions like Saltley was fully protected in new planning.

At the third meeting of the Delegacy in February 1948, the Director reported correspondence with the Ministry "about the closure of Emergency Colleges and the establishment of Permanent Colleges". The Director had received a letter of 16th December (the dating seemed highly significant to the Director) containing "copies" of letters dated 1st November, and 9th December 1947 to the Chief Education Officers of Coventry, City of Worcester and Staffordshire respectively. These letters referred to the establishment of Permanent Colleges . . . as follows:-

City of Coventry — Women's College, first entry January, 1949.

City of Worcester — Mixed College, to open with a half entry, October, 1948.

Nelson Hall (later Madeley) — Women's College, to open with a half entry in September, 1949.

The Delegacy Minutes make no reference to discussion of this momentous news, which meant that there was now to be an L.E.A. college established in each of the Diocesan areas covered by the Governors of Saltley. But the next day the Director wrote to the Principal of Saltley :

"Dear Platten,
I had no opportunity of saying anything to you after yesterday's meeting, but I would like you to know that I personally very much welcomed your intervention on the subject of the stablishment (sic) of new colleges, and I hope that you will not hesitate to express your views when the matter comes up again, which it is bound to do.

"It was not possible at yesterday's meeting to explain all that has led up to the present situation. In brief, the Ministry began negotiating separately with Local Education Authorities about the closure of Emergency colleges and the establishment of Permanent colleges a long time ago, before any of the Institutes had come into existence. When we and Bristol got ourselves on the map the negotiations had already advanced beyond the point at which it was really possible to ask for them to be re-considered. I have made it abundantly clear to the Ministry that I think the Institute could and should have been brought into the picture earlier, and there is really no doubt now that we shall be properly consulted in future and, what is even more important, that the Local Education Authorities will work as a regional team in consultation with us.

"It is obviously of first rate importance to keep the goodwill of the L.E.A.s. If they will work in consultation with us, all is well. If they won't, it is no good blustering to the Ministry about our right to be consulted. I am now morally certain that the L.E.A.s will play, but there is a risk of losing their goodwill if one presses a resolution which they would have to take to their committees for formal approval. That is why I thought it best to soft pedal the thing yesterday. . . .

"As regards the three colleges scheduled for establishment, I am quite sure that we have no option but to accept the situation.
                    Yours sincerely,
                    M. V. C. Jeffreys."

In reply, the Principal wrote merely, "I was afraid that I had perhaps said more than I should have done at the Delegacy meeting, and am glad to know I have your approval". In July, the Professor returned to the subject in a further personal letter to the Principal of Saltley :

"The Ministry's publication of circular 174 (supply of teachers) will give us an opportunity at the Delegacy meeting on July 20th to discuss the question of the establishment of new colleges. . . . I think that. . . the point of view of the permanent colleges ought to be expressed. You know my view that we are more or less faced with a fait accompli as far as the immediate plans for . . . the establishment of certain permanent ones are concerned and we can do no good by trying to claim a share in decisions which have already been made for better or worse. There are, however, ways in which we might do something to secure the more distant future. . . ''

The files do not reveal whether a meeting which Professor Jeffreys hoped to arrange with the Ministry and two Principals ever materialised.

In August 1948 a draft scheme was received from the Ministry of what was at first known as the Central Council for Teachers, but by its final draft as the National and Advisory Council on the Training and Supply of Teachers. There was plenty of public debate on this, the last link in the new structures for teacher supply, and few found it wholly satisfactory. It was to operate as two Standing Committees, one dealing with teacher training and qualifications, the other with recruitment and distribution. One criticism was that these committees seemed to be responsible directly to the Minister rather than to the Council itself. More serious, perhaps, was the fact that it was advisory and exercised no power on its own behalf.

Its subsequent history was chequered ; it usefully provided a national forum for educationists to discuss teacher education and it fed information from government to A.T.O.'s and colleges ; it may be that administrators, both central and local, found its deliberations tedious and its conclusions unnecessary ; eventually, in 1966, its advice became redundant and no more meetings were summoned. It had been no substitute for a real Teachers' Council whereby teachers controlled their own professional standards.

Chapter 4

The most important part of reconstruction was rebuilding the academic staff. Much of this was done by Principal Cooper whose judgment was remarkably sound ; but we may guess that the Vice Principal, Major Jimmy Chance, exercised some influence over the new appointments made. In any case, he, more than the Principal, influenced the way the newcomers settled down and adjusted themselves to the pre-war traditions. He dominated the Staff Common Room more than any other member subsequently, exercising much personal charm, which scarcely concealed an indomitable will. In his capacity as Master of Method, he reigned supreme over the professional work of the College. He was himself a superb teacher, especially of mathematics. One of the tributes paid to him in the Salt Magazine at the time of his retirement deserves repeating :

"The Vice Principal has never been happier than when in schools. To go round a Junior School with him, with gales of happy laughter marking his progress from classroom to classroom, was indeed a tonic. There are not many visitors who evoke spontaneous applause from a class of children as they leave, though some well might at the relief of their going. I have seen and heard the Vice Principal cheered to the echo from room to room in a manner most of us only experience on those occasions when we act as School Father Christmas. A born teacher and quite inimitable, he has a charm of manner that endears him to children."

Jimmy Chance had been greatly loved by the pre-war generation of students and it was above all through his personal contribution to the professional values associated with Saltley that pre-war traditions and ways of proceeding were reaffirmed, and that the College continued to enjoy its high standing in the Schools of the region.

By the same token Willie Burrow (W.B. to many students) was hardly less important and was held in similar esteem, especially by his colleagues. He was a Yorkshireman with a sharp wit and devoted the major part of his active life to Saltley, for which he maintained a deep affection :

"I shall have one consolation, that their spirit, the Saltley Spirit, will be with me, and as I round the corner of Bridge Road in the car, I shall feel myself to be surrounded by a host of ghostly witnesses who have laboured term by term and have helped to make Saltley what we know it to be, a great College with a great tradition."

(Thoughts on Leaving the College, W.B., June 1954).

He had been at Saltley since 1928 except for the war years and he hastened back in 1945 from Caerleon, where he had been acting as Master of Method. When Chance retired, W.B. was offered the Vice Principalship ; he must have been tempted to accept, but promptly rejected the temptation since he was himself on the point of retirement. During his last years he worked tirelessly to bring the Old Students' Association back to life and was responsible for the publication and maintenance of a College Calendar of Old Students. When W.B. died it was discovered that he had endowed an English literature prize and left Saltley College as his residuary legatee ; in due course when the new English block was built, it was named after him.

Tom Fowler had been tutor in Art since 1934 and he too was back in harness after exciting times in Birmingham's Civil Defence. He was a most friendly person with wide interests and tastes. His influence in the Senior Common Room was an important one since he was essentially a conciliator and was invariably generous as well as fair-minded. At the same time, he was one of the pre-war group who had worked closely together in nearly all aspects of teacher training and he expected the standards with which he was familiar to be maintained.

E. T. Norris, with a First Class Honours degree in Mathematics, brought distinction to Saltley nationally as well as within the Midland region. He first came to Saltley in 1936. He was outstanding as a teacher and his influence upon the teaching of his subject through Saltley students was considerable and widespread. He believed that the learning of mathematics should be logical, active and enjoyable ; that children were taught too many gimmicky rules without the proper understanding of the processes and concepts involved. He would have liked children to be taught mathematics by genuine lovers of the subject who had, for preference, taken substantial mathematics courses ; but he accepted realistically that most Saltley teachers, whatever their special expertise and whatever age of children they hoped to teach, would in their early years find themselves teaching some form of mathematics ; the professional courses which he devised to serve their widely varied needs would have been a model to any college in the country.

W. R. Middleton was the last of the pre-war group to return and to discover that there was already another P.E. Tutor on the Staff, Jack Osborne. Bill Middleton had sat at the feet of Jimmy Chance with the others and in a vigorous and out-spoken way and with sound judgment he continued to make his own contribution towards the preservation of the professional standards of the College. In the end, he remained the only member of staff, whether academic, administrative or domestic, to retain his post full-time during the whole period under review in this book.

In the meantime Principal Cooper had set to work to fill the gaps ; three of these were to be filled by Old Students of the College, each in his way unique, but also able to maintain those same traditions of which we have already spoken. Jack Osborne, known to generations of P.E. students as the "Major," lived in one of the college houses at Stechford and played a most active part in many sides of the college life and work, extending his interests to professional and student matters at national levels. He took real pride in the achievements of the P.E. courses and of the various college sporting clubs and the students reciprocated with much devotion. Jack Cornwell had been one of the outstanding students of the thirties ; as Senior Student he had had the unenviable task of presenting Principal Cooper with a student protest and ultimatum and it must speak well for the Principal's judgment that he was prepared to offer Cornwell a post on the staff ; but his record showed him to be a brilliant teacher and Jimmy Chance probably had already spotted him as a potential successor to himself. Thirdly was J. B. Grayson, home at last from P.O.W. Camp. He was appointed as a tutor of Arts and Crafts, but was able at an early date to fill the gap left by the departure of the part-time Music Tutor. Barrie Grayson's talents were exceptional and he was rapidly to become a well-known figure in Midland music circles ; Saltley was, perhaps, fortunate to retain his creative genius as long as it did. Although these three were old students, they did not suffer from parochialism, nor did they in any respect apply a conservative brake to progressive ideas ; but they were all familiar with Saltley's professional standards.

Among a number of other appointments, two need to be mentioned, those of Philip Dunn and Dick McDonogh. Philip Dunn, with a wide teaching experience in the Black Country and Birmingham, came to Saltley to support Burrow in the professional and academic English work and to open up Drama within the college curriculum ; he was to become as important to the teaching of speech and language as Norris was to mathematics ; he rapidly assimilated the teachings of the Vice Principal and threw himself with drive and fervour into the tasks ahead. Dr McDonogh was a scientist of wide interests, who believed profoundly in

Commander W. Heathcote

Brian Strand

Senior Administrative Officers

the desirability of teaching general science in secondary schools and delaying as long as possible the advent of narrow scientific specialisation ; at the same time, Dick McDonogh was not prepared to allow science to become superficial and fought tenaciously to preserve the proper scientific depth for those who were to teach the subject in school ; if, for example, science was to be taught in Primary Schools, then it must be done by competent teachers or not at all. In these matters "Dr. Mac" had the warm support of the new Principal, himself a scientist of wide interests, believing it essential for a men's college to offer science courses.

During 1948/49 the Ministry of Education conducted a General Inspection at Saltley and among their comments they recommended that much more generous staffing than the existing ratio of 1 : 14.2 students was urgently needed. This made it possible for Principal Platten to build up the staff ; he proceeded cautiously along the lines suggested by the Inspectors and within his first three years he made five appointments which may be said to have completed the staff cadre, the basis for subsequent expansions. The first of these in 1948 was of major significance — W. F. Caldbeck was appointed to be a Lecturer in charge of Craft courses. Caldbeck was a most able and intelligent teacher with a wide craft background. He had considerable gifts in planning and a fertile imagination and restless ambition. His own specialist expertise was in pottery and he soon struck up a good working relationship with Tom Fowler. In 1937 the Governor's memorandum to the Church Board of Supervision had stressed before all else the importance of the Advanced Course in Handicraft offered by the College and the special arrangements by which students were able to "pursue their course of training at the Birmingham Central Schools of Arts and Crafts". Caldbeck determined, with the Principal's approval, that all this work must be done at the College and so persistently and efficiently did Caldbeck set about building up Handicraft on the College premises, that the Ministry was to declare a Handicraft Wing at Saltley.

In 1949 Arthur Duval, a man of many parts with a fearsome reputation at the wheel of a car, became a second science tutor, but with specialist concern for physics and chemistry ; Principal Platten's eye was very much on building up the science courses. At the same time John Hamnett, brought in to handle French teaching method and to support the work of education, established close relationships with Jimmy Chance and Jack Cornwell, which were to have far reaching and beneficial results.

Finally the Arts were strengthened when John Murray was appointed to teach History and Religious Education and John Taylor became the College's first Tutor Librarian. Both were to play a major role during the whole of the subsequent history of the college ; both were to become Heads of Department : and both were to become Governors of the College at vital moments in its history.

Slowly over the next few years the numbers of students were to rise to between 200 and 250 and the staff slowly grew. Apart from the retirement of the Vice Principal and W. B., there were no departures from the names above until Duval left in 1958 ; this led to great stability of practice and confidence in the institution among both staff and students. The staff was hardly departmentalised ; there were two status grades and it was recognised that if there were two lecturers operating in one subject area, then the Senior Lecturer had the responsibility. But all met daily in the Staff Room, where there was a set of lockers for the Day Staff (which was the greater proportion) to keep their personal papers. No minutes of Staff Meetings have survived from the post-war period and 1959 remains the earliest date for Academic Staff Minutes. But there was much informal discussion from day to day and from meal to meal. It would be quite wrong to suppose that there were no clashes of temperament or conflicts of opinion ; they were all men of strong personality and deeply concerned for the job they were doing. Perhaps, above all, their strength lay in their small numbers, since there were no real difficulties of communication among them and, if any one of them failed to pull his weight, all the rest became aware of it.

In 1947 the Principal had also to create a new administrative team. All the administration was carried out from one general office where the Bursar had his table and there were two highly competent secretaries, appointed by Principal Platten ; but it was a tiny team to deal with all college business. The Bursar was also new — Major W. McLean, a rather excitable but lovable man. In practice Principal Platten like his prede cessor did much of his own administration for himself, keeping the books, dealing with the architect, typing his own letters ; he might be seen late at night working in his office. He felt, perhaps, that his colleagues ought to exercise the same independence from administrative assistance, and it was many years before it became practicable to offer them clerical aid.

Domestically there were fewer immediate problems since Saltley offered a fine source of labour for the kitchen and for cleaning the rooms. There were age-old friendships between the women who came in daily and the 'boys' whose rooms they 'did' or meals they prepared. The warmth and friendliness of these women, who had to be driven almost to desperation before they grumbled about their 'boys', was a factor in making Saltley such a congenial place.

One noted event that deserved recording was the marriage of the Porter, W. Sides. He had been an employee of the College for over 40 years and lived in a little room next to the Lodge. He was a spastic and much admired by the college ; among other qualities he was a splendid chess player and always represented the college staff in matches against the students. The new Mrs. Sides was a college servant, having been a maidservant to Canon Blofield, Principal Cooper's predecessor, and they were found married quarters in the building behind the South Lodge. Sides continued to act as Porter for a number of years more.

Chapter 5

It is possible that old students, visiting the College in 1947, would have observed little change from the Saltley of their own day, despite the bombardment of the war years. The rubble had been cleared away and gaps in the lines of terraced houses denoted where there had been direct bomb hits. The Ministry Inspectors thought little of the area:

"When the College was founded in 1850 Saltley was presumably a relatively pleasant place, but for many years now the College has been completely hemmed in with industrial development and relatively poor dwelling houses. There are no attractive open spaces within several miles, and the centre of the City can only be reached by traversing more than two miles of very dismal streets."

Certainly the approach to the College from the City by tram or bus, along Ashted Row or Great Lister Street, past the Gas Works and over Saltley Viaduct to Saltley Gate, was slummy and depressing. But as one climbed Alum Rock Road towards Highfield Road and College Road, there was at least on the right hand side a distinct improvement along Edmund and Ralph Roads and the others leading towards St. Saviour's Church which had been planned by Lord Norton 80 years before. College Road and the roads over the bridge, like Pretoria Road, maintained an urban respectability and quality, full of good working class families with some semi-professional people. The worst feature of the district was the air pollution which was very bad. Most factories and the railways were still powered by steam and they released volumes of black fumes into the atmosphere at all hours of the day and night; the aroma from the paint factories in the Bordesley Green Road was especially unpleasant when the wind was in the wrong quarter. It was a sad feature of urban development in the 19th century that our large industrial cities seemed to acquire an 'east end' deprived of 'attractive open spaces', theatres, museums, colleges and recreational amenities. After Saltley had been swallowed up into the jaws of the city-monster, Birmingham's city fathers did little to improve the communal life of its new inhabitants, to whom the College was a mysterious but agreeable oasis in their background.

In autumn 1946 there were 234 students in all, but by summer 1947 this had been reduced to 214, of whom 193 were classed as resident students; this difference was provided largely by ex-service men who had commenced their training before their call-up but had been unable to finish it; they were now allowed to do so. By September 1947, most of the students were commencing their course from its beginning, but nearly all of them were ex-servicemen; the Inspectors reported in 1949 that of the 125 entrants in that year "only one was below the age of 19, while 30 were 22 or over". The general policy then was that wherever possible students should be resident, since the residential life with its opportunities for religious and social fellowship was thought to be an essential element in the personal development of the aspirant teacher. In consequence there were few day students even though the larger proportion of them came from Birmingham and the West Midlands. The aim was that each year-group should be between 90 and 100, but in practice this was difficult to achieve, and once the two years were out of balance, to bring them together again would have necessitated taking "lodgers" or more day students.

The ex-service students were rated very highly by the staff ; most of them had seen "active" service overseas and this continued to be the case for several years, since a number of Salts served in Malaya and some in the Korean War. Between them they represented all the services and many ranks and responsibilities.

Most of them were eager to prepare themselves fully for what they deemed to be a most worthwhile profession and were equally ready to return to academic study, matured as they were by their active but sometimes monotonous experiences in the Forces. Many of them discovered that they needed to make personal adjustments to their new way of life ; the disciplined ways of service life were not appropriate always to school situations, and teaching methods were usually different and involved different values. Most older men made the adjustments successfully but a few — very few — had to accept that they were not suited. At the same time, especially in the collegiate life, adjustments were necessary for the academic staff and this was more easily achieved by the younger members of staff, themselves with recent forces experience, than it was by their older colleagues. It must have been especially hard for Principal Cooper, accustomed to the somewhat severe regime imposed by the College before the War upon its young men coming straight from school, and Principal Platten gave a high priority to the re-establishment of good relationships between himself and the students.

> "Here then we have one hundred and twenty-five men, most of them strongly individualistic, all of them mature. Hitherto the College has nurtured youths fresh from school, youths whose experience has been confined within the four walls of a classroom, but now she has become a sanctuary for men whose experience is as diverse as the four cardinal points of the compass. These lives have not been directed by fond parents but rather by the impersonal hierarchy of War Office, Admiralty, and Air Ministry. To them this is a strange life with only the communal living as a common denominator. Most have a complete abhorrence of close living yet all realise that such a way of life demands controls and regulations. They are men hoping and expecting to be treated as men, and those in authority, the mysterious "they", respect this and act accordingly. Thus the goodwill and understanding, the keynote of their two years sojourn."
>
> *"The Salt" (June, 1950).*

There was not and there never has been an easy solution to the problems posed in the paragraph above. Ideally, discipline should rest on the voluntary self-discipline and sense of responsibility of each one of the members especially in a Christian community. In practice, individuals interpret their responsibilities and liberties differently and

32

in the end a Principal has to accept a compromise between his own vision of a purposeful society and the personal freedoms demanded by his students. Principal Platten's clear understanding of what would be acceptable to students stood him in good stead ; he knew, for example, that they would not tolerate being spied upon. But he was still recognised (as were other Principals in Church Colleges) as a 'father figure' and was concerned that the community should be hard working, good living, and with a full social life. Tutorial staff should be readily available to students at all times and, since there were so few resident tutors, he instituted a scheme whereby non-resident tutors should sleep in college in turn ; this was unpopular with the non-residential staff and particularly their wives. There were inevitably some grumbles about the meals, especially the evening meal, which was always a problem at Saltley since the women staff who cooked and served the "high tea" had their minds on the need to be home to cook for husbands and families. But ex-service students probably recognised better than those straight from home that communal life imposes inconveniences which must be suffered with a grin ; on the whole, therefore, there were fewer complaints than in pre-war times and the students were much less "politically" agitated about their rights than many who succeeded them.

One major step towards liberalising the life in a Church College was taken immediately by Principal Platten in his decision to abandon compulsory attendance at College Chapel, a bold but sensible decision for 1947. The Chapel was not thereby relegated to a minor element in college life ; Jimmy Chance, preaching at an opening-of-term service in April 1950 said :

> "I like to picture our community life here as something in the nature of a five-point star, Chapel centred, with its outgoing points our quadrangle, dining hall, common room, library and gymnasium, the whole providing a spiritual, intellectual and physical opportunity from which to draw our sustenance as Christian teachers and equip ourselves for the responsibilities which we must shoulder on behalf of coming generations of the nation's children."

It is clear that many students still saw it that way too. The Inspector's Report commented upon a "short, voluntary service in Chapel at 8.45" and there is plenty of evidence that it was well supported at the time. On Sundays there was Holy Communion (said) at 8 a.m. and a Morning Service at 10.30 a.m., enlivened by the presence of several of the non-resident staff with their young families. The college year was punctuated by a number of set pieces in the Chapel and if the preacher was a visitor, the Principal could hardly be blamed for exercising some pressure ; but no sanctions were ever employed against any student who consistently absented himself whether for reasons or conscience or pressure of other events ; occasionally he would discuss with a student his objections.

In March 1949, Evensong was broadcast from the Chapel and from all accounts it was very well supported by the students. The Principal preached the sermon, the Vice Principal and the Senior Student read the lessons and the College Choir sang a motet by Palestrina. In 1949 it became customary to hold a special service for the Sports Clubs once a term, which gave suitable opportunities for members of the college staff to give an address ; other social events were fitted into the pattern of what came to be known as a College Weekend.

The daily routine was carefully structured, although not as tightly as before the war. There were rising bells controlled from the Lodge and students were expected to attend breakfast at 7.45 a.m. At night lights were put out by the tutor on duty. If this would seem to resemble the regime in a boarding school rather than in an institution for higher education, it should be remembered that about half of the students living in the West and North Blocks still slept in cubicles which were dormitories rather than study bedrooms and that without a strict code of rules all could have been chaotic. Breakfast and midday dinner were formal meals with the Principal, Vice Principal, W. B. and any other tutors available seated at High Table and preceded and ended by Grace :

"May God bless this food to our use and us to His Service, for Jesus Christ's sake. Amen."

"For these and all God's mercies may His Holy Name be praised."

Students had places allocated to them at table and their absence could easily arouse comment. Those who were late were expected to apologise to High Table and receive its acknowledgement ; this was a most unpopular tradition. There was waitress service at table and when the Hall was full, it was particularly noisy ; tutors at High Table often complained that they needed to shout to their neighbours if they wished to be heard above the hubbub. High Tea when the elected students' council occupied High Table was, if anything, even noisier ; the chief complaint was that this meal was too early, since there was only a hot drink to follow it before bed.

The working day was timetabled into 50 minute periods and most students were kept with a full programme of lectures. After the evening meal, they were expected to work for two hours, when common rooms were placed out of bounds ; Principal Platten, as a first priority, had provided studies for the room-less students of North and West, so that any students who were encountered in the corridors during this period could be challenged. It was indeed a tribute to the enthusiasm of these students how well they settled down to their labours. At its conclusion, there was a loud banging of doors and everyone relaxed ; it was not till then that many of the societies flourished.

There was a programme of lectures billed for Saturday morning, but none on Wednesday afternoons, so that the sports clubs were able to blossom. The Principal and Vice Principal attended meals on Saturday mornings, but normally W. B. had gone home to Stratford. Principal Platten agreed that resident students need not remain in college at weekends unless they were "College Weekends" ; but they must give notice of their intention to be absent to the Vice Principal with the address at which they could be found.

It might be supposed that the regime described above was exacting and unpopular, and needed to be enforced by stern disciplinary measures. The reverse was true. Generally, external discipline was a matter for the personal relationship between tutor and student and most tutors were entirely capable of expressing their displeasure effectively ; as W. B. said, "A tutor does not order ; he merely requests." Any particularly obstreperous or nonconformist student could always be asked to see the Vice Principal. Jimmy Chance explained to his successor that a confrontation was usually sufficient to ensure conformity, but he found that to write something in a book (which no one was ever allowed to inspect) was successful if done rarely.

Principal Platten instituted or re-instituted a round of Christmas cheer which became most popular. Indeed, once established, it rapidly became a tradition which always threatened to disturb good relations when it had to be changed. There was a Christmas Ball, in which the whole staff joined with the students ; the college provided a sit-down supper and the students a dance band from among their numbers. There was a Carol Service on the last Sunday afternoon of the term for which the Chapel was crowded out with visitors and students. The Dinner was the climax ; the wives of the staff and the lady members of the administrative staff were invited and each was escorted to her place by a student union office holder. The staff themselves were scattered around the Hall, the Vice Principal, by tradition, sitting directly below the clock ; he it was who proposed the Loyal toast, and further toasts to the College and the Ladies were proposed and replied to by the Principal, Senior Student and others. This was followed by an informal and unrehearsed concert, providing a suitable opportunity for students to satirise aspects of their life and work.

Then followed the Link. This was a student affair and visitors and staff might be present but they were expected not to participate. The ceremony may have changed its routine from time to time, but never its character or symbolism. As it was revived after the war the students silently assembled in the field and the whole college was shrouded in darkness ; they then shuffled, each with his hands on the shoulders of the man in front, along the main corridor, sometimes up the stairs into Lower East and North, but more usually through the old Common Room and out into the Quad, where they glided like ghosts into a circle round the Holy Acre, sang one verse of "The First Noel", of "Hark the Herald Angels Sing" and of "Home, Sweet Home" ; then the Saltley rocket was lit, soared and fell, and, finally, the silent departure. From the beginning until the end of the post-war period, this tradition was adhered to ; students always claimed that it was most moving to participate in and it was usually moving to watch ; as a body they would be angry with any of their members who made a less than serious contribution.

"Going Down" at the end of the summer term was also an emotional experience for many. The last Sunday of the year was devoted to a College At Home which contained the inter-year cricket match on the field, a Garden Party tea, exhibitions of work, chiefly art and craft, and dramatic and/or music performances. The Assessors and Examiners came and went. There was a "Going-Down" Service. There were last parties in the "Country Girl" and the "Station Inn", and on the final morning departing students said their farewells to each other and to Jimmy Chance and W. B. in the Quad.

Under the new Principal in 1947 things settled down very quickly and work and school 'prac' were the order of the day. In June 1948 the first post-war edition of "The Salt", the official magazine, was published, the production of a group of students with staff advisers : Mr. W. Burrow, Mr. P. Dunn. It welcomed the Rev. T. G. Platten :

"Under his direction we look forward with confidence to a flourishing College, happy in its many activities, and successful in helping many future teachers to give of their best in the varied fields of education."

"The Salt" reveals the existence already of a full programme of social and sporting events, a fact confirmed by the Inspectors in 1949 who had been most impressed to find the following events all going on at once : duplicate bridge at the Bridge Club ; a play reading, which included ladies from an outside dramatic club ; a photographic society meeting ; a choir practice ; a general business meeting of the G.S.C. ; and weight lifting and training in football skills. In particular the Inspectors praised the quality of the drama and music performances which they witnessed. In March 1948, the Dramatic Society had performed J. B. Priestley's "Desert Highway", despite "outstanding difficulties in the provision of stage furnishings, costumes, lighting and even scripts." But all was well ; "Superlatives are necessary in describing the work of the actors. They were all excellent." Nor could the concluding paragraph have been improved upon : "All in all this was a fine play finely produced, and a welcome sign of the return of the College to pre-war standards." Who were these fulsome theatre critics ? None other than those doughty and renowned authorities, J. O. (Jack Osborne) and J. C. (Jack Cornwell).

All the traditional sports clubs were at work, although the cricketers were too late for the printer. They had all fought St. Paul's, Cheltenham, but only the Hockey Club and the Harriers had won ; the Rugger Club had enjoyed a less successful season, having had "difficulty in obtaining the large amount of practice needed by the XV, the field being required also for soccer and hockey". The Soccer Club boasted the best season, having scored 80 goals against opponents' 42, 9 of these being against Dudley College ; but who may wonder at the club's superiority, when one sees that their captain was H. W. Hassall, the only Salt to win a full professional England cap in the post war period ? A couple of sentences from the Soccer club report deserve quotation :

"There were many keen to renew acquaintance with the leather, yet unable to join in team matches. These were catered for by an ingenious system of "inter-corridor" games which rapidly became so popular that they had to be curtailed because of the almost daily wear on the precious field. We hope these games will continue, all the same."

Chapter 6

Two events during the period 1949/50 reveal how successfully Saltley Training College had risen from the ashes and was poised by 1950 to move forward from its traditional base : in February 1950, the panel of visiting Inspectors presented their report to the Governors and in July the Centenary of the College was celebrated.

Reference has already been made to this Inspection. Once the new University Institutes became fully established, the Ministry recognised that such General Inspections were no longer appropriate and this Inspection of 1949 was therefore the last official public examination of its institutional strengths and weaknesses that the College enjoyed. Nine H.M.I's were involved and the inspection period lasted between 22nd February and 7th October 1949 with further meetings with the staff and the Governors in the following year. Normally with school inspections the visitation was concentrated over a few days, but in this case it was necessary to prolong the agony so that the effectiveness of the various types of school practice could be assessed. Now since the University alone was concerned in the examination of students the Inspectors may have felt the need to walk delicately. There had, indeed, already been a slight misunderstanding in 1948, when visits arranged by Inspectors to watch school practice were cancelled, because "I am no longer directly concerned with the assessment of the students". (Inspector, in reply to an enquiry by the Principal).

The Inspectors were skilled at putting both staff and students at ease and, although the scrutiny was a close one, relationships were most pleasant throughout. In October 1949 the presiding H.M.I. wrote to the Principal expressing gratitude for the warmth of the reception and enclosing a donation to the College Centenary Appeal Fund. On the whole the conclusions of the Report were good and certainly helpful, although it would be idle to suggest that they approved of all that they saw, academic or material. They praised especially the close association with the schools and the thorough nature of school practice tutorial supervision. They were most interested in the possibilities existing for the college to extend its facilities for training secondary school science teachers. They felt the college to be understaffed and in need of a considerable programme of building, conversion and re-equipment. They gave valuable advice about the way ahead and the Report proved most useful to the Principal in his subsequent dealings with the Ministry. The College might feel reasonably confident about its future.

In the meantime the preparations for celebration of the College's Centenary had gathered momentum. The proposals for this had first been presented to the Governors in May 1949 when the Chairman, Archdeacon Michael Parker, agreed to serve on a Programme committee which had already become active. By the next meeting, it was possible for the Principal to report that the date had been fixed for 8th July 1950, and that the Archbishop of Canterbury would be the chief guest. Staff, students and former students were at one in their desire to pursue the project vigorously; it was hoped that it would lead to a regathering of Old Salts into an effective association, which had inevitably lapsed during the war; it was hoped that such a festival would give publicity to the college in the schools throughout the Midlands and would assist recruitment in the years ahead; as an essay in public relations it could also strengthen the links between the parishes and the dioceses and Church Training Colleges in the light of the financial burdens that had already been accepted by the Church Board of Finance. It was hoped, too, that students and friends of the College would contribute generously towards a Centenary Appeal Fund to provide for a War Memorial, reconstruction of the organ, the building of a Pavilion at Stechford or other suitable object; a target figure of £5,000 was proposed although, more realistically, it was later lowered to £2,000. The Midlands Press responded well. "The Birmingham Gazette" had a splendid article on 12th May with large headlines and two pictures:

"This year, in July, one of the most famous teaching colleges in the country will celebrate its centenary. For a hundred years Saltley College, in the middle of industrial Birmingham, has been turning out a high proportion of Britain's best teachers, for it has concentrated on quality rather than quantity."

The article described the main points of interest in the long history of the College, commented upon the difficulties facing the teaching profession and concluded:

"Long after these difficulties have been overcome, Saltley will still be turning out teachers. And despite all the pressures to do otherwise the emphasis will still be on quality. The tradition of 100 years will not be lightly thrown aside".

On the day itself, the Church House put out a special press release and the events were well reported; the "Birmingham Weekly Post", for example, gave pride of place on its picture page to two pictures about the Centenary, above a picture of Jack Ord's benefit match on the County Ground.

Everyone worked particularly hard to prepare. W. Burrow, for example, visited the Pensions and Salaries Branch of the Ministry of Education to obtain the up-to-date addresses of as many old students as it was possible to trace, so that they could be invited to the proceedings. Subsequently it was possible to publish a Calendar of Old Salts. It was decided that the College should cope with the load of entertainment through its own resources rather than invite outside caterers. Miss Cockburn, the Domestic Supervisor, managed with much skill the exacting tasks demanded of her with the assistance of the usual band of women who cooked, served, washed up and cleaned rooms and corridors. Miss Cockburn left the College three weeks after the Centenary was over to everyone's regret.

One of the achievements in preparation for the Centenary was the publication of the history of the College. This was also a piece of self-help;

a committee of Old Salts with Jack Osborne as secretary produced a volume of 150 pages of fascinating interest ; a limited edition was sold to subscribers, handsomely bound and engraved with the College crest in gold, for the sum of 8s. 6d.

The Centenary itself was a tour de force for Archbishop Fisher. Friday 7th July was the last night of the college year and the Archbishop was entertained to dinner in Hall, where he met the departing students and the staff. In reply to the welcome from Senior Student, E. McCarthy, and afterwards in the Students' Common Room, the Archbishop was witty and at ease and passed a most pleasantly informal evening.

The next morning there was Communion in the College Chapel celebrated by the Archbishop and assisted by Principals Platten and Cooper. This was followed by a service of thanksgiving in the Cathedral. A procession of Clergy, Governors, Old Students and present students and staff assembled at the Union Club, Colmore Row, and at the appropriate time moved to the Cathedral headed by the Officers of the Students' Union. A large crowd was naturally attracted by this unusual spectacle which included five Bishops and one Archbishop, and a large following of notable persons, which contained three Principals of the College — Blofield, Cooper and Platten. A great congregation of over 1,000 persons in the Cathedral included the Lord Mayor, and they heard the College Choir sing the anthem, "Let us now praise famous men", and the Archbishop preach a sermon on the text from St. John VIII, 31/32 :

"Then said Jesus . . . If you continue in my word then are you disciples indeed ; and you shall know the truth, and the truth shall make you free".

The Archbishop set out to explain and perhaps to justify the role of the Church in teacher education and he ended with the words :

"So above all, it is the supreme end and glory of this College to teach teachers to find their vocation, that blessed word — their calling, — so that in the end, where they thought they were following their instinct . . . or even a choice made for want of better, they may find the sober joy . . . of knowing that in truth they are being called by God to be teachers and pastors in the family of Christ . . . Here is the greatness of the teacher's vocation . . . He sees himself and his pupils and the bond between them in the light and liberty of eternal things, of the eternal spirit, of the redeemer Christ, of the God and Father of all."

Buses had been ordered to convey guests from the Cathedral to the College, where a large marquee had been put up in the field. About 750 guests, including the Lord Mayor, sat down to lunch and speeches, and all agreed that it was a sparkling and brilliant occasion ; besides the Archbishop, who brought "suitable brevity with suitable levity", there were speeches from the Principal, the Bishop of Bristol (Chairman of the Council of Church Training Colleges), Professor Jeffreys and Jimmy Chance.

After lunch the Memorial Tablet was unveiled and dedicated by the Archbishop during a simple and moving service in the College Chapel. Old Students then filed past the Memorial while one of their number, Alan Walker, gave a recital on the new organ. There were forty-five names of Old Salts on the Tablet.

The Centenary celebrations were most memorable for all who participated and in the staff room it was a topic of conversation for many years ; it presented the College at its best. At their next meeting the Governors, in an attempt to recapture the spirit of the occasion, agreed "that an annual festival should be held towards the end of the summer term, including a Chapel Service for students and invited guests in the morning, followed by luncheon for guests and a public meeting in the afternoon". This was the genesis of the St. Peter's Day service that was instituted thereafter. The Old Students' Association had received a most welcome stimulus and under the chairmanship of George Ison it continued to flourish with its own annual reunion. The influence of the Centenary upon student recruitment proved to be disappointing and the hope that such publicity would encourage the parishes of the five West Midland dioceses to send their young men to Saltley had hardly materialised. The Editor of the "Salt" deserves to have the last word :

"Last July, however, our hundred-year old routine erupted into the splendour of a Centenary, and many of those who had been part of the routine in years past came back to the College to share in the celebrations. Their numbers testified impressively to the place the College commands in the affections of its old students — but what of its present students ? They were perhaps, a little too concerned in the vast preparations for the Centenary for the event to break with full solemnity. Further, do not centenaries, if they are to be savoured to the full, presuppose a certain mellowness in the participant ? Few of us are mellow yet, but surely our memories of that great day will wait on this gift of the years."

2 THE QUIET YEARS (1950-60)

Chapter 7

The Fifties showed a transformation in British life. In 1950 we were moving slowly away from the deprivations of post-war years, retaining ration and identity cards, and conscious always of the 'cold war' and the threat of atomic destruction. By the end of the decade, Super "Mac" was the Prime Minister acclaiming the affluent society. As a nation we had passed through a number of crises — the Korean War, the Suez 'invasion' and various economic stop-go's. Perhaps the death of Stalin had lightened our hearts ; at least, in 1955 Bulganin and Khrushchev passed along Bridge Road at 11.55 a.m. one morning and received a friendly Saltley welcome from a handful of students gathered by the Adderley entrance. Prime Minister Macmillan had warned about the "winds of change" that were blowing in Africa : similar storms were about to engulf the Training Colleges ; in 1960 there was no more compulsory national service and in September the first "three-year courses" got underway ; but already it was doubtful whether schools could cope with the population 'bulge', although the gravity of the problem was yet to become apparent.

The change in Government from the Labour Party to the Conservative in 1951 had little immediate consequence for education ; both parties were committed fully to spending whatever resources could be spared upon the educational system as laid out in the Butler Act. New schools, such as Alderlea and Long Meadow in Shard End and the Hodge Hill Schools, so familiar to many Saltley students, and Colleges of F.E. and institutions like the College of Advanced Technology, became new features of the landscape, evoking much civic pride. The limiting factor was finance as Britain continued to pass through recurrent economic crises no less disturbing under Conservative than Labour rule. But the economy was expanding and to splash money on education would bring a good return in later years.

Among the new buildings which were appearing were residential hostels and teaching blocks for the new local authority training colleges ; in some cases, like Coventry College at Canley, they were able to continue to use the wartime hutted encampment which had been the centre for the Emergency Training Scheme and build permanently on the same site. In Birmingham, however, the Emergency College had been on a very restricted site on the Bristol Road, conveniently close to the University but not suitable for a permanent College. At the time the College applied to the Institute for recognitition for full constituent membership it was projected that the new College would be built at Knowle in Warwickshire. Later this idea was abandoned and the College was built on its present location in Westbourne Road, in Edgbaston. In List 172 (1957) published by the Ministry of Education, the list of officially recognised Training Colleges in England and Wales, Local Authority Colleges within the Birmingham University Institute were established at Dudley and

41

Hereford (both pre-war Colleges but with new building programmes) Birmingham, Coventry, Shenstone (still hutted), Stafford and Worcester; of these, only Dudley and Worcester accepted men students, although, it was stated, "Coventry will temporarily admit men", so that there was no immediate cause for apprehension about local competition for men students. By the time the 1959 issue of List 172 was published, however, all the local authority colleges were billed to admit both men and women students. Inevitably Saltley with its environmental drawbacks faced a growing competition for what seemed a limited pool of suitable men candidates.

However, the Fifties were for teacher education (at Saltley at least) a period of relative stability. Most of the students had completed National Service, which had been reduced to one year, but unlike the immediate post-war intakes few had been involved with hostilities. Perhaps this is why Principal Platten in October 1952, reporting to the Governors about admissions, stated that he "did not expect so many exceptional men in the final qualification". Earlier that year he had been much blunter in a letter to the Ministry :

"With reference to the above circular (R 501/322) I assume that the Minister of Education is aware of the substantial fall in the number of men candidates for September 1952. In the case of this College only forty places so far have been provisionally filled out of 100 vacancies and very few candidates remain to be interviewed. Of the men provisionally accepted eleven will not have completed their service by September next and were hoping to obtain out of turn release. Of these, ten will have completed their service by the end of October so that if they miss the 1952 entry they will have to wait for nearly twelve months before commencing their course of training . . . This situation is very disquieting and unless some special steps can be taken it seems improbable that all places in the College can be filled.

I understand that many of the men's Colleges are in a somewhat similar position."

Perhaps the letter was unnecessarily alarmist, since every year there was something of a scramble to fill the last places in September. Curiously some of the best students were late applicants. We should be wary about making too hasty generalisations about the quality of student intake. It is possible that during the Fifties, Saltley's tail grew rather longer, but not appreciably so and the college could boast a succession of really first-rate students and teachers.

The college sustained the shock of losing by retirement both Jimmy Chance in 1953 (succeeded by the author) and W. Burrow in 1954. But by this time Principal Platten was firmly in the saddle and Jack Cornwell in charge of professional activities. There was little change in the staff otherwise. In September 1956, T. E. Hughes from Moray House, Edinburgh, made a third Education tutor with special concern for the

Primary School, and he thus satisfied the recommendation of the Inspectors' Report and at the same time provided a permanent member of the resident staff. T. E. Hughes took up his abode in the flat at the end of Middle South and resisted all attempts to entice him away from these quarters for twenty years ; in the end he retired prematurely owing to ill health ; he was much loved by residents of South Block during these years. Geography tutors came and went in those days more frequently than others ; W. Dickens was a delightful young man, also resident, who played rugger regularly for the College First XV (being dropped for matches against other colleges, although he could easily pass for a student in the mauls) ; he married an Anstey girl who taught at Saltley Grammar School. They left at Christmas 1954 to take up a post at Makerere College, Uganda. He died in 1958 from high altitude pneumonia when he was leading his students on an expedition to the "Mountains of the Moon" ; he had one child and when his wife received the news she was expecting another ; we were much saddened by this loss.

The college had usually mustered a few students who wished to offer a principal subject course in French and these were catered for by Lecturers from the University ; this was a most pleasant and friendly contact with the University, but eventually after the development of the postgraduate course it was decided that we ought to cope with French courses out of our own resources and in January 1957 David Turner arrived. He stayed at Saltley for three years ; he had been a one-year student on the first postgraduate course. He was a man of restless energy and inspiration and a notable member of the community. After the success of the B.B.C. T.V. production of the Black Country play, "The Train Set", which David wrote and to which he introduced a young star actor whom he had spotted while supervising teaching practice, he decided to abandon teaching for authorship. He reached the West End and even Broadway with his play, "Semi-detached", but his main writing continued to be for T.V. and Radio.

In 1959/60 the staff began to grow slightly in anticipation of the three-year course, but it was still possible at the end of the fifties for the whole staff to sit round the table in the Old Staff Room (later to become the Foyer with Bursar's and Vice Principal's offices attached). This provided great strength. Most of the contacts remained informal, although regular meetings were held once a month on Wednesday afternoons ; such meetings were rarely popular, especially with the Principal who bemoaned the fact that they invariably coincided with the home rugger match against Cheltenham, where he would usually be seen at his most belligerent. Formal minutes of staff meetings were not preserved until May 1959, when John Taylor was appointed Minutes Secretary, from which time a splendid account of meetings has survived. Much of the business concerned teaching practice, its conduct and its consequences. Discussion was frank and, if at times the Chairman seemed inclined to allow his concentration to wander, he was always there to offer the caution, "Gentlemen, remember where you are" when statements of opinion became too sharp. Thus, all were present and able to share each other's views and values and profit from experiences with headteachers and students ; one may only conjecture how difficult Heads of Education must have found it later in colleges with more than a hundred staff to bring professional standards into any sort of line. Such meetings made it possible for a Church College Principal to guide his colleagues consistently towards a common understanding that they were members of a Church College and all engaged upon a common task, necessary reminders as the College was to become, like all others, increasingly departmentally minded and structured.

A part of the Minutes for 29th May, 1959 was typical of Saltley democracy :

"The Style and Title of the College."

The Principal reminded the meeting that at the time of the Centenary, the question had been mooted that the College should include in its title a Patron Saint, and that recently the name of St. Peter had frequently been used in the College title. He suggested that the inauguration of Three Year Training in the College might provide a good opportunity to make official and permanent some such change. The alternatives that suggested themselves were : St. Peter's, Saltley ; Saltley College of St. Peter ; and College of St. Peter, Saltley. Opinion was divided on the merits of these titles, and on the need to change the present style. No unanimous decision was reached, but there was considerable support for the title, "St. Peter's College, Saltley", which title, Principal said, would be used in the Prospectus".

The Principal had in fact, in March, already received permission from the Governors to adopt this same title, provided that the five diocesan Bishops had no objection nor the Ministry of Education. This became the new designation of the College and the Principal had skilfully persuaded interested parties to follow his lead. At a later date, before his retirement he admitted that he had doubts whether it was a wise move : the adoption was followed, it seemed, by an increase of applications for admission from Roman Catholics, but also many young people failed to understand that this was the Saltley Training College about which they had such good reports.

During the fifties the College managed to increase the courses that it was offering ; the first and most significant of these was the one-year postgraduate course. This was a delicate issue requiring most tactful handling, since postgraduate training was normally handled by University Education Departments, which were, after all, much older than Institutes of Education. Here Saltley was fortunate in its own older relationship with Birmingham University and in the advice and guidance received from Professor Jeffreys. The question of postgraduate training first came up for consideration by the National Advisory Council at its meeting of July 1950. Since by long acceptance a university degree was in itself a licence to teach, it was as yet not obligatory for a graduate to obtain a teacher's certificate and, although there was some need to expand the

The Chapel, Centenary Service 1950

output from the University Education Departments, "the necessary increase in facilities for training graduate teachers in general would not put any undue strain on the training institutions in the next ten years" (Professor Jeffreys — Report to Delegacy). This, of course, assumed that the Secondary Modern Schools would continue to be staffed by generally trained certificate teachers. Professor Jeffreys did stress that it was anticipated that there would be a serious shortage of teachers of mathematics and science, but that this problem could only be resolved by producing more graduates. Canon Stopford had already shown interest in the way in which Church Colleges could become involved in the training of "Grammar School Teachers", although his interest was primarily in teachers of religious knowledge.

It was at this point that Principal Platten, after careful preliminary soundings, made his proposal. On 27th September the Governors approved a one-year course with "a maximum of 20 and a minimum of 12 students... provided it does not involve any heavy additions to the financial budget of the College".

He had meanwhile applied to Professor Jeffreys for permission to revive at Saltley the pre-war one-year postgraduate course which had been available for students who lived in Saltley College, but studied at the University for their three years as undergraduates. At the same time application was made to the Ministry. Professor Jeffreys agreed to prosecute the matter further, and sent out a letter summoning a special meeting of the Delegacy. The Ministry approved, provided :

"(a) the one-year course does not operate to the detriment of the two-year students and

(b) it would not involve an uneconomic addition to the teaching staff or other resources."

Principal Platten was unenthusiastic about the Delegacy Meeting :

"It seems regrettable that we should have to have a special meeting of the Delegacy for what after all ought not to be a contentious matter, as we are only proposing to resume a pre-war practice. Do you think an actual meeting is necessary ? . . . . "

The Professor was adamant :

"Thank you for your letter. . . I quite see the argument for not calling a meeting of the Delegacy to consider the question of a post-graduate course at Saltley, but on balance I still feel that it would be better policy to have a meeting. It is true that Saltley has given postgraduate training before but there is a general policy involved in this . . . Since the whole question of postgraduate training in two-year Colleges is being discussed at more than one national body at this time, it seems to me that we ought to accord the matter the dignity of a meeting of the Delegacy. I am anxious to avoid the possibility of anyone thinking that we are trying to slip something through unobtrusively which raises such an important question as the national supply of graduate teachers."

In the outcome the meeting was held, the course was approved and Professor Jeffrey's sympathetic guidance was deeply appreciated.

The benefits to the College from a close association with the University were considerable. From the beginning the Education Department agreed to give the College prospectus "as much publicity as we can" ; on Fridays, Saltley students were able to attend University lectures on Psychology and Principles of Education and the group seminars that went with them. Saltley tutors were invited to assist in the final teaching assessment at the University and tutors from the U.E.D. equally came to Saltley. The same University examiners were appointed to examine the two courses and they insisted that the Saltley graduates' results made a satisfactory comparison with the University, but that the graduates themselves much appreciated the less academic approach and the more intensive school supervision that they enjoyed at Saltley.

The first year **17** men were recruited for the course, but thereafter numbers were disappointing until the increase of the Sixties ; indeed during the Fifties only rarely was the minimum number of 12 equalled or exceeded. But the College persevered ; many more were recruited than arrived, since they were often tempted away from training by last-minute offers of teaching posts or alternative postgraduate studies. The abilities of those who did come covered a wide range, from Oxbridge First Class Honours to Polytechnic Ordinary Degrees, but they mixed together well and usually maintained good relations with the two-year students, being keen to participate in the activities of the clubs and societies, especially rugger and drama. More than one had to retire to the East Birmingham Hospital with a fracture sustained at Stechford. It was a pity the original plan did not visualise day as well as resident students and women as well as men, since there were probably many living on the northern and eastern sides of the city who might have chosen Saltley in preference to the daily trek out to Selly Oak, once the University had moved from Edmund Street.

Principal Platten had been eager to establish other one-year courses but here success was much more difficult to achieve. In 1950 the concept of "in-service training" had hardly developed, except through university diploma and postgraduate degree courses. Carnegie and Loughborough had "supplementary" one-year courses for two-year trained P.E. students. During the Fifties and before a final decision had been taken over the three-year course, some Principals, especially from Church Colleges, suggested that the three-year system could be arrived at piece-meal by extending supplementary courses into other areas — maths and science, for example, — where there was a need for specialist teaching in secondary schools. Principal Platten warmly supported this idea and believed Saltley to be well placed to offer such courses, as the following requests to the Ministry of Education demonstrate :

"2nd January, 1950. This College is prepared to provide supplementary courses, if sufficient demand exists, in
1. Dramatic Art
2. Art and Craft (with special references to light crafts)"

(*From the* "19th December, 1950. I am looking into the question of a
Ministry) course in Handicraft, Physical Education or Religious Instruction and will let you have a reply as soon as possible."

"18th January, 1954. I desire to submit a proposal for establishing
in this College a supplementary (third-year) course in Educational
Psychology."

(*From the* "28th May, 1954. . . about your suggestion for an extra science
Ministry) course at Saltley College. H.M.I. Dr. Tricker, who is giving
a good deal of attention to this question of shortage of science teachers,
hopes to be able to call upon you during the coming term . . . "

Alas, all these attempts proved abortive ; at that time the University
had not become involved in organising in-service work for the colleges
and decisions stayed in the hands of the Ministry.

Finally, the College was requested by the Ministry to offer Supplementary Courses in Craft and in Mathematics, which it was well equipped
to do. Unfortunately it was not always easy to recruit students whom
Local Education Authorities were prepared to second for a year on full
pay, since it might have been difficult to fill the gaps they were leaving
in school. We reached the conclusion that it was probably easier to run
supplementary courses in colleges under L.E.A. control. The Craft
Course commenced in 1957 with four students and the Mathematics in 1958
with 16, one of whom was the first woman student, Mrs. Bate, from
Wolverhampton ; she fitted into the everyday life of the College without
fuss and in due course became a life member of the Old Students
Association. The courses continued for over ten years and provided another
useful link between the College and schools ; one never heard any
comment from the teachers who attended them but praise for the stimulating and practical value of the work that was undertaken.

Chapter 8

The University instituted in 1947 a structure for the examination
of the work of the college committed to it. With each element that
comprised a student's course, assessment was initially the responsibility
of the college tutors, but this had to be supported by examiners (usually
from other colleges in the Institute area) appointed by the appropriate
Boards of Studies. The work of these examiners was co-ordinated by
two External Examiners whose duties included :- approving the final
signed copies of the mark lists ; reading work and interviewing students ;
holding a meeting with the academic staff of the college ; and, finally,
submitting a written confidential report to the Director, a copy of which
would in due course be received by the Principal.

The External Examiners were invariably distinguished educationists,
University Professors or retired Headmasters or Chief Inspectors, whose
judgment would carry weight professionally. Normally they made two
visits to a College during the year, when they would stay with the Principal

or Vice Principal and have the opportunity to meet whom they wished. The first visit would be to preside over the assessment of final teaching practice, normally in March, and the second of forty-eight hours or longer to review the academic work of the two years. This latter process was a task of monumental proportions which perhaps explains why it was abandoned at the start of the three-year course. Staff and students took pains to prepare themselves for these annual visitations and although they came so late in the academic year the contacts which they gave with these cultured and charming elder statesmen of education were of real benefit to all.

Not all the reports that the Examiners submitted were uncritical:

"It is perhaps worth mentioning, however, that occasionally a certain lack of mastery of the basic abilities of sentence construction could be found. . . . " (1960).

"The integration and unified purpose. . . has not been achieved equally well in all the areas where combined studies at present operate. Some linkages have proved intractable and we think it wise that they should be dropped. . . . " (1951).

Perhaps the opening paragraph of the 1959 report can be taken as a fair appraisal of the College at its best :

"We were greatly impressed by the quality of the supervision of teaching practice, both in general and in detail. The work of every student was thoroughly known and the greatest care had been taken, by the whole of the Staff, in fixing accurate and sympathetic marks in practical teaching, together with careful assessments of the quality of the achievements and potentialities of each student. The arrangements made for inspection of teaching were well-planned and most helpful. We noted close and willing co-operation between the College and a number of carefully selected practising schools. We were happy to observe the immense understanding and care with which each student had been helped by his tutors. We were aware of the effective blend of theory and practice in all the work in Education. The standard is sound and good and reaches a level which is by no means common to all colleges."

In the two-year course the Saltley students' routine was dominated far more by teaching practice than in the later three-year course and it follows that it occupied far more of the nervous and physical energies of the staff. During a student's first term he completed a programme of school visits, occupying a half day a week, to nursery schools, infant schools and special schools of different character ; he was required to write an account of these visits in his note book. During the second term, he was a member of a group of approximately 8 students with a tutor engaged in an "instructional" practice at a Junior School for one afternoon a week. The group undertook a "scheme of work" with one class, the first lesson or lessons being taken by the tutor himself and the others by the students in turn ; in addition the tutor was required to organise the distribution of the students during the second half of the afternoon into other classes where they might obtain some expeience in simple teaching techniques, like story-telling, black-board work, group work, including reading games of different types. In many ways this instructional practice was the most vital part of his training, since it introduced him to the techniques of lesson and scheme preparation and guided him in his early classroom contacts with children. It implied that the college saw the need for all its students to become general classroom teachers whatever their specialist expertise and this in turn most certainly improved their pedagogic powers and made it possible for them to teach in Junior and Secondary Schools to meet the demands of the market. Many in fact taught in both during their careers.

They commenced their third term with a three-week or four-week "block" (or continuous) practice in a Junior School under the supervision of a different tutor. During this period the college required them to draw up three schemes of work and to write in their note books an average of two sets of lessons a day ; at the same time, all their lessons were to be fully prepared with suitable teaching aids; they were not to teach a complete time-table, but "free" periods were time for observation, marking and lesson preparation. It was a rigorous challenge and, if the children were getting out of hand or if the student had not yet grasped the essentials of planning (and these two 'ifs' often went together), the practice could be a traumatic experience.

Many students found planning and lesson preparation difficult and time-consuming and the college, in order to encourage systematic and effective teaching, found it necessary to encourage students (even graduates) to work out their schemes and lessons along prescribed lines of thought, almost as a young subaltern used to be taught how to mount operations and draw up battle orders for his platoon. Two elements seem now to have been of paramount importance ; that all the work should be purposive, in the sense that every scheme and every lesson within that scheme should have its limited and clearly defined and understood objectives ; and secondly, that in each stage of the development of the work there should be a conscious search and preparation for the most effective methods. Both these elements should show through in all a teacher's planning. Most probably other colleges operated in a similar manner, but, by and large, this was the way Saltley trained its staff and its students to teach. It might be objected, and sometimes was by colleagues from other colleges, that the guidelines laid down for the "Teaching Note Book" were too strict and that student responses were not sufficiently spontaneous ; there was in fact a wide range in the level of response, but with sympathetic and understanding tutors at a student's elbow, the system probably helped large numbers of average students to survive more than it hindered the able ones from self-development.

In addition to teaching and keeping a note-book, the education department asked each student to undertake a special study of one pupil in his class and this might involve a range of special tests and return visits to the school after the practice was over; most students besides hoped to accompany a school trip and perhaps play a part in running the school sports, so that the summer term was always busy for a first-year student.

During the second year the attention was upon the secondary school. During the first term there was an instructional teaching practice for one afternoon a week, although one year an experiment was tried by having one continuous week ; the real difficulty was in taking so many tutors as were required out of college for so long a period while there was a whole year group remaining in college to be taught. The practice tended to become a specialist subject practice ; but the tutors of the education department insisted rightly that most secondary children were still taught for most of their studies by one person and that it remained essential for all Saltley students to obtain the general flavour of secondary school life.

The final practice was continuous Block Practice of four weeks at the end of the fifth term. This was a more exacting version of the first year's block practice with the needs of a final assessment thrown in. Some students were allowed to take their final practice in a primary school, but probably more than two-thirds of them operated in secondary schools. The college took its responsibilities of assessment very seriously and in addition to the routine visits by the normal tutor whose function it was to propose a final mark there were also appearances in the classroom from either Principal Platten or Dr. Cornwell or both. The marks were on a 15-point scale and the University put forward mark distribution lists as a general basis for the marks. Staff room debate about the marks, even about the addition of pluses and minuses to the grades, often provoked hot dispute in what was, after all, rather a subjective judgment and may have involved a number of factors outside the student's control. The "assessment" also involved a visit from a panel of colleagues from other colleges who saw only a sample of the students, but whose comments were listened to eagerly. Where these differed markedly from the College assessments, Saltley staff clung tenaciously to their opinions !

The role of the tutor in teacher training was all important and was time-consuming. Not all school teachers welcomed the arrival of college tutors, and tact and a sense of humour were useful perquisites for the tutor. Saltley tutors had notable advantages, especially as many of the schools that were used for practice had old students as Headteachers and the long reign of Jimmy Chance had resulted in a most friendly — almost family — relationship existing between the College and its schools. During his two years, a student would normally be placed under a different tutor for each of his practices and for obvious reasons this was welcomed by all and was a source of much strength for the College. Tact and good humour were necessary, too, in the relations between the tutor and the student ; students often (and rightly) took offence if they had prepared their lessons carefully and the tutor 'took over' after the lesson had been running five minutes and this may have happened too frequently with some tutors ; but it was necessary sometimes that this should happen. All tutors, whatever their background experience, were expected to conduct

51

instructional practices in junior schools and this was normally put to new staff applicants at the time of interview. One new tutor, most distinguished in his specialist field, put himself at the mercy of his Headmaster at the start of an Instructional Practice ; together they worked out "a scheme" ; both taught lessons within the scheme ; and thereafter they became firm friends.

Much of the work in college was designed to complement the school practice. The University Regulations allowed a mark to be awarded for "Other Work" ; this was not subject to external assessment and at Saltley it was made up from a group of what were sometimes called "professional courses" or "basic courses" ; in truth they were a bit of both, involving some fundamental teaching know-how and experience and some equally fundamental knowledge and understanding ; there were four courses which were compulsory and lasted for most of the two years ; English language and speech ; mathematics ; physical education and health ; and religious knowledge and education. Work undertaken here was usually in the hands of some of the most experienced members of the staff, including the Principal himself who insisted in taking a major share in religious education, to which he had much to contribute. One of the advantages offered by these courses was that all students had a chance to meet with new and challenging ideas in teaching as well as receiving a grounding in important techniques.

The University Professional Board had decreed that all students should take two 'main' subjects — these were areas of work intended to encourage a student's personal development, although of course they would also be a well of knowledge and interest from which he could draw in his teaching of older children. A student who studied Handicraft or P.E. would certainly hope to prepare himself for teaching those subjects in secondary schools. For the purposes of his certificate, however, his assessment in this work concerned only his "academic" performance and a few students were able in the limited time available to them to attain high levels of achievement in the subject work. It seemed to many of the tutors at Saltley during the Fifties that it was not in the best interests of the two-year student that he should spend too much time on purely academic ploys. In 1955, therefore, the College obtained permission from the University for students to substitute a grouped course for one of the "main" subject courses ; the grouped course, which was to contain two subject areas, was to be assessed by the same procedures as the main subjects, but would clearly remain at a lower academic level. In practice, these courses were advertised to the students as being orientated towards the classroom and involving considerations of methodology. Under this mantle, the College introduced a technical drawing course and it became possible to undertake a wider range of general science teaching by using this more flexible approach. All subjects offered these lower level courses except the four "basic" subjects described earlier and this must have been one reason why Saltley-trained students were generally popular in schools during this period. Even the main subject courses benefited from the "professional" approach which Dr. Cornwell, as Head of the Education

Department, called for ; in all the studies there was a sharp lurch away from the accumulation of what Principal Platten called 'inert knowledge' and a concern for the ways in which learning was to be stimulated. It was of little worth to preach to the students that they should emancipate themselves from talk and chalk when they reached the classroom, if they remained totally submerged by them whilst in college. Perhaps this was the most notable gain from the Fifties.

One further element in the student's profile was a 15-point character and personality assessment, which was accompanied by a rider that if a student was awarded an 'E' mark by his college there was no further opportunity for a reappraisal. Saltley College did not use this 'E' Grade at all, although once it came close to doing so ; in this case, the matter was strongly contested since, although the man under review was competent both in the classroom and in his college studies, he had revealed to all the tutors who had dealings with him certain character weaknesses which might make him an unsatisfactory colleague. Eventually Principal Platten determined to take a vote and the staff divided equally about the award of an 'E' ; the Principal rightly used his casting vote in the student's favour. When the three-year course started, it was agreed to drop the personal assessment and we have therefore no means of knowing how the executive of the N.U.S. would have reacted to the existence of this "character" mark. At the same time this issue raises a question on what safeguards exist, if any, to prevent unsuitable persons from entering the ranks of the teaching profession.

The two-year students at Saltley had little time for reading and reflection, since their timetable had few intermissions except Wednesday and Saturday afternoons ; within that background, the comments of the External Examiners in 1957 deserve repetition :

"We have no adverse criticism to offer. Wherever we observed what might be weakness, we found in our individual discussions with the Staff that these were already recognised and were either inevitable by reason of circumstances, or were being considered with a view to effecting improvements. . . .

"The academic and practical aspects of the Course are well balanced and the connection between them is never forgotten. Education occupies a central place in the thought and work of both staff and students. We were particularly impressed by the way in which the professional subjects were dealt with. Students' note-books showed that in these the students' own knowledge of the subject is reviewed in the light of class-room needs and practice. There is no suggestion of teaching techniques as having validity and effectiveness independently of the content of the lessons. On the other hand there is no encouragement of the notion that any method (or lack of method) will serve as long as a certain body of knowledge is put before a class. The tutors co-operate admirably in pursuit of a common aim but each deals with his subject and his students as he thinks best and the result is a stimulating sense of freedom and a great enrichment of the mind of the individual."

Two issues which disturbed the even tenor of the academic life of the Fifties deserve to be placed on record. In August 1956 the threatened shortage of men teachers in Birmingham's secondary modern schools reached crisis proportions.

"The city", reported the Daily Telegraph, "has a shortage of over 1,000 teachers. Head Teachers have said that classes may have to be sent home because there is no one to take them."

In a pre-term staff meeting it was decided to offer to put the second-year students out in school for the whole autumn term if the L.E.A. thought that this would be useful to them. The Principal consulted the Chief Education Officer at once, the offer was accepted and Dr. Cornwell made the detailed arrangements with the L.E.A. staff officers. The students themselves were at some disadvantage ; indeed the only practice most had had was in a primary school ; nor had they had the benefit of a term and a half's professional courses in the fundamentals of secondary teaching enjoyed by previous students undertaking their final practice ; they were required to teach for a longer period and at the level of full class responsibility, and at the same time were subject to the usual pressures associated with T.P. and its assessment. Further, only the lucky ones were placed in Saltley's normal practice schools and some found themselves in unfriendly surroundings ; one student, under the tutorial supervision of the author, was told by his Headmaster that he would be sent back to college if he brought a tape recorder into school again. The college staff helped the students as much as they could and some, in particular, spent long hours in college in the evenings assisting with the preparation of lessons. The second-year students under the leadership of Norman Francis responded magnificently and managed positively to enjoy their experiences. At the same time they somehow kept all the college clubs and societies going strongly, and produced a Revue in December with their accustomed verve. The experiment was not repeated and one wondered afterwards whether the crisis was quite as urgent as it had been presented in August. It is odd that there is no reference to the practice nor any expression of gratitude in the Governors' Minutes, despite the fact that both Alderman Mrs. Smith and Sir Lionel Russell were College Governors. There had been some criticism of the College, especially from the Inspectorate who probably saw this as an undesirable precedent. However, the issue was resolved by the "Times Educational Supplement" in a leading article, untypically friendly :

"A Training College is being criticised for deciding to help Birmingham in its shortage of teachers. The criticism would be stupid if it were not mischievous. As is well known, the Birmingham education authority are desperately worried that lack of teachers may lead to a breakdown in the education service of the city. To help out, Saltley Training College is extending the teaching practice of its students. The idea presumably is to put the students for a longer period at the disposal of the schools. It is a simple gesture that can do no harm and Birmingham hopes to benefit from it. But eyebrows have been raised and there has been talk of unpaid labour. The talk, of course, should rather be of how rare and welcome a thing it is for a training college to make so practical an offer."

The other issue, which made Principal Platten very angry, was the publication of Ministry List 172 in 1959. This official document contained a new index, clearly intended to convey Ministry blessing for certain prestige colleges and courses, which was headed :

"Index to some courses at "main", "special" or "advanced" level at colleges with special facilities for these courses and to certain other special features at particular establishments."

Saltley was included in a list of Colleges for Handicraft, but excluded from both Physical Education and Science. These two exclusions were especially bitter, since courses in these two subjects had always been offered at Saltley and were, surely, essential features of a men's teacher training college ; besides it was not easy to see where students were to come from in the face of such competition. The Principal picked up his pen once more and wrote in angry terms to the Ministry :

". . . I can understand that certain Colleges are being encouraged to develop a "wing" in particular subjects, so that they may acquire a special reputation and have more extensive facilities for the subject than other Colleges. Nevertheless, other Colleges may have quite adequate facilities for training specialist teachers and may be covering just as extensive a syllabus. For example, this College proposes to offer a three year course in Science and in Physical Education, both of which should equip a student to be a specialist teacher, but we do not appear in Index A for these subjects. It is certainly anomalous that under the heading "Physical Education (Men)" should appear the County of Stafford College, which has not even the germ of such a course in existence at present, and yet no reference should be made to this College which has turned out up to twenty physical education specialists a year for a generation or more. Similarly we should certainly claim, within this Institute, to be offering just as substantial a course in Science as the City of Worcester College. The work done by our men is of as high a standard and I trust will continue to be so in the future. There is obviously a great confusion of intention here which must be cleared up at the earliest possible moment."

He was unsuccessful and the teacher training jungle being what it was, this is scarcely surprising. What is surprising, is that Saltley continued to recruit, particularly in P.E., if anything more strongly than before, and, despite such rebuffs, its reputation for secondary "specialists" remained as firm as ever.

Chapter 9

It has been related in an earlier chapter how the Principal had extreme difficulty in obtaining permission for building to bring the college up to date after the war ; this was due, at least in part, to the fact that priority was given by the Ministry of Education and the Church planners to filling the gaps in Primary education and in the provision of women teachers. In the Fifties there was more concern for the men's colleges, but Saltley remained near the end of the queue and it required much patience and good-tempered persistence before the Principal's aims were realised ; indeed they were achieved only by decreasing Saltley's requests from major to minor projects (£10,000 being the line between the two) and by battling away at these one after the other. It must be said that the Church gave every support to these requests, which were much more modest than most of its other colleges and which envisaged modernisation only and not expansion — support both in supplying necessary capital and in persuading the Ministry to sanction the projects.

Before the summer of 1959, by which time the brakes had been taken off, there were six minor projects that were fought over successfully and each contributed notably to the improvement of the College. In 1952 two tutors' houses were completed at the entrance to the college playing fields in Flaxley Road and they were occupied by two senior members of staff and their families — Jack Osborne and W. F. Caldbeck.

In December 1950 the Ministry agreed to a building project on the College site to be "started whenever you are ready to begin it" provided it could be kept under £5,000. The Principal seized upon the gift horse with alacrity and reported to the Governors in January 1951 "the new scheme for the Hostel block which it is proposed to erect on Staircase principles". He advised the meeting that he would be visiting the Ministry of Education, together with the Architect, the following day when it was hoped to discuss the possibility of erecting two portions at a cost of £5,000 each in the very near future.

He was able to report by the next meeting submission of sketch plans to the Ministry. But only one staircase had been agreed and building progress was slow. It was eventually occupied by students in September 1952.

From the old college the new building looked distinctly odd, standing alone and incomplete, with its staircase and its gable end, three storeys high, three windows to each floor. There were four rooms to each floor plus the necessary wash and lavatory areas. Each room had built-in cupboards and wardrobe, and, unheard of luxury, its own electric fire, because it would have been impracticable to link the staircase with the existing heating arrangements. The rooms overlooking the college field were most pleasant and became the most sought-after of all the rooms in college ; the other rooms looking out over the railway embankment towards Pretoria Road were only slightly less desirable.

Three weeks before the occupation of 'A' Staircase the college had received further welcome news :

"I am directed by the Minister of Education to say that she has found it possible to include the remaining stages of the new hostel in the building programme for 1953/54."

At the same time, since there was now some spare accommodation, it had become possible to convert the cubicles in the West Wing into study bedrooms without having to transfer students into lodgings. Once more the Principal, assisted by architect Hobbiss, got to work. In October 1952 he reported to the Governors that he was endeavouring to obtain permission for a tutor's house to be included and that during the summer Canon Stopford had visited the college and had discussed the whole project. Originally it had been proposed that the 'new' block should contain 60 study bedrooms, but because of rising costs this was reduced to 50 ; in February 1953 the Ministry approved the sketch plans for the completion of the hostel with a tutor's house and at the same time agreed to the conversions of the West and North Wings ; it seems probable that the college owed this to the good offices of Canon Stopford. The starting date for both projects was delayed until June 1953. By January 1955 the conversions in both West and North Wings and the "New Block" and Warden's House had been completed a term late, which had necessitated the Warden's House being used as an extra hostel until all the rooms were ready. The New Block had 51 rooms with five on each floor of C Staircase and these were all a great success, giving their occupants a little more privacy and comfort than others, and it brought the whole campus into better use than at any time since the war. Philip Dunn and his wife, Ida, came into the Warden's house, where they remained until retirement some fifteen years later ; they played a full and invaluable part in the evolution of residential life. The room conversions could also be accounted successful, but with some reservations. Life in the Old Block was never quite the same afterwards, the students no longer being thrown together in so overt a manner as before the war and something of the intimacy of residential life was lost ; the new rooms, especially in the West corridors, were small and gloomy, especially those which looked out over the roofs of the Morris Commercial factory. There were few grumbles from their occupants, however, except about the wattage of the lights that were provided.

The Central Board of Finance paid 50% of the costs of the New Block and the Conversions, together amounting to just over £24,000 ; to this figure should be added the contributions made in the period 1949-1951, amounting to £1,850 and £2,423 towards the Gymnasium in 1959. The Church Information Board published a paper, C.A. 1213, in 1957, entitled "The Capital Needs of the Church Training Colleges", in which it was stated :

"The position, then, is that since the War the Church has made available some £1,300,000, of which about £425,000 is being provided by the Diocesan Gifts Fund, for capital improvements to her

Training Colleges. This will all have been spent or committed within the next three or four years and a further sum of £450,000 will still be required to complete the programme, making a total of £1,750,000."

In these circumstances, Saltley's expenditure must be accounted modest.

The next objective for the Principal was a new pavilion at Stechford ; although the ground was well used in the winter terms, it was rarely used in summer, while the grass at Saltley suffered grievously from over-employment. The Principal wrote first in January 1956 to the Ministry requesting the Government to pay 50% towards a "modest Pavilion at a cost of approximately £8,000". After a delay of several weeks, he received a dampening reply — "We are not fully convinced that it is absolutely necessary . . . to replace the existing changing accommodation which despite its faults, has apparently not reached the end of its useful life . . ."

The Principal was much roused and replied the next day, having already decreased the proposed price to £4,000 :

"The hut which was purchased second-hand from the Territorial Army immediately after the war when nothing else was available, has never provided adequate facilities for a College such as this, and bears no comparison with the accommodation available on the Sports grounds of similar Colleges elsewhere. It is now in a dilapidated condition and considerable expense will have to be incurred in repairing it and improving the ablutions if it is to be retained. Even then it would be barely adequate as changing accommodation for the winter games, and it is totally unsuitable as a pavilion for cricket. Because of this we are unable to use the ground at Stechford for Cricket, although the latter was laid out at considerable expense with a Cricket 'square' when it was reconditioned in 1953. I do press therefore that the very modest proposal which we are now making should be accepted.

"Although is it not strictly relevant to the present application I feel justified in pointing out that we have been very restrained in our proposals for capital works in the College, in comparison with many other Colleges. We have erected a new hostel at a cost of little more than £600 a place as compared with the figure of £1,000 or more a place which I believe has been incurred elsewhere ; and what we are now asking for on the playing field is the very minimum of accommodation for a College of this size. Many schools have much more lavish accommodation for the purpose."

The Ministry capitulated in July. The Pavilion was opened in October, 1957, by Sir Stanley Rous, then Secretary of the Football Association. Sir Stanley, who had been a Church training college student, captivated the large gathering assembled at Stechford by his charm and his humour and capped his performance by presenting £200 from the F.A. towards the cost of the Pavilion. The matches planned for the occasion against an Aston Villa Youth XI and a West Midlands representative XV were both lost by the College teams but provided superb entertainment. From this time Stechford became much more the focus of sporting activities and no more cricket was played at Saltley, except the very light-hearted variety. The pavilion was handsome in appearance and gave reasonable changing rooms with shower and toilet facilities and somewhere to boil a kettle. It was a pity that the means had not been available to build a pavilion large enough to establish club-house service which would have attracted later students to use the grounds more than they did.

By this time work had at last begun on the Gymnasium, promised since the 1930's. In order that it could be accepted as a minor project, only the gym hall itself would be built, with changing rooms and showers to be added later. The Ministry letter which gave this permission fore-shadowed things to come :

"We are anxious that you should have this additional accommodation as soon as possible and our approval is given on condition that the extra teaching space will make possible the admission of a substantial number of day students . . . I should be grateful if you could let me know later this month about the possibilities of increased admissions next year . . . "

This was the term when Saltley came to the rescue of the Birmingham L.E.A. by staging its final teaching practice for a whole term in Birmingham schools, where an acute shortage had arisen. The new Gym was ready for use in September 1958 and the 'old' gym could be put to other uses. The Principal reported to the Governors :

"that the new Gymnasium was completed and was in use. The lack of changing rooms was a great disadvantage and he had asked for permission for their provision at an early date. No reply to his request had been received and he was continuing to press the matter."

This was the last piece of modernisation to be completed in the Fifties, although the College had already committed itself to an expansion for the Sixties. The Governors were able to pay their 50% for the Pavilion from their own resources and for the Gymnasium from the balance of money left from the War Damage Commission as compensation for the loss of the Practising School. Although there had been no further call on the Church Central Board of Finance for funds, the relationship between the College and the Council of the Church Training Colleges had developed to an interesting and important point in the history of the College and this requires a separate chapter.

Chapter 10

The modernisation of the Church colleges with the financial support of the Church Assembly had the welcome effect of drawing the Church and its colleges closer together during the Fifties. The Council of the Church Training Colleges was a part of the Church of England Council for Education (later Board of Education) but possessed its own full-time secretary, Robert Stopford ; in 1955 Canon Stopford became Bishop of Fulham and, subsequently, Diocesan Bishop of Peterborough and finally Bishop of London. He retained a close interest in the work of the colleges and he was a real friend to Saltley, visiting the College in November 1954 to preach on Founders Day and, in January 1961, to lay the foundation stone of the new Library. He was succeeded as Secretary by R. J. Harvey, a man of wide experience as an administrator in the Colonial Service and of practical knowledge of the operation of the training colleges.

Annually the Secretary organised the Standing Conference of the Church Training Colleges, which lasted for two days and brought together Principals and Governors of all 26 Church Colleges with a number of representatives from the Council. This provided an opportunity for a Secretary's review of the development plan as it applied to the whole group of Colleges and for informed discussion of current issues of a more general character, which affected Christian and teacher education. Governors were thus able to report back to their constituent bodies problems, anxieties and ambitions shared between them all. In addition the Secretary organised staff conferences in different colleges which combined devotions with discussion of current topics of concern to educationists ; these usually came during the vacations and were quite well supported and much appreciated by members of the Saltley staff.

A Council of Principals of Church Training Colleges also met three times a year under its own chairman with secretarial assistance provided by the C.C.T.C. Many matters were handled which must have proved of inestimable value to the Principals, sometimes detailed points of administration like how they could obtain adequate pensions for non-teaching members of their staffs or persuade the Ministry to agree to fix student fees at an earlier date ; sometimes delicate and confidential questions relating to student discipline and the powers that Principals exercised ; through the Church secretariat it was possible to obtain informed opinions or to press a point of view strongly to the Ministry. In 1950 the C.C.T.C. advocated the appointment of an Accountant who should act as a confidential adviser, each of the colleges contributing towards his remuneration. Principal Platten was unenthusiastic :

" . . . my own first reaction is to doubt whether a person who could really be of any use to the Colleges could possibly be found. I should be very much against merely appointing someone who would be yet another administrative official making a job for himself. I should have thought that the best solution to our problem of budgeting would be found by a conference among ourselves in which we could compare the figures under the various items of expenditure. Dare I suggest that separate conferences for the men's and women's Colleges might be advisable ?"

Nevertheless an Adviser was appointed for three years and he reported to the annual conference ; after three years the Ministry expressed reservations and the appointment does not seem to have been renewed.

One of the functions which the C.C.T.C. performed for the colleges was that of publicity, especially in the Church, which in general during the Fifties became increasingly indifferent and in some quarters openly hostile. In February 1952, the C.C.T.C. published a pamphlet, directed to the parish clergy :

"Church Training Colleges
Christian Teachers — The Need and the Opportunity."
"The Church relies on all Incumbents to awaken the responses to Christian vocation in teaching . . . We hope that clergy will encourage candidates who are active members of the Church of England to apply first to the Church Training Colleges . . . "

These and other appeals were made throughout this period but those who made them were increasingly aware of their ineffectiveness. A few of the clergy from parishes close to Saltley showed interest in the College and its students and certainly there were students who arrived with strong personal convictions and wished to contribute actively to the religious life of the College. Year by year their numbers diminished. In admitting students to Saltley one always hoped to be able to select a fair proportion of young people with a good Christian and Anglican background ; but all students were now supported by public grants and it was not, of course, practicable to select on grounds other than general suitability for the teaching profession.

In 1955 Canon Stopford, both at the Standing Conference and at a Lecturers' Conference at Whitelands College, expressed his anxieties that in the Senior Common Room "most Colleges were carrying passengers who would be equally happy in a secular College". This was an issue which much bothered Principal Platten, although he believed that other Church colleges were less fortunately placed than Saltley. Certainly the staff in the Fifties supported the ideals behind the Foundation sincerely enough but many of them lived too far from Saltley to be able to participate actively in the religious life of the College. The difficulty arose with the appointment of new members of staff, especially as few men in the Fifties seemed to want to make a teaching career in Birmingham unless they already had roots in the area. The problem of finding suitable men to come to Saltley to study or to work was plainly and forcibly set out in a letter from Principal Platten to one of the Clergy on the Governing Body :

" . . . I realise that many of the Clergy are much concerned about the large expenditure on the Church Training Colleges, but I am bound also to say that we, in the Colleges, are beginning to feel very upset by the constant sniping and suspicion to which we are subjected. Of course, we do not in these days turn out 100% of young teachers who are fully committed Churchmen, but what parish organisations can do that either ? On an average Sunday morning, we have about 40-50 Communicants in our College Chapel. I could name half a dozen parishes in East Birmingham in which the total attendance at an early Communion Service of all combined would probably be no greater. If the expenditure of money is to be measured in statistical

The Chapel, O.S.A. Reunion Service 1977

terms of this kind, one might as well suggest that all these six parishes should be closed down and the stipends of their Vicars diverted to foot the bill for the Training Colleges. No doubt such a suggestion would be regarded as flippant, but it is no more than applying to parish life the sort of yardstick which some incumbents seem to apply to our Colleges.

"The suggestion that we do not take care to appoint churchmen to the staff whenever possible is very hurtful. Again and again I have agonised over this matter, but what is one to do if no reasonably qualified churchman applies? I have now advertised three times for a Lecturer in Mathematics, and I have not yet had a single decent application. If I do eventually get one, I shall be forced to appoint him whether he is a churchman or not. The fault will not lie with the College, but with the Church of England which is apparently unable to produce decently educated laymen willing to serve in the Colleges."

As criticism of the Church colleges became more vocal in the Church press and among the parochial clergy, the Central Board of Finance and the C.C.T.C. suggested, very reasonably, that the colleges should be seen to be helping themselves and that the best way would be for them to send money regularly to the Central Board which would be able to fund loans for capital development on favourable terms. In February 1950, Principal Platten obtained the approval ot the Governors for £110, ten shillings for each student at College, to be donated from the Foundation Account. Thereafter, until the closure of the College, the Governors maintained this yearly subscription, assessed according to student numbers. In 1954 when the C.C.T.C. was in some dilemma about finding money for many Priority III demands from colleges, a further appeal was made at the Standing Conference; the Saltley Governor at the meeting wrote at once to the Principal, who was absent :

"The point of the gathering was really due to the fact that the total requirements of the Colleges as recently sent in is about £2,000,000 and the most likely available sum is £800,000 so that more than half are bound to be disappointed . . . One of the important decisions to be made by each College is whether or not they will be able with the help of the students to raise money . . . I asked what would be the position of those colleges whose requirements were not included in the final list and was told that it would be a matter of indefinite postponement."

Despite the Governor's apparent pessimism, Principal Platten now turned to the Old Students Association for help, under the long and popular chairmanship of George Ison. At their Annual Meeting in July 1954, they agreed, but could not of course guarantee, the payment of £100 a year from their limited funds for as long as possible. The issue of "self-help" was to become more urgent in the Sixties, when once more the College responded, so that altogether the Central Board of Finance and the Board

of Education received a loyal and consistent response from Saltley, payments being made annually by both Governors and Old Students for
more than twenty years.

The new secretary in 1955, R. J. Harvey, seems to have approached
more closely to a vision of a federation of colleges in which it might become
possible to devise an overall design for the Church colleges. At the Standing
Conference of 1957, he addressed the Conference at length on the subject,
"Towards a Strategy for Christian Education"; he pointed out, "Something
like 80% of the Church's educational resources are concentrated in primary
schools, most of the rest in secondary modern, very little in grammar and
technical schools and nothing in the universities or technical colleges . . ."

He stated his thesis : "there is a real danger that the needs of the
Church may go by default unless we think out the future of our own Colleges
as a group and not just individually . . . we must get on with our own
planning and it seems worth while to outline, as it were a first draft of
what might be done."

He spoke of the University sector and suggested certain colleges
which might specialise here ; then he said, "Some colleges that might
consider a specifically technical bias are Saltley, King Alfred's Winchester
etc."

He wished, he said, the rural specialisation of Colleges like Culham
to be further developed. He then considered some of the implications
for the Colleges of his ideas :

"Even a small reduction of subjects in a number of colleges will mean
that some members of staff will become redundant, but they may be
needed somewhere else in the group, and we ought to provide the
machinery for Colleges to let each other know about redundancies . . .
We must ensure that the teaching in our colleges is fully up to requirements, but we also owe every consideration to members of staff who
have served our colleges well."

The Saltley staff would have had much sympathy with this speech
after 1974.

In June 1957 Principal Platten reported to his Governors the
receipt of a letter from Harvey on his suggestions for the development of
Saltley as a Technical Teachers college ; unfortunately no copy of this
letter remains in the college files, but it would appear that Harvey had
ascertained that the Ministry was contemplating the extension of its
Technical Teaching Institutions to the Midlands (colleges already existed
at Bolton, Huddersfield and in London) and presumably might be ready
to do a deal with Saltley. The Governors appointed a sub-committee to
"prepare a Report" and the Archdeacon of Aston, the Venerable M. R.
Dunlop, who had recently joined the Governing Body, suggested "that

64

the terms of reference be extended to consider the entire future of the type of training offered by the College — not only the possibility of becoming the fourth Technical Training College." Harvey was to be invited to attend the next meeting.

This was held in September ; there were twelve Governors present, above the average, although they included only the Bishop of Birmingham from the five Diocesan Bishops. For the first time, "the future of the College" appeared as an item of the agenda. The report of the sub-committee was laid before the meeting, but unfortunately no copy remains.

Secretary Harvey presented his ideas which were substantially similar to those which he had developed at the Standing Conference in June. The Principal felt that our first duty was to bring Christian influence into teacher training and that this would be difficult to achieve in "such a short period as one year". But Sir Lionel Russell's voice was decisive ; he "expressed the view that our aim should be to put men into schools and not into technical colleges" ; the Minute continues : "All Governors took part in the discussion, and the unanimous opinion was that the three-year course commencing in 1960 should be framed to include the training of men able to teach technical subjects in Secondary Schools, without excluding the possibility of conducting a one-year course for a number of technical teachers if the need arose." Harvey was disappointed and it was clear that neither the Principal nor the Governors were prepared to consider a change in role for the College which would have involved ceasing to train school teachers. The question was not put to the academic staff, but they could hardly have disagreed with the Governors, since few of them had experience of work in the field of Further Education. There remained some correspondence between the Principal and the Ministry in May 1958 in which the College made a bid for the establishment of a one-year course for a group of 40 students "technically qualified" ; the Ministry replied that the College seemed to be confusing training teachers for school and for technical colleges. This was the end of the matter and the Ministry decided to open its fourth Technical Teachers College at Wolverhampton. Later the one-year course for F.T.C. students was opened at Saltley in the Sixties and this was close to what Principal Platten had in mind at this time, although on a smaller scale. In the light of subsequent events the Secretary of the C.C.T.C. had certainly shewn himself to have vision, although he lacked the power to implement his ideas.

It was strange that the Central Board of Finance did not at some point insist upon an overall plan or strategy for the colleges before it disbursed these huge sums of money or agreed to sponsor the building of two new colleges. It might be tempting here to accuse the Saltley Governors of acting timidly, but such a charge would be unfair, since they could hardly have been expected to fly in the face of the advice given them by the Principal and by Birmingham's Chief Education Officer or to act contrary to the terms of their own foundation.

Chapter 11

The hallmark of residential life at Saltley during the Fifties was solid achievement rather than innovation. Each year (or almost) there was a College Revue in the Autumn Term which engaged the maximum effort from a large number of students and thereafter with Block Teaching Practices and Summer Sports, time flowed on smoothly and rapidly till final assessment in a programme which varied little year by year.

The College Revue started in 1949 and became a tradition lasting until the early Sixties. It would be difficult to exaggerate the popularity of this annual show among the students or with the crowds of visitors, mostly Birmingham school teachers, but also including dignitaries of the Cathedral and high ranking officers from the City's Education Department; nothing else in post-war history brought such admiring crowds to Saltley. Its excellence arose from the fact that it combined all the vitality associated with student performances with the professional expertise of the two unusually gifted staff producers, Dunn and Grayson. Speaking generally, one may say that Dunn was responsible for the production, Grayson for the music and Mrs. Dunn (Ida Priest) for the dancing. But in truth they operated as a team and the contribution made by each was hardly to be departmentalised, although there were times when, as in other theatrical partnerships, they pulled in different ways and finally, exhausted by the colossal effort which they put into their shows, fell apart.

It was, of course, an all male show, and the producers insisted that every act, especially where female impersonation was involved, should be performed 'straight' and without burlesque ; this was especially important in the dancing, with perhaps, some slight latitude for the P.E. Groups. The show was never allowed to last too long and the producers pruned quite ruthlessly when they felt standards were not being maintained. Many of the sketches were written by students or staff and they were presented in impeccably good taste. If jokes and songs may have had a Saltley flavour and an especial interest for the world of education, 'in' jokes understood only by Saltley students were avoided. Two examples are worth quoting : first, the song with which each Revue opened and closed:—

"From North, South, East and West,
Here we come with zeal and zest,
For we know that learning's best
At Saltley by the Rock.
In specs and checks, the slow and fast,
In flannel bags worn at half-mast,
All hormic drive and mnemic past,
At Saltley by the Rock.
Working morn and noon and night,
Hounded by the bell,
    Lectures,
      Worksheets,
      Timelines,
      Notebook A
          And notebook B as well."

Secondly :   "In Eighteen Eighty-nine
We all came here as students ;
In Eighteen Eighty-nine
We were as young as you, gents —
Posing for our photographs,
Scowling, glum or grim,
In attitudes unnatural,
Stiff in every limb . . .
In Saltley, Saltley, sixty years ago
We cultivated learning and let our whiskers grow ;
Though very serious-minded we weren't exactly slow,
In Saltley, Saltley, sixty years ago."

The students rose magnificently to the occasion and the shows must be an abiding memory to all those who participated, and they were legion. Perhaps Paul Wightman deserves a special mention. He appeared outside the Principal's office the day term started in September 1953, to enquire whether there were any vacancies in the new intake, as a teaching career attracted him. He was then at the age of 47 older than most of the staff. At one time he had been a regular soldier in the Horse Guards and had escorted Princess Marina to the Abbey when she was married to the Duke of Kent. He was a most gifted entertainer and was one of the stars of the Revues of 1953 and 1954. When he left college, he returned to Old Students Reunions and enlivened their smoking concerts with his Revue successes, like "Jellied Eels". He became a member of the Old Students Executive and travelled to meetings from Leicester where he had become Educational Drama Adviser. During the Sixties his son, Andy, joined the three year course. Between them, father and/or son, must have been well known to more students than any other post-war Salts.

On St. Peter's Day, 29th June, it became customary to hold an annual College festival and in 1955 this was coupled with the formal opening and blessing of the "New Block", which retained that title until the building of another new block necessitated that it be named "Adderley". It was the most publicised event of the Fifties and the guests included the Lord Mayor, Governors and Head Teachers to meet the Director-General of U.N.E.S.C.O., Dr. Luther Evans, who had been invited to perform the ceremony. The Bishop of Lichfield preached in the College Chapel in the Festival Service and in the evening at a public meeting Dr. Evans and the Principal were the main speakers. Dr. Evans put events at Saltley into a world perspective by emphasising the vital tasks of teacher training in under-developed countries, where many children would become adults before it would be possible to find the teachers to give them any schooling. He spoke, too, of the need, recognised by U.N.E.S.C.O., to re-write text-books without "nationalistic and chauvinistic lies" ; he used as illustration "the case of a United States geography book which describes Costa Rica as a little banana republic which assassinated its Presidents. In fact Costa Rica had assassinated fewer of its Presidents than the U.S.A."

A yearly feature during the Fifties was the Ryland Lecture. In 1874 Miss L. A. Ryland had left an endowment to the College to promote the teaching of the Laws of Health. By 1945 this needed no special action since it was an integral part of the college course and the trustees decided that the money should be spent to support the giving of a public lecture in college by a person eminent in some field of knowledge which could broadly be fitted into the spirit of the Trust. The series commenced in June 1952, by an address on the nature and testing of intelligence by Dr. Cyril Burt. Although Dr. Burt was an acknowledged authority on the subject, he disappointed the audience which contained many Head Teachers and Education Administrators. The most entertaining and popular of the series were, "The Ascent of Everest" by A. Gregory, the photographer of the Hunt/Hillary Expedition in 1953, and the "Olympic Games, 1956" by Harold Abrahams, famous athlete of the Twenties who had himself won two gold medals. In 1958 the College was fortunate to obtain the famous physicist, Dr. Edward Appleton, to lecture on the "International Geophysical Year", but it was apparent by this time that the lecture was losing its appeal to students and was attracting fewer visitors. As a result the Trustees decided to divert the endowment into prize money for suitable performance in the course.

Professor Jeffreys and the Institute Secretary, W. A. C. Berry, were concerned that the Institute should appear to students as something more than a body concerned solely with examinations and assessments and tried to cultivate a sense of corporate awareness among the students. In 1947 they proposed the "Association of West Midland Training Colleges" and they sponsored an inaugural meeting in November:

"... with the aim of promoting the closer union which it is hoped to secure between the University and the Training Colleges, especially as, under the new scheme, members of Training Colleges will be attending short courses at the University. It should also make it possible for valuable University facilities to be extended to Training College students, probably as affiliated members of the Guild of Undergraduates. We hope to publish regular and more detailed reports in future issues." (*The Salt*, 1949).

The Saltley "Senior Student", W. J. Rees, was elected as President of the new organisation. After this promising start unfortunately no more was heard of the A.W.M.T.C. A proposal to hold a concert of "Combined Choirs of Colleges and Departments of the Institute" in Birmingham Town Hall in May 1951 met Principal Platten's firm non-co-operation. But a suggestion made by the Principal of Leicester Training College for "a religious service to be arranged by the Institute during the coming session" was taken up and Institute Day became a permanent annual feature in the College Calendar and lasted almost as long as the Institute. In alternate years the celebrations were held in Birmingham and in 'the provinces', the central element being an Institute Service, the region being well endowed with Cathedrals and Birmingham with nonconformist Chapels suitable for very large congregations. Every effort was made to ensure that the Service would be memorable, the music being provided by the local Colleges, the Academic procession by the Delegacy and academic staff, gowned and hooded, and the congregation by Second Year Students, who, in the case of Saltley, were expected to attend although no effort was made to reproach truants. The preacher was specially selected for the purpose, but, alas, was not always able to meet the occasion with a suitable address to what was undeniably a difficult and critical audience ; some were excellent, notably that by the new Bishop of Birmingham, Dr. Wilson, in Hereford Cathedral in the summer of 1954. It is recorded that in May 1953, "our own choir gave an excellent performance of Dr. Christopher Edmunds' anthem, 'Where the spirit of the Lord is there is liberty' ". Events during the rest of the day varied with the location. In Birmingham the usual pattern was that the visiting colleges were given hot drinks at lunch time while they consumed their packed lunches in suitable places — a rare sight, indeed, for those days for the Saltley field to be adorned by hosts of young ladies munching their sandwiches. Should the afternoon events be rained off, as they were in 1955, the host college improvised entertainment, which never presented any difficulty to Saltley students. If the weather were fine (or in any case at tea-time), the coaches moved off to the University for an athletics meeting and various other associated events, which were not to be 'inter-Collegiate' ; they were not highly competitive but were enjoyed by all and certainly fulfilled their social objectives. Tea was in the Great Hall and after the debris had been removed, there were folk dances and concert items. Saltley usually participated whole heartedly in the fun and we read in the 'Salt' that in 1953 "special mention must be made of John Boylan who compèred the evening's entertainment and Ken Leeming who brought the Great Hall down with the aid of his ukelele". This latter-day Samson later joined the academic staff for a year or two.

Students changed their character hardly at all during these years at any rate until the later Fifties when exemption from National Service became possible. Student Union organisation was simple, comprising a committee of 12, 6 from each year ; at first, they met rarely and with the Principal in the chair, assisted by the Vice Principal, but in 1952 the 'senior student' K. Bowskill himself took the Chair and established a clear precedent followed in 1953 by Vernon Spicer. The Students used to mutter that they didn't know what the 'Union' did anyway, with good reason because they had no union funds and no union premises to supervise. As a result meetings without agenda or minutes became occasions for student grumbles chiefly about food, or staff grumbles about the state of the Student Common room. Such meetings were often lively. But membership of the students union committee and in particular the office of Senior Student were held in high honour by staff and students, and were usually occupied by men who had already won a good reputation for ability and leadership.

"I think there was always interest in the election of student councillors. Very few men were on the Council for two years largely because first impressions were amended in the light of experience. The election of senior student was intriguing. The candidates 'emerged', reminding one in a sense of the old style Conservative leader 'elections'. I was very surprised and quite terrified when told that I was under serious consideration as a candidate. The theory was that a senior student had to be acceptable to the bulk of the students and at the same time thought by them to be a candidate acceptable to the Principal and Staff . . . The theory was a sound one bearing in mind that the senior student's role (if I interpret rightly) demanded liaison between students and staff as an essential ingredient. One of the worst jobs I had in this line was to tell the Principal that students were very unhappy about one of the 'year' lectures they were receiving ; that the standard was so poor that very few men were even attempting to listen . . . the Principal was very understanding as far as I was concerned."

(Norman Francis : *Senior Student* 1956-57).

There were a number of significant developments during the Fifties in student affairs. In 1953/54, the students started a "canteen" for the sale of coffee and biscuits ; by the end of the year they had made enough profit to purchase themselves some curtains for the new Common Room. In 1954/55 a new constitution was formulated which created an 'executive' and established a Council on a corridor/block basis, the intention being to improve communications among the students. One of the Officers on the executive was to be a Union Treasurer who received a block grant for clubs and societies from the College Bursar. Among the earliest of the Student Treasurers was Harry Jones, later to become the Head of Music Studies.

In 1956/57 the Students Union decided to join the N.U.S. which had a much milder reputation than it was to enjoy later. The comments of Norman Francis, whose duty it was to implement this decision, are interesting :

"I remember telling the Principal about our proposal to join and he was rather disturbed. I don't think he was over-concerned about the political implications, but anxious in case 'students' rights' as opposed to responsibilities would become a big issue. . . The student council were keen for us to be affiliated to the N.U.S. more for the concessions that membership conferred than for active participation at that stage. The Council did send me as their representative to an N.U.S. week-end conference at Avery Hill Training College. . . We talked a good deal about the extent to which students' freedom might be widened. . . I recall that the Principal of Avery Hill College said to the N.U.S. Secretary, "If you think Mr. — that I am going to allow girls at a London College to have sexual freedom, you must think me very irresponsible"."

Coming events cast their shadows before them.

Clubs and societies flourished during the Fifties and their sporting and athletic reputation steadily climbed, despite the absence of outstanding performers. The only international was D. W. Field (1955-57) who represented England on a number of occasions in the Hop, Step and Jump. At one time there were two students able to run 100 yards in ten seconds flat and they did so one evening in an athletics match against the University and R.A.F. on the University track, the sprint being run as two races and Saltley easily winning both.

The student body was made more colourful by the presence of a number of overseas students. One of these, Bequalie Getahun, stayed for two years, he came from Ethiopia and was distantly related to the Emperor, Haile Selassie ; he found Saltley bitterly cold and during winter months could rarely be persuaded from his bed, where, cocooned in blankets with only his face visible, he chain-smoked dangerously, to the terror of the cleaning ladies ; years later he called at the College on his way to New York where he was due to represent his country at a U.N. Education Conference. The College conducted what became known as the Headmasters' Course, of one year, for up to six students a year from the still far-flung Empire, from Borneo and Singapore to Barbados. Especially to be remembered among these was J. L. Byer, a tall and fine looking Barbadian, the Headmaster of a Secondary Modern School. The story was told, surely unique in Saltley history, that on the final day of his school practice in Tile Cross, he received a gold cigarette case from his pupils and there was a queue right round the school hall for his signature. Byer was a friend of the three W's, Weekes, Worrell and Walcott, and these three distinguished cricketers visited the College during one Weekend At-Home.

3. THE EXPANSION: THE THREE YEAR COURSE AND THE ROBBINS ENQUIRY (1958-64)

Chapter 12

In February 1959, a strange event occurred which was a mystery at the time and remained a mystery thereafter — an "informal visit" by the Minister of Education, Geoffrey Lloyd. This was the only visit to the College by a serving Minister of Education during the post-war period, since even in 1974/75 the Minister did not find it necessary to see for himself before deciding the fate of the College. He gave one week's notice:

> "The Minister of Education would be most grateful if arrangements could be made for him to pay a short informal visit to the Saltley Training College on the morning of Friday next . . . This visit would be part of a tour of training colleges which are to expand under the Government's programme for increasing the size of the teaching force. The Minister will be staying in Birmingham for the night of 5/6th February, and has in mind arriving at Saltley College at about 9.15 a.m. He would then be free to remain with you until about 10.45 a.m. when he would wish to leave for a visit to the City of Birmingham College . . . The Minister has in mind a very informal visit and would particularly value opportunities for discussing with yourself, with the staff and with selected students, the coming change from a two year to a three year course and the problems which will arise in increasing the size of the College . . . "

The Minister was to be accompanied by the Under-Secretary in charge of Teacher Training, besides the Press and L.E.A. Officers. In the circumstances described above, the Principal and staff wisely decided that the only way to provide the desired informality was for 'business as usual' and the normal programme of lectures and classes was maintained. Few places in England can show themselves at their best during the first week in February and Saltley had its environmental problems. There was little time left to spring-clean the College. At least the Principal could make sure that the Minister and his retinue would be able to penetrate the College, which was not always easy:

> "To General Manager,
> Morris Commercial Cars Ltd.,   2nd February.
>
> Dear Mr. Spires,
>   On Friday of this week . . . we are expecting a visit from the Minister of Education to this College between 9.15 and 10.45 a.m. I should be very grateful if you could assist us by ensuring that the road to the College is not congested at that time with vehicles, particularly by the heavy carrier lorries waiting to take body parts into the Works. I am afraid that your instructions to these vehicles not to wait on our side of the road are again being disregarded. At the moment of writing two of them are parked firmly on our side between our main entrance and your gate . . . "

One may assume that Mr. Spires was successful, for the Great Lodge Gates were thrown open and to celebrate this unique occasion the Minister's Rolls Royce was allowed to park in the Quad itself. The visit seemed to proceed according to plan, but it is only fair to allow the Special Correspondent of the "Times Educational Supplement" to tell the tale in his own words :

"In the visit to Saltley . . . Mr. Lloyd had toured the College buildings and had informal talks with students and lecturers. Saltley was built in 1850, and the long procession . . . threaded with difficulty the tortuous passages of the science block and filled to bursting the dank laboratories in one of which one could discern the bleached skeleton of a piano . . .

"At the City of Birmingham Training College the atmosphere was understandably different. The College is only five years old and is the most modern complete training college in the country. One could surely hope for no better prototype for the new training colleges to be built in the future . . . "

It is, however, significant that the only photograph of the whole day's proceedings was that of the Minister talking to a science student in the Physics Laboratory at Saltley — despite the piano. As the Minister departed, he joined in the following duologue :

"Principal : Now you will be going from the oldest College in Birmingham to the newest.

Minister : Ah, but you have something else as valuable. I can see that".

He followed up this oral appreciation with a letter :

"I should like you to know how very much I enjoyed my visit to Saltley Training College last week, and how grateful I am to you and your staff for all that you did to make my visit so interesting and useful. I was very impressed by the good work I saw being done in the College and with the high quality of the young students whom I met. I should like to send my best wishes for the future of the College and my thanks for all that you are doing to provide the country with first class young teachers.

Yours sincerely, Geoffrey Lloyd."

At the end of his visits the Minister held a press conference in which he announced a planned provision of 16,000 extra places in Training Colleges, but that, to reach the objective of reducing all school classes to under 30, the number of places would need to be doubled. As it was there were 70 projects for expansion under way, based on five principles :

"The average size of colleges is to be increased considerably ; the colleges are to be made more akin to university institutions ; new places that will be created are to be sensibly distributed throughout England and Wales ; emphasis is to be placed on training more science and mathematics teachers ; and the number of mixed colleges is to be more than doubled."

Somewhat ominously and controversially, the Minister enunciated the new prevailing philosophy in the Ministry about Colleges :

"Large colleges have many advantages. They can offer a wide range of courses, employ more specialists as lecturers and offer first class opportunities to students for social and intellectual developments. They are also more economical to run."

It seems a safe deduction that the Minister's visit was not unconnected with two Governors' meetings in 1958/59, at which Birmingham's Chief Education Officer, E. L. Russell (soon to become Sir Lionel) had made a strong contribution. In June 1958, the Principal reported receipt of a letter from the Ministry calling for an immediate expansion of the Saltley intake and a long term consideration of proposals for future expansion. The subsequent discussion was dominated by the 'Chief' :

"Mr. Russell suggested that the Governors must consider a long term policy and decide on the maximum capacity. The day of the large College was coming and, as many of the governing factors suggested by the Ministry as necessary for larger Colleges already applied to Saltley, we should decide if we wished to be included in the Ministry list of Colleges to be permanently expanded. He proposed an immediate interview be sought with a Senior Ministry official to ascertain the possibility of future development." (Governor's Minutes)

The next meeting in September 1958 was crucial. The Principal reported that the Ministry had not replied to his request for them to receive a Governors' deputation, but that there had been a further letter calling for proposals for dealing with the teacher shortage. He then out-lined his suggestion : "A three year course demanded a minimum of 300 students to continue the present number of subject courses economically", although "the Ministry directions clearly favoured a policy of Colleges being not less than 400 students with a preference for a higher figure if possible". After some discussion the Bishop of Aston moved from the Chair that the Principal be authorised to submit to the Ministry and to the C.C.T.C. schemes of development for a college of a minimum of 300 students. There was no indication of the length of the discussion or of the points that were made. There was no recorded vote on the Chairman's motion and it is left to us to conjecture the reactions of Alderman Mrs. Smith from the City Education Committee or of its Chief Officer.

This Governors' resolution should perhaps be set against events elsewhere in the West Midlands. In July 1958, Professor Jeffreys announced to the Delegacy that new figures for other colleges included 200 men for the City of Birmingham College, 180 for Coventry and 100 each for Dudley and Worcester. In January 1959, the Director announced the project of building a permanent college at Bromsgrove to include the existing Shenstone, and the construction of a new college "to the North of Birmingham". There was much contention between the Local Authorities about what should be the order of priorities and Birmingham's Chief argued for the new college to be in Birmingham. In January 1960,

Wolverhampton Day Training College was proposed, although "it was not expected that the College would remain in existence beyond a period of six years". If Russell had failed to get his way over the location of the new college, which was finally located in Walsall, becoming known as the West Midlands College, the City gave its firm backing to a day training college sited in the old Camp Hill Grammar School buildings, despite the publicly expressed opposition of Miss Rigg, the Principal of the City College at Edgbaston, and to a newly projected Roman Catholic training college somewhere in the city.

It is tempting to conclude that Geoffrey Lloyd wished to look for himself before he approved the details of the expansion programme, and that, as far as Saltley was concerned, the Governors had made the decision for him. It is tempting to suggest that the Governors failed to exploit the situation and fairness requires that we should examine the position from their angle. It seems probable that, very properly, caution was inspired by financial considerations ; at the meeting in September 1958, Canon Platten had revealed that the modest expansion to raise the numbers to the "minimum 300" was going to cost between £130/140,000 ; in fact, it was to cost less than this and the Ministry share had risen from 50% to 75%. The Principal himself and many of the Governors were deeply sensitive to the criticisms and alarms that were sounding in the Church, which would have to find the money. Or it may be that the long battle which Canon Platten had waged during the past fifteen years to achieve the improvements that had been accomplished had convinced him that the sort of expansion that would satisfy Russell was no more than a pipe dream. Further, fresh rebuffs had been received during the previous two years when he had written calling for money to provide more teaching accommodation :

"I have been approached by the Chief Education Officer of Birmingham in connection with the possibility of taking more day students in this College whose homes are in Birmingham, and who may, therefore, be expected to teach in Birmingham Local Authority's area. Our problem is teaching accommodation . . . With the 195 resident students, the total of 215 strains our accommodation to its reasonable limits". (*September*, 1956).

and

"The limiting factor on numbers in this College hitherto has been not only residential accommodation, but also teaching accommodation. With our existing lecture and tutorial rooms we cannot accommodate more than about 240 . . . we wish to submit a proposal for erecting a small teaching block . . . We estimate that such a block might cost about £10,000." (*June*, 1958).

It is well to remember that Saltley's site was little more than seven acres and few, if any, could have visualised in 1959 the possibility or desirability of 700 students on the site. Indeed when Canon Platten thereafter considered further major expansion his first thought was to supplement the site itself. In any case the Principal and Chairman and probably most of the Governors would not have accepted Geoffrey Lloyd's arguments in favour of large colleges, but would have replied to the Minister that he was ignoring the character-building value of small colleges in contributing to the quality of life, and that the main reason for Saltley's past effectiveness was its smallness. Bishop Parker gave his opinion at that time to the Vice Principal that so long as Saltley maintained its reputation for well trained teachers, it had no need for anxiety about the future.

Although few, if any, realised it at the time, the College had passed through a crisis in its history in 1958 ; the future of the College had been determined as well as the nature of its probable relationship with the Birmingham L.E.A.

Chapter 13

The issues related in the last chapter posed problems in planning, both tactical and financial. Originally it had been supposed that the advent of the three-year course would mean a reduction in the annual college intake and that there would be no increased burden on residence or upon board. If, however, the intake remained constant, then both residential and lecture space would be inadequate for a three-year course. The changes that would be needed would be complicated, controversial, but, above all, costly, even for an increase which brought the College to a "minimum of 300".

Quite remarkable to relate, the Church Assembly and Board of Finance came once more to the rescue of the whole group of Church colleges, persuaded by the Bishops of Bristol and Peterborough yet again that "on a long term view of the Church's educational responsibility, there could be, in his judgment, only one answer as to the decision which should be taken". (Bishop of Bristol, at the Standing Conference 1958). R. J. Harvey was still Secretary of the C.C.T.C. and he devoted his considerable administrative drive and vision to provide room in Church colleges for as many as possible of the 16,000 new teacher training places that the country needed. There was some conflict with "ministry officials" who, pursuing their objective of large colleges, would have been content to put all the new places into eight colleges and leave the rest. Not so Harvey, who was most concerned to ensure the future of the whole group of colleges and was happy to persuade the Church to build, if necessary, a new college rather than to exceed a figure of 500 for any one — a policy with which Canon Platten heartily agreed but which may have been unpopular in some places. He gained assurance from the officials "that there was no danger to any Church college of early closure" (Harvey, Standing Conference, 1958). Harvey achieved agreement at the Ministry and the expansion was put in hand, including the construction of a new college at Canterbury. There were in the Sixties none of the prevarications of the Fifties ; there was firm pressure from the Local Education Authority on the Ministry to fill the gaps in the supply of men teachers in Birmingham and keen support from Harvey and the C.C.T.C.

There was less agreement about the details and Harvey grew restive if he felt that decisions were taken without full consultation. In general the Principal was determined to retain as much of the familiar and traditional as possible, while Harvey would have preferred to strike out anew with fresh architects and contemporary design. For example, urgent decisions had to be made about the kitchens and dining hall ; Canon Platten desired to modify and extend the existing kitchens and hall, where there was little room to make effective extension if one wished to retain the 'family service' for meals ; further, the extension of the kitchens was complicated by floor levels, which would require fresh foundations to be dug out and the roof to be supported by a steel girder — an expensive business. Harvey would have liked to scrap the existing kitchens and hall and build anew somewhere else on the field ; the Principal proposed that new teaching premises and a hostel block should be constructed at points still available on the periphery of the College and should be built in brick (stone faced where necessary) to be in keeping with existing architecture ; above all, existing amenities should be disturbed as little as possible, particularly the green field, along two sides of which buildings extended and the tennis courts, one of which would have to be sacrificed ; Harvey would have suggested different structures in new materials and design, probably encroaching upon the field.

The Governors, staff and students overwhelmingly supported Canon Platten and no one seriously proposed alternative plans. It should be clear, however, that the expansion that was effected probably prevented the later implementation of that massive expansion that Sir Lionel had in mind at the Governors' meeting in 1958. It is worth stating that the College's visiting H.M.I. observed to the Vice Principal at the opening of the new library that, much as he admired it, it was "already too small", (although twice the size of the old one).

The buildings and adaptations were completed in two phases in time to accommodate the three year course operating fully in 1962/63 for the first time. They involved changes to almost every part of the College. The new buildings included a handsome residential block, built parallel with Bridge Road ; it had four storeys with 50 rooms arranged on a corridor principle, but was less institutional in appearance than South Block.

The north wing of the College was extended so that with the new library and the Chapel and the old East wing, a second quadrangle was created. The north wing housed the James Chance Lecture Theatre on the ground floor and a number of pleasant study bedrooms on the floor above, where originally it had been planned to move the Music Department ; on the southern side, the new flat-roofed building comprised the Hobbiss Memorial Library on the ground floor and the Burrow English wing on the floor above. There was much necessary reshuffling of rooms, in which the students' union fared less well than others ; the "New" Common Room, built by Canon Blofield before 1914, was needed as a supplementary dining hall (the Refectory) since it had not been possible to increase the dining hall, and the "old" common rooms on the ground floor of East Block became lecture rooms ; the old billiard table discreetly disappeared during the long vacation. In their place the students acquired the old library at the bottom of South Block, which was to remain until 1978 as a new focus of student life. On the other side of the College field, the Handicraft Department had become a "Wing" and the whole of the ground floor was converted to its original purpose, a well-equipped wood and metal workshop ; this meant the end of Room 14, which had been used most unsuitably for 'year' lectures since the War.

The idea that the Chapel should be extended was considered but abandoned, although there were still a few rare occasions when it was filled to capacity. Instead, the Chapel had a thorough renovation. Kirkland Bridge himself arrived to give advice, clad in morning dress and accompanied by a particularly chic secretary to take notes. As a result, the chevron ornamentation on the columns and the dado on the lower walls disappeared and the choir stalls became less roomy ; the stonework was cleaned, the chapel redecorated, the capitals at the head of the pillars were painted, a curtain was hung over the arch above the altar concealing the paintings, which had become badly flaked, and a large cross was suspended on the wall above the altar. At the same time, the College received the gift of a Jacobean table, to replace the existing altar, and communion benches and silver candlesticks in memory of Mr. Percy Lea, who had been Diocesan Surveyor from 1925—59.

In October 1960, a special service was held in the newly decorated Chapel, when the gifts were dedicated and the College itself was officially renamed St. Peter's, Saltley. The renaming was done by the Bishop of Hereford, and the dedication of the gifts by the Chairman, but the most memorable feature of the day was a great sermon delivered by the Principal on the text on the Chapel War Memorial "Keep this for ever in the imagination of the thoughts of the hearts of thy people", a sermon which was printed in full in the "Salt" of July 1961. A few weeks later in January 1961 the Bishop of Peterborough, then Chairman of the Church Board of Education, preached at another special service, opened the James Chance Lecture Theatre and laid the foundation stone of the new library.

In the meantime, thoughts had turned to paying the bills. The Ministry now paid 75% of capital projects but it was already being estimated that by the time the expansion had been completed, the Church would have paid out through central or diocesan funds nearly £3 million since 1945, of which Saltley would have received £68,000, more than half of it during these two phases of expansion. Criticism, long dormant, was becoming outspoken, for example a resolution of the Manchester Diocesan Education Committee in 1960 :—

"That this Council . . . is concerned about the functions and responsibilities of those Teachers' Training Colleges in this country which are controlled by and are in receipt of financial assistance from the Church of England, and would welcome information about their par-

78

The Staff at the Centenary, 1950.

P. Dunn, A. E. B. Duval, T. H. Fowler, W. F. Caldbeck, Rev. K. A. Fraser, Archbishop's Chaplain, D. A. Clee, W. R. Middleton, Major W. McLean (Bursar), J. E. B. Grayson.

J. H. Hammett, Dr. J. Cornwell, W. Burrow, Major J. Chance, Rev. Canon T. G. Platten, Archbishop Geoffrey Fisher, Bishop Michael Parker, J. Osborne, Dr. R. S. McDonogh, E. T. Norris.

ticular contribution to the work of the Church as distinct from their ordinary training work which is similar to that undertaken by Training Colleges not controlled by the Church . . . "

In his speech to the Standing Conference in 1958 Harvey "stressed the need for all colleges to see if they could increase their contributions to the Central Building Fund, and also if any further capital could be provided". Canon Platten certainly felt that there was a compelling obligation on the College to make a satisfactory response to this appeal and promised to do his best. In the "Salt" of 1959, after describing the proposed new buildings, he wrote :

"WHO PAYS ?

Every Church member is being asked to contribute individually to extending our College. Is not this a challenge to us to do something directly ourselves and reduce this burden ? The Staff and present students have opened a Building Fund. It has begun modestly with some individual contributions . . . On hearing of the fund one of the present students spontaneously contributed £1. If every present and former member of the College would give only that sum we should have some £7,000. It is not really very much to ask that we should help ourselves to this extent."

The Principal was to discover that he had underestimated the difficulties in making an appeal of this nature and while Harvey persisted in his requests, he recognised that Saltley would find it less easy to respond than most colleges. The Governors, almost entirely clerical and professional men without financial substance, were in no position to head subscription lists, even supposing they had wished to ; the pre-war subscribers had long since disappeared — one had been the Prime Minister, Stanley Baldwin. By 1962, the Foundation Account, built up by vacation lettings, had £2,500 in the kitty, which the Governors handed over to the Central Board, as soon as they were sure they had enough cash in hand to pay their bills. There remained the Staff and the Students.

Here there was a deep reservoir of goodwill towards the College and a large majority showed themselves well disposed enough, after the situation was explained to them. Most of the students were now younger than their predecessors and fewer had any direct link with the Church ; they all received their grants through Local Education Authorities, like students at L.E.A. colleges, and few were curious about the foundation of their College. The Staff, academic and administrative, was growing slowly in numbers, but most of them had been at Saltley for a long time and had developed a strong attachment for the place ; their relationship with the College was, however, a professional one, which inhibited direct giving of money, although there were a number who responded generously to the Principal's appeal.

The attempt to persuade staff to make covenants in favour of the Building Fund was a non-starter. It was suggested most firmly to the Principal that his appeal would be much more popular if the money could be appropriated to some specific purposes — and there were numerous ideas, like repaving the Quad and decorating the Hall, now no longer a gymnasium. The trouble was that Harvey was expecting the proceeds to go to the Central Board of Finance :

"My dear Platten,   5th February, 1962.
.... how much capital are you likely to be able to let us have? I believe that you have some in hand and are also running an appeal. We would much prefer that you should hand over your capital to us and that we should pay the whole of the Church's share of any agreed schemes.

Yours sincerely,

Reginald Harvey."

A Building Fund Committee was set up in 1958 and at the end of a year's operations the staff discussed the subject afresh :

"Mr. Bailey reported that the fund now totalled £344 7s. 4d. Mr. Murray (Chairman) . . . reminded the meeting that this sum had been achieved from four main sources : the May Ball, the College Summer Play, direct gifts from the Staff and contributions from the student body. He suggested two further ways of raising money : a covenant scheme and a scheme whereby students would be given a sum of money and asked to double it. A short discussion followed on the merits and difficulties of covenant schemes."

The meeting agreed to reassemble at the beginning of the next term and thrash something out. The "May Ball" deserves comment ; a small committee of staff and students had formed to organise a Ball as a new major attraction to the Summer Term to embrace Governors and Old Students as well as those at present in College. For a few years in the early Sixties this proved most successful, until the advent of new fashions of dancing and of costly "beat" groups became the primary attraction for the students. Although the staff and Governors dropped out, the May Ball remained one of the calendar events for nearly 20 years. The May Ball was itself responsible for an even more significant innovation — the introduction of a college bar, at first as a special occasion with a special licence.

The reconvened meeting agreed to hold a "Gala" on the first Saturday in July 1960 and established the organisation for the purpose with all 24 members of Staff promising to assist ; there was indecisive discussion on the aims of the Fund and the minute concludes, "this topic was held over for future consideration".

The Gala was indeed a considerable effort, even though it included many willing helpers ; the Summer Term with its first year teaching practice, its frequent interruptions for examinations, assessments, interviews and farewells, was not an ideal time for a prolonged money-raising effort of this type. In organisation it comprised a number of projects, many involving schools, coming to their fulfilment on "G" Day. There were school handicraft and art competitions and exhibitions ; a girls' dress-making competition and fashion parade ; a stall (miscellaneous) run by staff and their wives ; a second hand book stall ; rides on a

81

penny-farthing bicycle ; innumerable side-shows, including a bingo stall run by the members of Lower West. For two or three nights before the Saturday, students toured the streets of Saltley and Bordesley Green, led by the College Dance Band, selling programmes.

It was difficult to find a suitable opener and those invited included Lady Isobel Barnett, Peggy Ashcroft and Billy Wright. Eventually, Miss Peggy Bacon, B.B.C. Midland Regional Organiser for the Children's Hour proved a most charming and welcome opener and Sir Lionel Russell (the only Governor present) presided over the Opening Meeting. Rain threatened during the Saturday morning, but it remained dry during the afternoon when the College entertained its largest post-war gathering except perhaps on the day of the centenary. For spectators the afternoon was enlivened by a programme of events which included Junior School dancing, the Band of King's Rise Boys School and a display given by the College Porter, Harry Taylor, with Solo, his handsome young alsatian trainee. No accurate financial statement of profit and loss was made, but results were disappointing ; the side-shows made a splendid profit, but there was a loss on the teas. Despite the large gathering, the visitors brought little money with them since a high proportion were children, and perhaps there was not enough for them to have spent their money on. High credit went to the student who brought some lads from his School Practice school and cleared up the mess afterwards.

The Building Fund was further swollen at this time by the first of a number of jumble sales, this one held on the South car park, and by a Prize Draw run by the Old Students' Association ; the distribution of tickets for the Draw had to be undertaken largely by post and it meant a lot of time and effort for those who did the work.

The Building Fund made little advance for some time after this. Not until September 1961 was the subject again debated by the Staff and once more there was division of opinion about its objects. At this time the Fund stood at £1,200. A sub-committee recommended that it be closed on 31st December 1962 with a target of £2,500, and made numerous suggestions how money might be raised, including schemes whereby technical expertise among staff and students might be utilised to complete jobs about the College which could be remunerated for the credit of the Fund.

In November 1962 Harvey wrote again :

"You have so far let us have £2,500 in capital and you have put your target at £5,000. I know St. Peter's is not a College which can raise money easily and I think £5,000 is very generous. I therefore hesitate to ask whether you are likely to be able to add to this from lettings or any other source over the next few years. If you feel you cannot do so I will understand."

It is pleasant to record that the final target was reached exactly on the day. It was assisted by some generous gifts from outside the College. One such gift ought to have been much more generous than it was and to have relieved us to all anxieties.

In May 1962 there had been a spectacular fire one evening at the Morris Commercial Works next door with a fine ringside view from Upper South. The "Birmingham Mail" reported thus :

"Students of the Saltley Training College turned out to push and drive nearly 70 vehicles from the blazing works. 'They did a magnificent job', said a B.M.C. spokesman. 'The company is immensely grateful to them for their voluntary services. Some must have risked burning and injury to save the vehicles. Many of the vehicles have been parked on the College playing field.' A student, Mr. J. C. Bamford, said, 'We saw the vans quite close to the flames. We broke the double gates down and about a hundred students moved the vans to the College playing field'."

The B.M.C. gratefully presented the Building Fund with £100.

Eventually a cheque for £2,500 was presented to the College Foundation account and its receipt was most gracefully acknowledged by the Chairman of the Governors in separate letters to the staff and the students. The "Building Fund" continued to operate and became a permanent feature of College life.

In 1961, Bishop Parker became the Diocesan Bishop of Bradford and he therefore vacated the Chair which he had occupied since the death of Lord Cobham in 1949. He and the Principal had established strong bonds of mutual understanding and he had shown throughout a close interest in the life and work of the College. His successor, the Diocesan Bishop of Birmingham, Leonard Wilson, agreed to hold the office, in his own words, "until we can find someone more suitable" ; he presided over the College in its era of expansion and was particularly successful in his relations with the students, although he never achieved quite the same intimate relationship with the Principal that Michael Parker had done. Another change which had a large bearing on further expansion was the arrival of Commander W. H. Heathcote, R.N., in place of Major W. McLean who had retired in 1961 ; Heathcote transformed the financial situation and therefore opened up the possibilities available to the Governors.

In 1963, the pressure to expand was once more raised and in March at the Governors' meeting the Principal reported the receipt of a further letter from the Ministry and asked the Governors to call in a deputation of senior members of staff — The Vice Principal, Hamnett, Head of Education, and Dunn, Head of English. The Principal then proposed the building of a new student union block which would release other parts of the college for teaching purposes and that the Governors should accept the idea that resident students spend one third of their time in lodgings. The staff representatives favoured more drastic measures, like the admission of women students and a more ambitious building programme, but despite the support of Alderman Mrs. Smith, they lost the day after a decisive intervention from Sir Lionel, who regarded the Ministry appeal as so urgent that they could not afford to wait the "long period to resolve

83

the difficulties in the College becoming mixed". It was thought that the new building would cost £40,000 and that the Governors would be able to find their share of £10,000, "if spread over a number of years". In November 1963, the Delegacy published a list of "approved target figures" of students for each College in the Institute ; these showed Coventry leading the way with 1,000, followed by Worcester with 900 and the City of Birmingham with 700. The new West Midlands College showed a target of 650 and the even newer "Cornelia Connelly" (later Newman) 600 ; Westhill's target was 260 and St. Peter's, Saltley 475 ; the Saltley students would be, of course, all male.

It was reasonable that the student facilities should be improved, if only as a reward for their efforts on behalf of the Building Fund. As described above, in 1963 the Principal put forward a scheme to increase the College to 475 and take advantage of a fund of £7 million which the Government had made available and this provided a suitable opportunity :

"Dear Harvey,   February, 1963.

I should be very grateful for advice concerning proposals for the further expansion of student numbers . . . we should need some further student cloakroom and common room accommodation at least. The question is, on what scale should I think of this ? We could probably meet minimum requirements for about, say £10,000, but some of my colleagues have noted that the Government has offered £7 million to create 15,000 new places which is roughly £500 a place. They therefore argue that we should put up a scheme for a sort of Student's Union building costing £40,000 or £45,000. I have told them that I do not think the Church could finance 25% of this, but they are inclined to feel that in previous negotiations I did not open my mouth wide enough and that this College has not had as big a share of improvements as some other Colleges received. Of course, there are answers to this, but I would like to know your views before continuing the argument further.

Yours sincerely,

T. G. Platten."

Harvey's reply was to advise proceeding on the more ambitious lines. This was how the Students' Foyer, Shop, Coffee Bar and second Common Room (T.V. Room) by the South Block entrance came to be projected. The original plan had been for a new Union Block located next to Lyttleton, but it was rightly decided that this site should be left for a later further expansion. Other developments put into effect were to build another group of study bedrooms above Lower North Annexe and a Porter's House near the main entrance to the College. This meant that the building near the South entrance which in its time had been used for a variety of purposes could be reconstructed to enable some "Day" rooms and studies to be provided, later to be known as 'South Annexe'. A project to build another floor over the College offices was not proceeded with.

84

Chapter 14

The first three-year course students arrived in September 1960. The extension of the course from two to three years had been recommended by the McNair Report and promised by Government on various post-war occasions. There had long been a powerful lobby in favour of a three year course ; it was seen as a step towards an all-graduate teaching profession and a healing of divisions that existed within the teaching ranks. Not everyone shared this full enthusiasm nor was there general agreement about how the extra year should be utilised. Among the 'don't knows' was Canon Platten, who had warmly advocated during the Fifties that the three-year course should be available for some, especially for teachers of science and technical subjects in secondary schools, but not immediately for others, more particularly in the primary field ; his views prompted quick reactions from some of his colleague Principals in the Birmingham Institute. Something of Canon Platten's doubts is portrayed by a letter to Harvey in June 1963 on an agenda for a Church Principals' meeting :

"What I would like to hear is the experience of other colleges on the working of the first three-year course. Has the third year proved really effective ? Is it justified by marked improvement in academic attainments ? Are the outgoing students more competent as teachers than the two year trained students of the past ?"

Good questions, but perhaps early in the day to ask them ! By the Seventies it was becoming commonly believed that it was unreasonable to expect a young man or woman straight from school to commit himself for three years training before a teaching career and that a situation which segregated those who had made such an undertaking was positively harmful.

However, the decision had been made and was warmly approved by all political parties. It provided an opportunity for the University together with the college Principals to make a complete reappraisal of the teacher education course. This was the time when the critics of the colleges could have presented coherently and positively their main grounds for discontent. The opportunity was lost. The Delegacy represented central and local government, a broad spectrum of university and higher education, the Inspectorate, teachers' professional associations and tutorial opinion within the colleges themselves ; only the college students were unrepresented ; in 1957 and 1958 Professor Jeffreys called special meetings of the different elements above. But little general change in direction was proposed for teacher education. In March 1958, the Professor reported to the Delegacy :

"That there was now a fair measure of agreement as to what should be the content . . . of the examination for the Certificate in Education. It had been stressed that, although the need for specialist teachers was recognised, such teachers should be able to teach some general form subjects in addition to their specialist subjects.

"That there was general agreement that one of the main aims of the course should be to improve the personal education of the students.

"That the option had been expressed that, after a three-year course of training, students ought to be more mature as persons . . . "

The new regulations offered some minor improvements, but there was nothing to suggest any university or general public disquiet about the standards that were current in the colleges. The new course was to be assessed upon a five point scale instead of fifteen; the course was divided into four sections instead of five, the old "character assessment" being abandoned ; under the old regulations it had been possible to fail if the all-round performance was mediocre, since the marks had to reach 70 on a numerical compilation ; now, two 'D' marks would constitute failure, even though 'D' was itself a pass mark. The old style External Examiners were replaced by a number of University education and subject external examiners, who were required to report confidentially to the Director ; these were supplemented by college examiners. In practice it may have become marginally easier for weak students to pass the course. Under a system of course assessment over a period of three years, it was very difficult in most of the studies to arrive at a final mark of 'E', unless course assignments had not been completed ; it was somewhat easier in a final teaching practice to achieve an 'E' mark, but before one awarded it, one had to consider carefully a certain subjective element in such awards and the varieties of good or bad fortune the student might have enjoyed in his school or tutor. The best means of removing unsuitable students from the teaching profession remained that of persuading them to withdraw on the grounds that they were unsuitable.

The different courses within the whole pattern were carefully reviewed by the University Boards of Studies. Each student was required to offer either one Principal Subject Course (three years) and one Subsidiary Course (two years) or two Principal Courses. In actuality only one student at Saltley ever offered two Principal courses, since the demands on a student's time in the third year were heavy, and after the B.Ed. course commenced it would have been to his disadvantage to have done so. If the History Board of Studies was representative, then subject courses followed the traditional lines for the first two years, but in the third year there were wide variations between the colleges, which provoked no University protest until later when they became part of the B.Ed. degree course.

Contrary to much student belief, the introduction of the three year course did not result in the Education part of the course becoming more academic, at any rate, at Saltley. It had always been the avowed aim to harness "education" work to children and to schools and to put the needs of the students first. The Education Department made a strong bid to persuade the subject departments to co-operate with them in a carefully planned approach to the study and solution of classroom problems. In the third year of the course there was little "academic" education study; instead, advantage was taken of Professor Jeffreys' request that all students should follow some special expertise such as school librarianship, remedial education, careers and counselling. One of these options became of mounting significance as the years passed and as Saltley and its environs became increasingly deprived. This was a course in Youth Leadership, which filled a need among the students and also in the profession, where there was plenty of scope for the employment of men and women who were trained teachers and had experience in youth work. The University agreed that a student who had taken this option should have his certificate specially endorsed.

It was generally hoped that one of the effects of the extra year of the course was that the student would enjoy more leisure, which would enable him to read widely and to think maturely. In practice it may not have encouraged either of these enough. The bookish subjects were able to reduce the amount of time in which students were listening to lectures, and to replace them by seminars and tutorials — not that they, too, didn't have their problems ; but many of the Saltley students offered courses, like P.E. and Handicraft and Sciences, which required a large measure of workshop, laboratory and practical activity during daylight hours. There was a tendency, too, to fit in extra professional courses when it was seen that the need existed. Students remained as busy as ever.

One major decision by the School of Education may have caused some raising of eye-brows ; the minimum requirement for school practice time was not increased as much as was expected — partly for fear that the schools would then be swamped by the increased numbers of trainees. Secondary head masters strongly favoured a whole term's practice :

Sir Wilfred Martineau School

"Dear Canon Platten,   8th July, 1960.
. . . One thing is quite certain in my own mind about Teaching Practice and that is the virtue of a complete term of practice under normal school operating conditions. In my experience this is far superior to the cumulative effect of a number of shorter periods.
Yours sincerely,
J. Herbert."

"Dear Mr. Herbert,   9th July, 1960.
. . . We found that a great many Head Teachers of Secondary Schools favoured the whole term's practice. On the other hand the Heads of most Junior Schools say that it would create too great an interruption to their normal teaching. It has also a detrimental effect on the general life of the College to have a large proportion of the men out for so long. I expect in the end we shall effect some sort of compromise.
Yours sincerely,
T. G. Platten."

The Principal was correct ; a compromise gave the three-year students a final practice during their third year of between eight and ten weeks. At first this was put into the summer term ; then into the autumn where it remained thereafter.

In July 1960 the Head Teachers of schools used by the College for T.P. were invited to a half-day conference, which proved most successful and the forerunner of many more. After a plenary session in which the Heads were briefed about the plans for the three-year course, they were divided into discussion groups under the chairmanship of senior members of staff and the suggestions they made were collated by Dr. Cornwell and copies distributed to all concerned. Nine suggestions were common to all groups and when the staff discussed them there was complete agreement, except, perhaps, about the length of the final practice. It was possible to implement all suggestions during the following years, except that which called for "a ruthless weeding out of unsuitable students in the first year", which was splendid in principle, but impossible to effect ; in fact, many weak students were persuaded to withdraw of their own accord. As a result of this request, the College instituted Head Teachers' reports on first year practices and made a serious review of its students annually, trying at the same time to avoid bitter complaints that one sometimes heard elsewhere of unfairness to students.

At the Standing Conference of the C.C.T.C. in 1959, Harvey had uttered something of a warning about the significance of a three-year course :

"Expansion and the lengthening of the course from two to three years are different sides of the same process, a process which involves a widening and redistribution of authority. It does not seem to be realised in the educational world in general and not fully even in the training colleges, just how much difference these two factors . . . are going to make in teacher training. It means the final end to the idea that teacher training is something tacked on to the schools . . .

"As for the students, there will be much greater continuity and so, in a sense, greater student authority . . . As far as the staff is concerned . . . there will obviously be considerable devolution of authority, particularly to the senior members. Yet the staff will have the opportunity of an even closer association with the students than in the past. With the swing in the pattern of teaching away from the large lecture into smaller group work, members of staff will have a personal responsibility for and knowledge of individual students which sometimes they have not had in the past . . .

"What is most important is that our colleges should be really adult institutions which will attract first class men and women as principals, staff and students and which will stand for something of real quality. That is where their future lies — as adult institutions, adult in every way, and of the highest quality."

It was a wise speech, although the pace of change at Saltley was slower than visualised by Harvey, partly, perhaps, because the College remained conservative in outlook with a long established staff cadre and a student body which retained a small but important element of slightly older men. Within the context of Harvey's speech, one noted the Editorial of the "Salt" in July 1963, when the first three-year students went down :

"We are indeed caught up in the web of transition and we feel that on looking back, we will find that these years were not only exciting ones in the development of the college, but also the foundation of the new outlook which the recent advances in our educational system demand."

In teaching methodology, Dr. Cornwell noted that by the College's use of small groups in education work, the H.M.I.'s constantly affirmed "how far in advance of most Colleges we were", although it meant an overloaded time-table for the education staff. In fact the flood-gates were not yet open.

For the time being attention concentrated more upon staff development. At one time there had been discussion at Saltley as at other colleges whether it would not be necessary to reduce the number of subjects offered by colleges and Professor Jeffreys had visited each college to discuss with senior staff where it might be practicable to effect some rationalisation of courses with other colleges. The expansion came before decisions were taken and one consequence was that Saltley moved slowly to a departmental staff structure ; this was assisted by the institution of a new salary scale which enabled the appointment of Principal Lecturers, although it was several years before each Head of Department was a Principal Lecturer. It is surprising that not until January 1960 was there agreement to hold regular staff meetings and then, one a month on Wednesday afternoons, which threatened seriously to reduce the spectators at Stechford when there were important rugger matches. At the same time it was agreed to publish a calendar of college arrangements on the Staff Room notice board.

However, proposals for the establishment of an academic board with its authority written into the constitution of the college had now been raised and desultory discussions continued throughout 1960 and most of 1961 before the matters were resolved. These discussions included Saturday morning sessions in which two senior staff met with the Principal, Sir Lionel Russell and Geoffrey Templeman to assist redraw the articles of Government. The Governors clung tenaciously to their power to control the "academic policy of the college", but admitted an Academic Board "to advise the Principal in the detailed administration of academic matters including the prescription of a curriculum" ; the Board would have the right to "make representations to the Governors on any matter affecting the college".

By 1961 the staff had grown to 30 and, although the new Academic Board consisted of "all full-time members of the Tutorial Staff", a Standing Committee of 17 was to make routine decisions ; there were some misgivings about this and one new colleague introduced the phrase "open government" ; another new colleague expressed public disapproval when the staff discussed a new student union constitution. There was, however,

89

little enthusiasm for representation on the Governing Body and the Principal, although he favoured such representation, did not press the matter.

This led to a sharp altercation between Canon Platten and Harvey :

"My dear Harvey, 7th March, 1963.

As I told you yesterday, we did not look upon the operation as creating a new constitution for the Governing Body, but only as incorporating an academic board officially into the existing one . . . The Governors had divided views over including members of staff on the Governing Body, but the staff themselves did not wisn to be so represented, feeling that a substantial voice in the control of academic affairs fulfilled their requirements . . .

I am afraid that the damage is done now, if there be damage, as I can hardly go back to the Ministry and ask them to revise again a constitution which has just been officially stamped. I do apologise if I have been discourteous to you . . .

Yours faithfully,

T. G. Platten."

"My dear Platten, 13th March, 1963.
. . . the really crucial factor is how soon you are going to retire. In recent applications for principalships I have found that some of the best candidates will not consider the post if they are not to be full members of the Governing Body, and also prefer that other members of staff should be on it. If, therefore, the post were to be advertised with your present Constitution, I am quite certain that serious harm might be done to the College, because some of the best candidates would not be interested . . .

Yours sincerely,

Reginald Harvey."

"My dear Harvey, 13th March, 1963.
. . . the Bishop read the copy of the letter which you sent him at the meeting of Governors which, as it happened, we had on Saturday . . . In the discussion which followed, the general opinion seemed to be that the present constitution works well in practice . . . Sir Lionel Russell . . . emphasised that although the Principal was not officially a Governor no meeting of the Board had ever taken place without him or could conceivably take place, and the Bishop asked me to mention this . . .

Yours sincerely,

T. G. Platten."

Nothing at the time was further from the Principal's mind than retirement ; but Harvey was right and Sir Lionel wrong, as a close examination of the immediate post-war history would have revealed. Before Canon Platten did retire, there were staff members of the Governing Body as well as the Principal himself.

90

Chapter 15

November 2nd 1962 must count as the high spot of the middle period of Canon Platten's Principalship. During the morning the Bishop of Hereford preached at a Founders' Day service, and in the afternoon Viscount Cobham opened the new Library and Burrow English Wing and Lyttleton House, the residential block. The first chairman of Governors had been a Lord Cobham and his large portrait still looked down benignly upon Saltley students in the dining hall. The afternoon's events commenced with a Public Meeting in Hall, which had been newly decorated and made to look much less like the gymnasium which Principal Blofield had built before World War I. The guests included the Lord Mayor of Birmingham and the Mayors of Solihull and Sutton Coldfield, four Bishops, Chief Education Officers, Church College Principals and dignitaries, Principals of local Colleges, Head Teachers and Old Students. The Bishop of Birmingham presided over the meeting, his first public engagement as the College Chairman; the weather was fine and the students supported the occasion in reasonable numbers. As usual the Principal opened the batting order, explaining to the audience the long family ties that linked Lord Cobham and the College and paying tribute to the Church Assembly which, by providing 25% of the capital, had made the expansion possible and had thus demonstrated its determination to retain a place in the national system of education. Lord Cobham, making his first appearance since returning to Britain from the post of Governor-General of New Zealand, came next. His speech was delightful; contrasting two views from his home, Hagley Hall, one across the wooded hills of Kinver and the other towards the Black Country, "an everlasting memorial to man's spiritual decay in his unseemly scramble after riches", he exhorted his audience to cherish the beautiful things in their inheritance:

> "So when I open these fine buildings today, I enjoin you to remember that your whole education is directed towards the production of whole men, whom adversity cannot daunt, flattery cannot corrupt, nor the search for worldly goods swerve from the paths of service. Britain can never become a second class Power so long as she is filled with first rate people."

Finally, Philip Capewell, the first three-year student to hold the office of President of the Union, thanked His Lordship in a composed and impressive little speech.

The Opening Ceremonies were then completed. The Library and English Block were dedicated in the name of Willie Burrow, whose portrait, drawn by T. H. Fowler nearly thirty years before, was hung on the wall. The ground floor comprised the Library in two rooms, one a teaching practice library and the other an ordinary working library, light and pleasant, still at this time under the authority of John Taylor, Tutor-Librarian. The special furniture from the Hobbiss Memorial Library, was installed in the new quarters. The Lyttleton Building was a fine asset and a notable advance upon all the older residential quarters; the rooms were equipped with wash-basins and drawer units; the corridors

91

supplied with utility rooms ; and the design skilfully combined the economy of a corridor lay-out with the intimacy of staircase rooms. They were much admired. The guests lingered over tea and conversed with friends and one by one departed. Principal Platten wrote to ask Lord Cobham to accept the Chairmanship of the College, but sadly, he declined.

The steady growth in numbers of the academic staff brought also increasing departmentalisation of the College. Two heavy blows were sustained ,but by good fortune the College was able to ride both of these. One was the departure of Dr. Cornwell in 1962 to become the first Principal of the newly-established West Midlands College at Walsall ; it was a promotion well earned and Saltley's loss was certainly Walsall's gain ; as Head of Education he had contrived to keep the work of the College in the forefront of progress while he retained the standards inherited from the pre-war college ; John Hamnett, who succeeded him, had been his close friend and confidant since 1949. In January 1964 Wallace Caldbeck died at the early age of 48 after a short spell in hospital. There was an aggressiveness in his temperament which may have led some to under-value his contribution ; he was the architect of the 'wing' course in handicraft and played as well a most active part in many aspects of College life, until slowed down by a severe heart operation. He was succeeded by Frank Brinkworth, who had been given a full-time appointment in the Craft Department in 1960. Frank was a superb craftsman, in both wood-craft and silver-smithing ; and by precept and example he was able to maintain the fine standards of craft education, which the D.E.S. and the West Midlands were so wantonly to dissipate in 1976.

With opportunities for promotion elsewhere, staff now came and went more frequently, but many remained for at least five years and some longer. One of these was G. Paget, Deputy Head of a Primary School, who was seconded to the College staff for a year by the Birmingham L.E.A.; so useful was he and so well did he enjoy the work that he stayed for 17 years. It was pleasant to be able to appoint a number of post-war old students to the staff ; one of these, Paul Lapworth, followed Dr. Cornwell to Walsall and became Head of English and eventually Vice Principal there; another was Steve Allatt, P.E. Tutor and well-known personality in West Midlands sporting circles, who after ten years at Saltley returned to school as a Deputy Head.

An idea much aired by the C.C.T.C. was that colleges should appoint a full-time Chaplain and in response the resident post of Assistant Lecturer for a three-year term was offered to the Rev. Alan Heawood, despite the fact the College had three staff in Holy Orders including the Principal, who held nominal responsibility for the Chapel. The experiment was only partially successful, for the role of Chaplain needed to be more carefully worked out. Alan Heawood was able to make a thoughtful and scholarly contribution in Chapel and with the Divinity course students. He was well liked in the Senior Common Room where he literally towered above his colleagues. But he was less at ease with uncommitted students, and the insecurity of his status doubtless worried him. He left after three years, and it was disappointing that he felt he must make public his reservations about the College when the Chairman was fighting for its life in the Church Synod in 1975.

The arrival of Commander W. H. Heathcote, R.N. to be the new Bursar in September 1961 was by contrast outstandingly successful. After he had been appointed the Principal informed him :

"I advertised for a Matron, a Senior Lecturer in Mathematics, a Lecturer in English and a Bursar. I received three applications for the Matron's post, two for the Maths, none for the English and 375 for the Bursarship."

The decline of the Colonial Empire and the run-down of the Forces had come at a good time for Saltley. Commander Heathcote had a fine record in the Royal Navy, both in war and peace, and by his skill as a trouble-shooter he had probably saved a number of service reputations. He enjoyed a challenge and, having discovered Saltley to be a friendly place with a strong character of its own, he accepted the post offered to him. He soon found scope for his talents :

" . . . having noticed with admiration the well-stowed fire hoses, with gleaming brass connections, at the Main Entrance, he then discovered that the hose connections were the wrong size for the hydrants. During his walk round the College he noted with interest, in the Boiler House at the rear of South Block, a comfortable armchair with at its side a mound of tobacco ash about a foot high in the shape of a perfect pyramid. This was the Headquarters of the electrical and boiler maintenance department and the chair was the site from which the maintenance man, known to staff and students as the Colonel, directed operations . . . At this time there was only one filing cabinet used for all administrative records, sited at one of the entrances to the Principal's office . . . "

Commander Heathcote led an administrative revolution, and now took responsibility for all maintenance. He decided that an attitude of "financial stringency was no longer necessary" and set to work to improve the environment, especially for those who had to work in the College. He negotiated an eight-year plan with the Ministry to rehabilitate the old buildings and £30,000 became available for this purpose. Sadie Ward, cleaners' foreman, stated that for the first time the cleaners found themselves with some proper equipment for the job.

"The plan also provided sufficient money to permit proper washing-up facilities to be installed in the kitchen, and the removal of the galvanised sinks in the darkest corner where teams of women employed part-time worked for twelve hours each day under Dickensian conditions."

Heating was converted to oil which certainly helped to clean the air and would have been a distinct advantage if the boilers themselves had been less prone to break down during the colder week-ends.

One important administrative change had been effected before Heathcote's arrival and that was an agreement with Birmingham Corporation for their Restaurants Department to take charge of catering. It was a curious arrangement : the Corporation provided caterers and met the College requirements for food, using the low prices they had negotiated for their very large contracts ; in return the College paid the Corporation 10% extra on all food purchased (later changed to £1,000 annually) ; the College paid the salaries, provided the cooks and waitresses and equipment and offered advice about the menus. Heathcote found "that the scheme worked very well ... To improve the standard all that was required was an adequate allowance from the Government for the purchase of food." Unfortunately Canon Platten fought a long and indecisive battle with the Ministry on this issue, protesting that the allowance was inadequate for a men's college :

"Dear Harvey, 17th April, 1962.
We have this morning received instructions from the Ministry concerning estimates for 1962-63 ... I am much perturbed at the figure suggested for food. They propose, as a norm, 28/- per student week, which is considerably lower than that at which we have been running ... I do not believe it possible to satisfy men students at this rate of expenditure. I have already had a brush with them (the Ministry) over food costs as they said that we have been consistently high in this respect ... Apparently they refuse to recognise the fact that men eat a great deal more than women ... "

"Dear Harvey, 11th July, 1962.
For the moment I have suspended the battle over feeding costs, but I would like to know whether we are going to make any concerted effort to insist that men do eat more than women. Perhaps they would like to have their attention drawn to figures supplied in their own reports in order to convince them that men are : (a) taller, (b) heavier, and (c) usually more active physically, than girls of the same age."

Perhaps the most important element in Commander Heathcote's contribution to the later history of the College was the manner in which he relieved the Governors of any further financial anxiety in capital expenditure. This was achieved by intense and fruitful letting of the College during vacations and by the simple expedient of investing all money with the Church Central Board of Finance until it was required for use ; at first the Auditors were inclined to raise their collective eyebrows at this device, but the Commander, warmly and skilfully supported by the Principal, won the day. The Conferences which turned up and which demanded heavy duties from the administrative and domestic staff were varied and often colourful, including the English Association of Morris Dancers, the Algerian National Football Team throughout the World Cup Finals, Students of Thailand, and more than 250 nuns from many parts of Europe. The most celebrated visitors were doubtless the Red Army Choir, who stayed at Saltley during a bitterly cold week in April.

It didn't escape notice that the Choir, who complained that they couldn't sleep because they were so cold, had engaged rooms at the lower rate, in which heating was restricted, but that all the senior officers were billeted in hotels. In their leisure hours the Choir bought up large supplies of consumer goods from Saltley and elsewhere or took exercise by slowly pacing up and down the College paths clad in their long dark overcoats and trilby hats.

To the casual observer student life might have appeared to change little during this period. The round of dramatic activities, college plays, student revues, one-act plays in arena, continued to achieve high standards; in June, 1961, there was a memorable performance of 'Henry V' in the Quad with the Holy Acre as the central stage ; in 1962 there was a moving production of "The Long and the Short and the Tall" at which the dramatic tension was heightened by the presence in the audience of Bishop Wilson, himself so long a Japanese P.o.W. at Singapore. The three-year course gave a fillip to the general level of the Sports Clubs; all the clubs now ran two teams and badminton and basketball became major activities ; students who played together regularly for three years developed a fine team spirit and the performance of some sides reached a high level. The Soccer Team, 1963/64, was acclaimed by the 'Salt' as "the Team of the Year" having won 18 of its matches, which included opponents like the 'Colts' sides of Aston Villa, Coventry City, Wolverhampton and Walsall ; they were a delight to watch when they included Howard Riley, Leicester City's cup finalist outside right, John Mason and John Cocking, both Amateur Internationals. For a year or two an Easter Vacation tour in Germany was organised for the Soccer Club ; and tours in N. Devon or W. Wales for the Rugger Club. The Cricket Club were almost as exciting that year, although John Woodford, later to score a century for Yorkshire against Warwickshire, shone as a fast bowler rather than a batsman. Student societies were maintained at about the same level, although their leaders began to complain more frequently about student apathy. One society which lasted for a number of years was the Political Society, devoted to a general interest in politics rather than the pursuit of any particular philosphy ; this brought a number of well-known figures to Saltley — Roy Jenkins, Christopher Chataway, Sir Edward Boyle, John Stonehouse and the local M.P., Dennis Howell ; attendance remained small. During the Fifties the S.C.M. had flourished ; in 1963/64 the Christian Union was established and so successfully did it "unite Evangelican Christians of all denominations in one body" that it became a permanent feature of the life of the College, while the S.C.M. faded away. A College Dance Band still flourished and students organised Sunday afternoon concerts and a Dancing Club, which began as a vehicle of instruction but developed into one of the normal features of the social calendar. The 'stars' of the early Sixties were John Fyffe and Mick Jones, who formed the popular folk-singing group, the "Settlers", and eventually abandoned their course at Saltley for a life of recordings and professional music engagements, returning occasionally to entertain their old colleagues.

Senior Staff with Mr. Seaman, March 1978

W. Powrie, J. A. Kohler, B. V. Spence, C. W. Rowley, J. C. Kitchen, L. Raby, V. A. Mills, H. Jones, N. Cockin.
Rev. J. D. Murray, Miss P. A. Dixon, Miss A Brereton, R. D. H. Seaman, J. K. G. Taylor, W. R. Middleton.

"The Salt" for 1959 reads :
"The life of the Chapel changes little from year to year. The daily morning services have been conducted as usual by students . . . The normal Sunday service has been the Choral Eucharist, but this has not been attended as well as it might have been . . . "

"The Salt" for 1964 reads :
"We have been very discouraged in that attendance at the daily Chapel Services has not usually risen mucn above 60 . . . "

Later students might wonder why there was discouragement at such good congregations, but at least no one was complacent. In December 1959, the staff had a long discussion on "the Chapel in College life", but there was little agreement, except that the morning service should start at 9 a.m. to give non-residents a better opportunity to be present and that the proceedings should be known as College Morning Assembly. It is worth recording that on two occasions during this period full length addresses were given in Chapel by students and that in 1963 the annual Remembrance Day Service was organised by the Treasurer of the Students Union, M. J. Woodward, and that he successfully filled the body of the Chapel. One Sunday evening in February 1961, the B.B.C. Light Programme broadcast Suhday Half-Hour and a good congregation of staff and students sang lustily, especially Cwm Rhondda, which was always a Saltley favourite; what a pity that the Producer insisted on making the trite commertaries himself, since Canon Platten would have done a far better job ! The Institute Day Service in June, 1962 was held in the newly consecrated rebuilt Coventry Cathedral and was most memorable.

The Students Union celebrated the three-year course with a new constitution under which a succession of able students established a fair degree of administrative routine and autonomy, especially in financial matters ; much depended on the firmness and hard work of the Treasurers, who included in their number Gerald Haigh, the future author of four witty, informative and useful guides to a school teacher's life.

During the Spring of 1960, it had been decided that, following the success of the Bar at the May Balls, the College should obtain a Club Licence, a move much welcomed by the students but with reservations by some of the staff :

"Principal reported that he had received a request from the Students to give permission for the bar to be available more frequently. He asked members of staff for their views. It seemed to him there were three possible courses, namely : to open the bar only at the more formal College functions, to extend this facility to the informal fortnightly dances, or to allow the bar to open every Saturday night. In the subsequent discussion widely divergent views were held, but the idea of the remainder of the term being used as a period of experiment was generally agreed to. Nine votes were cast for opening the bar experimentally for the remaining formal and informal dances. Six votes were cast for reserving the bar for formal occasions. All other members abstained."   (Staff Minutes, 31st March, 1960).

As a result of this decision, a formal constitution for the St. Peter's College Union Society with the Principal as President and the Vice Principal as Secretary was drawn up and approved by the City Magistrates; members of the student union, 'paid up' members of the O.S. Association and members of the Academic Staff were members of the Society; the Staff protested when they were required to pay a subscription and this stipulation was withdrawn. Inevitably the constitution created anomalies about the control of the Student Common Room where the Bar was situated and difficulties in establishing agreement about Opening Hours, but it instituted what soon became a major amenity. The old Library on the ground floor of South Block became the club room and retained this function to its end.

"This year the profits of the Society are being used in the purchase of timber for a bar, which is nearing assembly in the craft shops. The bar is designed and constructed by second year craft students as a co-operative project; the lessons they learn from work of this nature they hope to apply to wood-working in schools . . . Anyone who has seen the work to date will agree that it has been designed and accomplished with great skill, a fact which will be appreciated by succeeding generations of students in this College." ('The Salt', 1963).

On a number of occasions Canon Platten stated that to him the strongest indication of a change to the Saltley order came when the College could no longer sit down together at meal times, and especially for the midday dinner. Breakfast had become a cafeteria meal in January 1960, although there was still a High Table with waitress service for the resident staff. Even before there was a third-year in existence, numbers at midday necessitated two sittings for dinner, but this proved most difficult to operate and in 1961 space-saving octagonal tables were acquired and the lecture room next to the Lodge became an over-flow for first-year students, while lodgers and day students of the second year continued to enjoy the dining hall. When the Student Union moved into South Block, the 'new' Common Room became a refectory for first-year dinners, but soon the refectory became the Senior Common Room and, with the greatest of reluctance, the students were left to a cafeteria meal in Hall while the Staff continued their formal meal in their new Common Room. which had been discreetly partitioned into two parts.

Desperate efforts were made to continue the traditions of Christmas Dinner with the staff wives as guests escorted by students; service was difficult but the overcrowding merely added to the conviviality of the occasion. Eventually, seats in hall were restricted to those students and staff who would be leaving the following June, plus the guests, while the remainder retreated to either the Refectory or the Assembly Hall under the presidency of the Vice Principal; communication was established between the two rooms so that speeeches and toasts could be enjoyed together, but on at least one occasion when the microphones broke down, the Vice Principal and his colleagues had to improvise. Everyone clung tenaciously to these customs.

This chapter would be incomplete without reference to a group of newcomers to Saltley in 1963, who rapidly established a firm place in everyone's esteem. This was the F.T.C. course, yearly from January to December. Most staff and students were somewhat vague about what F.T.C. stood for, but it was clear from their annual exhibition that they were men of very high technical and handicraft expertise, who were leaving industry or the Forces in order to become teachers. They were for the most part older men, whose contribution to the life at Saltley was valued by students and staff alike.

Chapter 16

While the colleges were in the throes of absorbing their three-year courses, the Government instituted a Prime Minister's Committee under the Chairmanship of Lord Robbins to :

"review the pattern of full-time higher education in Great Britain and in the light of national needs and resources to advise . . . on what principles its long-term development should be based . . . "

The Enquiry occasioned much consultation among College Principals, nationally and regionally and R. J. Harvey submitted a lengthy document by way of evidence, insisting that the Church of England was concerned to maintain its interest in teacher education and the colleges to which it had contributed £3,000,000 in capital since 1945, and making a number of suggestions, including the most tentative advocacy of "Liberal Arts Colleges". Canon Platten played his part in the public discussion, favouring some broadening of the basis of college studies by offering courses for "various kinds of social work — e.g. club leaders, hospital almoners, probation officers etc. . . . In Church Colleges a place might be found for ordinands also to do at least a part of their training . . . " With real insight into the internal politics of teacher education he wrote :

"One danger to which the country should be specially alert is that of parochialism — local students trained in local colleges to go back to work in the same locality. It would probably be better to free all Colleges from control by L.E.A.'s and place them under some nationally constituted body analogous to the University Grants Commission." (January, 1961).

"I am told there is a strong movement afoot to destroy the whole connection of the Colleges with the Universities and to include them with Technical Colleges and other Institutions under Regional Boards or Councils of Higher Education. The controlling voice in these Councils would be the Local Education Authority's. This development would be deplorable . . . " (July, 1961).

By 1976 these dangers had become realities.

The Report was published in October, 1963. It reflected the optimism of the Sixties and forecast booming conditions for Higher Education :

1962 — 216,000 students in Higher Education; 1973 — 390,000; 1980 — 560,000. Its proposals would increase public expenditure from £206 million to £506 million, but,

"we are convinced that no economic consideration need hinder their adoption if we as a nation desire the educational changes they will make possible".

Indeed, future developments were seen only in the context of expansion :

"In Chapter 11 we . . . recommended that by 1980 the number of students in the colleges should increase from the present total of about 50,000 to about 130,000 . . . we are convinced that in the long term a college with less than 750 students should be regarded as exceptional." (*para* 319).

These forecasts were reasonable for ten years and were made in good faith ; but it would have been interesting to have known the reaction of the Robbins Committee to different arithmetic, or to the need for retrenchment to meet an economic slump.

The Training Colleges were well satisfied by the main body of the recommendations. In future Training Colleges were to be known as Colleges of Education and should have independent Boards of Governors. Their enhanced status was linked to the revival of the old McNair proposal that they should be members of University Schools of Education who would take over the functions of the Institutes and, further, organise four-year B.Ed. degree courses for suitably qualified students of the colleges. The most revolutionary proposal was that Colleges of Education should be brought within the orbit of University administration and financed by a Grants Commission which "should not be accountable in detail to Parliament". This proposal never had a serious chance of adoption. One member of the Commission made his note of reservation :

"It may well be that some local education authorities have not shewn a sufficiently liberal attitude to the colleges ; if so, it can and should be changed. On the other hand, in many material respects . . . the Ministry of Education and local education authorities have no need to apologise for their record ;"

Both main political parties rejected this proposal and Local Education Authorities, some of which like Birmingham were due to lose their Colleges of Advanced Technology, would doubtless have resisted strongly losing control over the Colleges of Education that they had nurtured with civic pride. This was disappointing for the Voluntary Colleges which would have welcomed the close association with University administration and would have avoided the interminable and detailed communications which passed between the College and the Ministry. When the subject was discussed by the College Governors in June, 1964, when unfortunately Sir Lionel was unable to be present, Professor Jeffreys expressed the opinion

"that although stronger University representation on the Governing Body would undoubtedly be required it was not likely that any

100

difficulty would attach to maintaining the Anglican character of the College". (Governors' Minutes)

Most attention was concentrated upon the degree courses, the recommending of which was a triumph for the colleges. In a staff meeting held at the University shortly after the publication of the Report, Miss Rigg, Principal of the City of Birmingham College, who had been invited to speak for the Colleges — somewhat strangely, since she was certainly not the senior Principal available — pleaded for the adoption of the academic proposals, and expressed anxiety that if the University failed to respond the better students might be diverted to colleges outside the West Midlands. Indeed it was widely believed that there was no enthusiasm in the University at large for any closer association with the colleges or for a new type of degree ; some Principals of colleges hoped that the University would raise the status of the School of Education into a Faculty, able to take responsibility for the degrees, and of the Director to be a member of the University Council. Doubts about Schools of Education were not confined to Birmingham and they were echoed in a document presented to the Church Assembly by the Church Board of Education in January, 1964 :

"If the new policy is to work the Schools of Education will not only have to be accepted as a responsibility by the Universities but accepted ungrudgingly and gladly. This is asking much of the Universities."

It is interesting to speculate what would have happened if Robbins had opened widely the door for College of Education degrees to be made available through the National Council for Academic Awards, the formation of which the Report also proposed. Many hours were exhausted during the next few years in creating the new B.Ed. degree and these will be the theme of a subsequent chapter.

It was, however, the Robbins paragraph 319 stating that "a college with less than 750 students should be regarded as exceptional" that attracted most attention at St. Peter's. It was an unguarded and inflexible statement and at once caused the academic staff to become anxious about the security of the College. It made Canon Platten angry since it elevated academic values far above other values in teacher education, the argument being that only large colleges could provide that variety of academic expertise suitable for establishments preparing students for degrees. However, the paragraph certainly precipitated once more the problem of the long term future of the College and at once absorbed much of the Principal's time and effort, as will be seen.

"Dear Harvey,   26th February, 1964.
    Some of my colleagues are very anxious that we should consider the possibility of future expansion to something approaching the size which the Robbins Report thinks necessary for running a B.Ed. course, and although the actual implementation of such a scheme would

obviously depend upon financial conditions, at present quite unknown to us, they think we ought to be ready with an overall plan for putting the maximum possible buildings on present site . . . "

Perhaps there was some reassurance from this letter from the Ministry of Education (now overprinted — Department of Education and Science) :

"Dear Canon Platten,   10th July, 1964.
. . . . Perhaps I should say at the outset that because of the ideas put forward in the Robbins Report that in future colleges of less than 750 students should be regarded as exceptional, it does not follow that most colleges must expand to that figure in order to survive. There is nothing sacrosanct about the figure of 750, and although in the future many colleges will undoubtedly expand to that level and beyond, we see no reason why some of the smaller colleges should not continue without going much beyond their present size or effect a small expansion to a size below 750 . . . "

4 THE EXPANSION BECOMES AN EXPLOSION (1964-1968)

Chapter 17

At the Church Standing Conference of June 1967 Canon Herklots made his farewell address as Moderator of the Church Colleges and he chose as his theme the pluralistic society in which the colleges were now operating :

"they (students) may find it rather odd that the College to which they have come happens to be a Church college. They find the language of Christianity strange and unreal . . . They come also from what is at least partially a permissive society. Some of them may be specially on their guard here ; because they think that the Church exists to stop people doing things. They are at the same time against paternalism yet in favour of a close relationship with the members of the staff.

". . . And there are few things they dislike more than the sense of being got at. Some, at least, of the younger members of staff have similar characteristics. The situation has been complicated by the great increase in the size of the colleges. Principals and Chaplains face together, not one situation, but a series of overlapping and contradictory ones. Nor does time, in any recognisable way, appear to be on their side . . ."

A few months earlier at the Church Principals' meeting, one Principal "wondered if it were possible for colleges to have a common policy with regard to moral standards among young people seen against the back-ground of an increasingly permissive society. He found himself in a dilemma, for instance, with regard to the treatment of unmarried men who became fathers at College and were allowed to complete their courses, whilst young women who became pregnant were often forced to abandon their College careers".

After discussion the Principals wisely agreed "that no common policy could be determined and that, from a moral standpoint, each case should be viewed individually." These are but two examples of the remarkable pace of change in social 'mores', affecting all, and particularly young, people in Western Europe during the second half of the Sixties. It was the period of the first Wilson Labour Government, although many of the changes did not spring from political action and, where they did, the previous Conservative Macmillan government had also been equally responsive to the winds of change.

The diverse social upheavals were difficult for pre-war generations to assimilate and often created discord in the home as well as in university, college or school. Conflict was accompanied by challenge to existing authorities, religious, political and institutional, and showed itself in withdrawal from participation or in personal idiosyncracies in dress or appearance. It would have been undesirable for the Established Church or a Church College to be sheltered from the consequences of change and writers like John Robinson, Ronald Goldman and Richard Acland challenged both accepted beliefs and religious teaching principles and methods. Governors, Principals, staff and often many students themselves needed to adjust their values and to beware of striking moral attitudes about discipline or sexual behaviour, if they were to hope to achieve any sort of understanding with young people.

This need for resilience by those in positions of authority about matters long held precious may have appeared to be weakness and probably lay at the bottom of many of the criticisms levelled against students and young teachers in the early Seventies. "Revolting" students made readable material for the mass media, which seemed at one time to relish hostility and mutual confrontation. It is well to remember that many students in the Sixties emerged from social backgrounds which had no experience of higher education and did not understand its traditions. In the face of the cultural shock which young people could hardly avoid, it was right that Principals of Church Colleges should resolve that "each case should be viewed individually".

The explosion in numbers of students to be trained as teachers certainly complicated the difficulties, since it was achieved in an atmosphere of desperate urgency. The 7th report of the National Advisory Council, 1962, entitled "The Demand and Supply of Teachers, 1960-80" estimated that provided the Government raised the school leaving age, as it had undertaken to do, there would be a shortfall of teachers in maintained secondary and primary schools by 1975 of 76,000 : if junior school classes were to be reduced to a maximum of 30, then the shortfall would be 140,000. The figures were based upon forecasts in which birth rates and wastage played an important part and perhaps these were more imponderable than the assumptions warranted. In a letter to the Council's Chairman, the Minister wrote :

"I have already asked the training colleges to continue to crowd up their premises to the maximum and to forgo the measures of relief from overcrowding for which we had planned. I would hope that more could be done by taking in more day students into the residential colleges. I also propose to retain in being parts of training colleges and, in some cases, whole colleges at present scheduled to be given up . . . In addition, I intend to invite local authorities in the more densely populated areas to establish, as an emergency operation, some temporary colleges for day students in addition to the six so successfully opened last year . . . "

In fact these measures proved insufficient and subsequent Ministers, urged on by the urban Chief Education Officers, kept asking for more. There was a whole series of appeals to increase output during the Sixties — 1962, 1965, 1967 and 1968. In July 1965 the teacher supply situation seemed to have deteriorated so badly that the D.E.S. called on colleges to devise schemes with "box and cox" arrangements, or extra terms and indeed, the D.E.S. promised to smile upon any schemes which would cause the college "plant" to be used more intensively. This was discussed in a

Saltley Governors' Meeting in October when a little more warmth than usual may have been generated. Canon Platten proposed more lodgers and increased teaching accommodation but nothing more :

"Sir Lionel stated . . . that the shortage in the dioceses with which this College was associated were higher than the national average and some authorities were not able to provide the statutory requirements of education . . . he welcomed the action by the Principal but he feared that the D.E.S. would require us to do more . . . "

Sir Lionel was supported by Alderman Mrs. Smith who stated :

". . . unless we faced up to this challenge we should be failing in our duty, and the discomfort in College should be accepted, otherwise we should never have smaller classes and a longer school life for our children."

The Principal was supported by the Headmaster of King Edward's, Aston, who complained about the "drain of staff from schools" and by the Rev. G. R. Fishley, the Coventry diocesan representative, who was minuted as stating that "he did not recommend a lowering of standards in this College just to increase output". For once, the feeling of the meeting was against Sir Lionel and the Principal's recommendations went forward unchanged. The D.E.S. accepted them.

Undeniably there was a problem to be solved and possibly cooler judgment might have devised different expedients ; what happened was that new colleges were created, all existing colleges were expanded and some of them grew to mammoth proportions. Among the Church colleges, St. Luke's, Exeter was 300 in 1961 and 1,255 in 1968 ; St. John's, York 250 in 1961 and 954 in 1968. St. Martin's, Lancaster was a second new college to be built since the war (Christchurch, Canterbury being the first). In the West Midlands the local situation was even more startling ; we have already remarked upon the appearance of Wolverhampton Day College and the West Midlands College at Walsall ; to this was added Bordesley Day College and when the New Shenstone College was opened at Bromsgrove, the hutted encampment at old Shenstone was reopened as Summerfield College, which ran for a few years and then united with Shenstone.

Finally the projected Roman Catholic "Cornelia Connelly" College opened in 1968 at Bartley Green as Newman College. It is interesting to note that Westhill College with its long-standing Froebel courses was officially granted constituent membership of the Birmingham Institute in March 1964. Meanwhile the established local authority colleges had responded most positively to the appeals and had expanded at a great rate ; by 1963, Coventry's target was 1,000, Worcester's 960 and the City of Birmingham's 700, while their actual establishments in 1959 had been 360, 300, and 200 respectively. In 1967 colleges had been invited to submit further expansion proposals to the D.E.S. and they reported to the Delegacy in December ; Worcester proposed to go to 1,660, the West Midlands to 1,500, Dudley to 1,200, Hereford to 1,000 and Saltley to 750. In fact the D.E.S. could now see some prospect of reaching its target and reduced some of these bids. The expansion of 1968, in which Saltley shared, was of a more limited character.

The impact of this successful expansion upon the colleges and the teaching profession in general is controversial and outside the scope of this enterprise ; its effects upon Saltley are not. Much of the rest of the story will of necessity will be taken up by the changes which Saltley's own expansion wrought upon its life and character. There were for Saltley immediate problems in recruiting the numbers of new staff and students needed. The provision of suitable staff for the new colleges and the expanded old ones stretched the resources of the teaching profession to the utmost as the Advisory Council recognised :

"We must bear in mind . . . the claims of those other parts of the educational service which will (or should be) expanding at least as fast as the schools which are our direct concern. For example, the universities and the training colleges, given the expansion we have assumed, will need at least 10,000 extra teachers between them within this decade, while it is tentatively estimated that institutions of further education might need an additional 20,000 teachers by 1970."

Saltley's staff situation was complicated by the fact there was little suitable housing accommodation for families within two or three miles of the college and more than one tutor who had been appointed withdrew for domestic reasons before he could take the post. On a number of occasions Governors recommended readvertisement rather than make any appointments from those they had interviewed. In the circumstances Saltley was fortunate indeed to collect a body of staff as willing and as able as the team that Canon Platten was successful in assembling.

It would be idle to pretend that Saltley was a fashionable college and it may not have been high on the list of student choices ; this was less a reflection on St. Peter's than on the city of Birmingham itself which, despite its dedicated and progressive education department, found it hard to recruit the full number of teachers it needed. In addition, many of the buildings of St. Peter's hardly matched up to the post-war building that made new colleges attractive to students. It was only when students arrived and enjoyed the friendliness of the welcome and absorbed the ethos of the community that they began to understand the merits of the college. Again, it must be said that within these circumstances the achievements were remarkable and there was despite the slowness of recruitment, never any suggestion that Saltley-trained teachers were in any sense inferior to those of other colleges.

There was, however, no doubt in the mind of Canon Platten that the devices employed to increase the annual intake of the colleges would adversely effect both the colleges and the teaching profession. After the Governors' meeting in 1965 described above he wrote to Birmingham's Chief Education Officer :

"At the risk of being tedious I feel that I would like to continue a little the dialogue which we began at the Governors' meeting last Saturday . . .

"What we do fear is that all the schemes envisaged will have a deleterious effect educationally. We feel bound to be concerned about the quality as well as the number of teachers produced. I cannot help feeling that in some quarters this point is insufficiently appreciated. For instance, Mrs. Alderman Smith said that everything depended on getting the number of teachers as though number alone is all that matters . . .

"Actually the business of training requires far more than some personal expertise in teaching children, as we find with new members of staff. These of course are all recruited from the schools and usually on the ground of being good teachers, yet we find that they have a great deal to learn about methods of training when they come here. The suggestion, so often made, that we in the Colleges of Education are mere airy-fairy theorists is one which we greatly resent . . ."

Unfortunately there is no recorded reply to this letter.

One further chain of changes occurring during the second half of the Sixties was to Saltley's own environment. During the Fifties and early Sixties the process of slum clearance and relandscaping had been slowly progressing in the familiar areas of the 14 and 55 bus routes between Saltley and the city and this may have had the effect of making Saltley and Alum Rock almost 'inner ring' territory ; railway embankments, marshalling yards and derelict factories, like the 'three M's' factory in Arden Road, did not improve the environment although the atmosphere was certainly cleaner as steam trains gave way to electric. The "Rock" ceased to be a shopping centre for Little Bromwich, Washwood Heath and Ward End, and it tended to lose its air of lower-middle class respectability in favour of an uncared-for seediness. Most of the housing in the district was owned by landlords and in streets like College Road many of the leases were running out. This meant short-term lodging was cheap and comparatively easy to acquire, which was convenient for Saltley students who were seeking flats. But it also meant that Saltley became one of the down-town parts of the city to which immigrants, mostly coloured, were attracted during this period. It should be unnecessary here to dwell upon the social complications that the flood of immigrants brought, but it was not long before Saltley students came across them in teaching practices, youth work and other activities ; it made the tasks before the staff and students infinitely more challenging and, perhaps, more rewarding. It meant that the College became much more significant in its relationship to the community in which it was set than it had been before ; there was no comparable institution or group of buildings on the eastern side of the city once you passed Aston University.

The changes that have been described in this chapter provided the background for much of the last fourteen years in the story of St. Peter's College and although to the casual visitor it might not have appeared different from 1951 except for the extra buildings and the presence of women students, those who knew it well must have been aware of the efforts which were being made to adapt it to its new circumstances. It is interesting to read Editorials from the "Salt", written by some of its ablest students :

107

1966 "If the expansion envisaged is to be at all satisfactory in providing for the social, educational and individual welfare of the teacher in training, it is important that the liaison between all its members, which has always been a valued element of the Saltley tradition, should be preserved in the College."

1967 "The best get better, and the rest stay outside and rapidly lose interest. But the rest are always the most, and the prevailing mood becomes one of apathy and almost total non-participation . . . "

1968 "A warning to all 1st and 2nd years — it gets worse. Three years at Saltley have left me with an overall feeling of dissat- isfaction and disappointment . . . . Why don't the college authorities give up this absurd role of 'loco parentis' and leave the student body to arrange their own personal and moral affairs . . . " ("Saltette").

Chapter 18

If this narrative has succeeded in establishing any truths, one would be that planning of the sort called for in the mid-sixties depended entirely upon the initiative and the wisdom of the College Principal, aided perhaps by advice from his senior colleagues, from R. J. Harvey at Church House and, to a lesser degree at that time, from the Chairman of the Governors. It absorbed the last years of Canon Platten's Principalship. A number of interesting proposals were pursued and sadly they all proved abortive, but the story of the College would be incomplete without some account of them.

Of the most mysterious of these, no record exists in the College files, but when, in 1968, the Governing Body was being reconstituted it became known that the Chief Education Officer for Northampton had been nominated as a member by the Association for Education Committees and it was common knowledge that Northampton was interested in establishing its own College of Education. In fact he never took his seat, but it would be reasonable to surmise that someone, somewhere, had contemplated moving the College down the M1.

In 1961 when the Anglican Order of the Sacred Heart moved away from their buildings near the Pelham in Little Bromwich and their hostel was used by Saltley students as a lodgings base, Harvey suggested that the Governors might seek to purchase these buildings for use as a supplementary residential block ; but this was firmly vetoed by the Bishop of Birmingham who was one of their trustees. Also in 1961 it became known that the leases for the block of buildings opposite the College on the junction of College and Bridge Roads would be closing within a few years and that the College would have an opportunity to purchase the freehold of this bit of land. Canon Platten raised the question of borrowing the necessary money from the Church, but the Governors at their meeting of February 1962 agreed to accept the recommendation of their Finance Committee and take no action. Canon Platten was disappointed :

"Dear Harvey, 2nd February, 1962.

. . . . We have not taken any further steps concerning the possible purchase of property at the corner of Bridge Road and College Road. A report which we obtained from a firm of Surveyors was not encouraging and, unless there was a definite understanding that the Ministry would sanction the building of a further Hostel on the site, it would appear to be a risky venture for us to purchase it now. I still feel myself that a future generation may say we lack boldness, but my Finance Committee is all for caution . . . ."

The Governors' lack of interest still rankled two years later :

"I thought, at the time, that it was a mistake for the Governors to refuse the offer of the Bridge Road property which might have provided a site for a further building in the future, but as the lease does not expire till about 1970, they would not commit themselves. Now it looks as if we might be in a position of needing just such a site."

Seven years later the buildings opposite the College, including the familiar King's Removals Depot, were demolished and the land was levelled and turfed. Principal Buckmaster sought permission to purchase the land with a view to building a Sports Hall thereon as a joint venture between the City and the College Governors and he received some support from Denis Howell, the College's M.P. Unfortunately it was no longer available as freehold and the City Estates Office insisted upon a Ground Rent of £2,710 per annum for a 75 years lease ; on these terms it all fell through, and the site was taken by the Roman Catholics for an extension to their Rosary School.

In August 1964, Canon Platten submitted to the strong pressure of Harvey to have the College examined by a London firm of architects who had supervised the expansion of a number of Church colleges, and their report was duly received. It stated that :

"The disposition of buildings on the ground is rather unimaginative, too much space being allocated to the Principal's house, for example, and too much attention has been paid to the sanctity of the hockey pitch."

Neither of these statements was calculated to attract the report to Canon Platten nor was the main proposal :

"a new quadrangle is to be formed adjacent to Administration . . . No attempt should be made to match existing buildings except in colour tone."

This new quadrangle would have covered a significant area of the existing field, which was held by many, including Canon Platten and most

109

of the students, to be the best residential amenity which the College possessed. The Report must have reinforced Canon Platten's determination to find some other site which could be developed without the necessity of ruining the Saltley site.

Two desirable projects presented themselves. The first of these, about three miles from the College, was Castle Bromwich Hall, one of the lovely ancestral homes of the Earl of Bradford, an 18th century mansion, standing in grounds of 11 acres on the hill in the old village of Castle Bromwich well above where the M6 motorway now runs. The Hall had been occupied since the war as a hostel for apprentices of the General Electric Company, but they were not renewing the lease. The condition of this lovely 18th century house was "far better than he expected" according to the College architect and Canon Platten lost no time in marshalling support. To the faithful Harvey he wrote :

"If we are ever to expand to the size envisaged by the Robbins Report, we ought to keep our eyes open for additional land. I have learned that Castle Bromwich Hall . . . might become available for development . . . Had it been available 17 years ago, we might have thought of transferring the whole of our College to such a site. Now we have done too much building here to think of abandoning Saltley, but a second section of the College, only three miles away, would be quite practicable."

One advantage was that the Hall stood in a "green belt" area between the city and Warwickshire so that Lord Bradford was not subject to the temptation of selling the land at inflated value to house-property developers. The feelers which Canon Platten extended received a promising response. In July, 1964, the D.E.S. gave a cautious government approval :

"No expansion programme additional to the present one has yet been authorised, and you will appreciate, I am sure, that we cannot at this point in time come to any decision about the future development of St. Peter's. At the same time we recognise the necessity for further looking ahead especially where, as at St. Peter's, there are site limitations . . . We are not opposed in principle to the idea of the College operating on two sites . . . a distance of only 3½ miles between sites would certainly present no serious obstacles to a split organisation, but I must say that we have very serious doubts about taking on such a costly building as Castle Bromwich Hall. It often turns out to be less costly in cases of this kind to build new premises than to convert and maintain a "stately home" which, despite possible aesthetic attractions, may well have only a limited functional value."

A response from Harvey contained "a most interesting, I would say exciting, suggestion." He had received a visit from the Secretary of the Education Department of the Congregational Union, who, with the Presbyterians, had proposed a joint venture with the Anglicans in either founding a new college or making a major contribution to rebuilding

110

an old one ; Birmingham, with a large nonconformist tradition and a flourishing University seemed to be ideal for the purpose, which, once the Chairman had been informed, must remain totally confidential. Canon Platten, after his experiences in South India, was passionately in favour of church unity and, much attracted by the prospect of being Principal of a Birmingham Christian College, redoubled his efforts.

The Governors had responded with little enthusiasm and gave the impression that they would not support a scheme that left the College permanently divided upon two different sites. Canon Platten had discovered that Lord Bradford had a further piece of land, still within the "green belt" and up to 22 acres in all, which he might be persuaded to sell, so that it would become possible to redeploy the whole College in time.

Early in 1965 he received a quotation of £100,000 for the Hall and about ten acres of land. It seems that after years of legal squabble His Lordship's advisers expected the use of the land to be derestricted and their selling prices were therefore almost within range of the property developers. It was too much for the College Governors and for the Nonconformists. On 1st April, Canon Platten visited the D.E.S. and reported the next day to Harvey :

"As far as Castle Bromwich is concerned all he would say is that we should keep an eye on the situation and if necessary, revive the suggestion when and if the Minister makes a pronouncement about further expenditure. I suggested that if undue delay occurred we might lose the possible source of our share of the cost (without, of course, mentioning the nature of that source), but he replied that if for such a reason we pressed him for an immediate decision the answer could only be "No"—so that I think we have to leave it for the time being."

In November 1965 the D.E.S. "territorial officer" visited Saltley. Canon Platten was able to report that Lord Bradford had reduced his asking price, although he had been unsuccessful in persuading the "Council for Historic Buildings" to show any interest in sponsoring the repair of the Hall should the College complete its purchase. Finally, in May 1966 the D.E.S. objection to taking on responsibility for historic buildings caused them to reject any further consideration of the project. It was raised once more in slightly different circumstances in 1967, but really all hope had died.

Canon Platten continued, undaunted, to search for a new site for the College or for part of it. It was while he was looking in the Solihull/Warwickshire area that he came across "Sans Souci" in October 1966 and at once moved into the attack.

"This is a substantial modern house, built in 1920, which was recently presented by the widow of the original owner to the Borough of Solihull . . . It appears that the Borough does not know what to do with it and would welcome its use as a branch of a College of Education and would be prepared either to sell it outright or let it on a long lease with some of the adjacent land.

111

"The accommodation in the house includes six rooms which could be used as lecture rooms, a large well-equipped kitchen and a built-in garage of 88 sq. ft. which could easily be adapted as a refectory. The whole is in an excellent state of repair and decoration . . .

"There are about 5 acres of land attached to the house itself including a level grass area which could immediately be used as a sports field for any major game ; and it would be possible to acquire or rent on long lease up to 15 further acres mostly in the Green Belt."

In a number of ways this seemed an attractive proposition, especially the possibility of a ready-made playing field. The College had many contacts with schools in the Borough and was held in high esteem there ; it would have compensated for the decline in interest of the Birmingham City Education Committee and given Saltley a new advocate within the corridors of educational power. Unfortunately there were snags ; the site was seven miles away from Saltley and a much more difficult road journey than the one to Castle Bromwich. But the major snag was that a new piece of link motorway was projected which, though plans were not finalised, looked as if it would sever the proposed Saltley annexe into two parts. This was the chilling burden of the D.E.S. reply :

"I have been deliberately discouraging in this letter and put the objections which we see to your proposal. It does not mean that the matter is closed so far as we are concerned but if you want to go ahead with your proposal to acquire the house at Shirley, then clearly we shall want you to let us have a carefully reasoned justification."

The matter was discussed by the Standing Committee of the Academic Board and it was agreed that it would be unwise to risk the possibility of the motorway and the project was abandoned. For once Canon Platten's spirits were depressed. He wrote to the Chairman on 30th December, 1966:

"if this idea is abandoned we continue with the proposal to erect additional buildings at Saltley . . . Yet I must confess my own misgivings about continuing to build in this difficult and unattractive neighbourhood. Certainly had we been told in 1947 that within 20 years we should be erecting buildings at the cost of £340,000 we should have explored the possibility of moving to another site ; but the extensions have been piece-meal and each one has seemed as though it would be the last."

When Canon Platten wrote that letter he had no foreknowledge of the cost of the Library and Resources Centre to be built in the Seventies at a cost of a further £250,000. Seven months later, in July 1967, the D.E.S. published a letter inviting Colleges to submit schemes for the establishment of "Outposts" for mature students. As soon as he had assured himself that Castle Bromwich Hall and Sans Souci were still available, this time on a short lease, Canon Platten appealed for permission to undertake such an enterprise ; he put the case for either Castle Bromwich or Shirley and added :

The Old College.

"For either of the above sites we would contemplate having a group of 30—40 older candidates who would complete the course before another group was admitted. A member of staff residing in or near the house would be in charge and the remainder of the teaching would be undertaken by staff coming out from the College as required."

The Solihull scheme came close to approval before it was in fact rejected. Dudley Love, Director of Education for the Borough, wrote warmly :

"I have been considering the proposal for the establishment of an "outpost" of St. Peter's College in Solihull in terms of the number of mature students attending day colleges from this area, some of whom are students at St. Peter's. So far as we are concerned we should welcome any additional facilities for students from this area to train as teachers as near as possible to their homes and the outpost you have in mind in Shirley might well fill this need . . . May I say that we should be most happy to cooperate in any way that we can with you and your staff in the arrangements for setting up such an outpost. . . ."

The D.E.S. must have been impressed by the Director's support, and requested some further information in a letter dated 18th December, in which they flatly rejected once more the Castle Bromwich venue. Finally the issue turned upon the reaction of the Principal of Bordesley Day Training College to the proposal. This should have been considered earlier and it was no surprise when Mrs. Roe stated in forthright manner that indeed she would see such an outpost as an invasion of her territory. To be fair to Mrs. Roe she was probably correct and care ought to have been devoted to emphasise those aspects of teaching, both secondary and male, where St. Peter's could have acted in a complementary role to Bordesley College. It was sad that contacts established here between St. Peter's and Solihull could not have been developed and consolidated, since Sir Lionel Russell was on the point of retirement from Birmingham and a strong relationship with L.E.A.s was one of the cardinal necessities for all Colleges of Education after 1945. The final rejection of the Sans Souci Outpost scheme came in a letter in March, 1968.

The consequence of this failure to discover a suitable new site was that further adaptations and new buildings were required at Saltley. In May 1966 the Governors had agreed to admit women students (to be related in the next chapter) and this required adjustments in accommodation. But chiefly the need was for teaching and tutorial accommodation and improvements in Student Union facilities, since there would be increased numbers of day students and 'lodgers' who would still need to base their lives on the College premises. The stern men of Curzon Street were surprisingly generous in the allocation of public funds, as the nation staggered from one 'Stop-Go' crisis to another. Indeed it was remarkable how friendly relations were sustained, well illustrated by this short exchange of letters in September 1966 :

"Dear Platten,
I should like to thank you for giving so much of your time to Evans, Loyd (sic) and myself when we came to the College last Thursday. I hope to be able to write to you soon about the new building work which we discussed.
Yours sincerely,
E. B. Granshaw."

"Dear Granshaw,
Thank you for your letter of September 23rd. The gratitude is on my side for your willingness to consider our proposals for expansion and to offer us a share in the limited resources available for further building . . .
Yours sincerely,
T. G. Platten."

A variety of projects was embarked upon : a new teaching block, later known as the Michael Parker Building and designed to house Geography, Mathematics, French and Religious Knowledge Departments ; a new centre for the Art Department on a floor above the Gymnasium at the end of the Adderley Building ; a new house adjacent to the Principal's House for the College Porter ; a one-storey building parallel to the South Block for student common room purposes ; the enclosure of the South Lodge area in order to create a students' foyer ; old South Lodge became a set of small rooms, designed to be day student study rooms ; increased toilet and laundry facilities ; the extension of the biology laboratories. All these and other developments were effected during the last years of Canon Platten's Principalship, as well as a considerable programme for the maintenance of the fabric, arranged by separate negotiation between Commander Heathcote and the D.E.S.

By these means it was possible to squeeze a quart into a pint pot. It is curious that the students themselves, men and women, never complained about being overcrowded, although they were ready to grumble about other things. Certainly the College became a much noisier place to live in, but it was able more easily to retain its strong sense of togetherness.

Chapter 19

Before the end of 1966 Canon Platten had arranged to meet D.E.S. officials to discuss with them a teaching block "to house one or two Departments in conditions comparable to those of other Colleges". St. Peter's would stay at Saltley. But would the College succeed in recruiting enough students to justify its continued existence ? There had long been anxieties among the senior members of staff on this score ; in 1952 when Saltley held the field almost alone the Principal complained to the D.E.S. about the shortage of suitable men candidates. Since then there were many Midland competitors offering excellent living and teaching facilities, and, although the College entry had managed to keep up with the modest

115

expansion undertaken and although the students included many men whose standards and achievements were well in line with the past, there was also a long tail of weaker students. It seemed improbable that the annual entry could be raised to 200 to meet the Robbins minimum requirements unless the entry could be extended to women. There was, too, a feeling abroad that the introduction of women staff and students to the College would genuinely improve the character of its life and work.

Canon Platten made no secret of his opposition to the admission of women students to St. Peter's. His long and excellent experience had thrived on men's communities and he probably had little taste for the kind of problems thrown up by mixed ones. He sensed that St. Peter's traditions and ethos were masculine and he believed that it would be a mistake to depart from them. The "Salt" Magazine 1959, contained an article written by him and entitled : "The Future of Saltley" and its second paragraph was :

"Saltley will remain a College for men only."

When, in March 1963, the Governors had received a delegation from the staff, containing the Vice Principal, J. H. Hamnett and P. Dunn, they had firmly refused to consider the admission of women students.

The subject was next publicly aired during a Lent Term meeting, 1966, of the Standing Committee of the Academic Board and Canon Platten realised that the issue was serious enough to summon a meeting of the full Academic Board, which at that time consisted of the whole staff. A lively meeting followed in the College Library and, when the Principal called on the staff to vote on the issue of the admission of women students, only one vote was cast against it. The time had come to appeal to the Governors, who were summoned to a special meeting one Saturday morning early in May. The Principal wrote a letter :

"I have mentioned at previous meetings that we have been disappointed this year at both the number and quality of applicants . . . This is no doubt due in part to the fact that while the total number of male applicants for Colleges of Education over the country as a whole shows no increase, more women's colleges have been encouraged by the D.E.S. to become mixed and mixed colleges have been urged to admit a larger proportion of men . . .

"The majority of my colleagues have reached the opinion that in defence of its future this college also must become mixed. While it is a policy which I am very reluctant to urge myself, I feel that my colleagues must have an opportunity of presenting their views to the Governors . . ."

The Principal's letter evoked an unusually good response and 17 Governors were present to meet an Academic Board deputation of six, headed by the Vice Principal. A full account of the arguments advanced was included in the minutes of the meeting ; Canon Platten made no attempt to influence the discussion and one Governor only, Canon Fishley from the Coventry Diocese, suggested "that there might be some advantage in staying a single-sex College" ; the Bishop of Lichfield, making a rare appearance, "stated that the modern trend was towards co-education and he felt that we should welcome it." Sir Lionel Russell, returning to his oft-repeated theme, "felt that we should aim at becoming a larger College." The motion to admit women students into residence from September 1967 was carried and the Governors appointed a small working party to consider College numbers. An unexpected bonus was the proposal of Sir Lionel that the Governors should "invite the Vice Principal plus one member of Staff, elected by the Academic Board to attend future meetings".

The decision having been made, Canon Platten set himself to implement it to the best advantage; the Institute of Education agreed, perhaps with a few surprised Principals; the D.E.S. agreed without hesitation and despatched their experts to discuss the necessary plumbing arrangements. The changes were made with little fuss and because of the demands for day-student places it was possible to phase mixed education into St. Peter's gradually. It is true that there had already been one or two women engaged on shorter courses and non-resident : a number, for example, on the one-year supplementary mathematics course ; Annette Houghton in 1961, on the post-graduate course, who starred in the College performance of "Tiger at the Gates" as Helen of Troy ; Betty Gaukroger, who after a spell as a missionary in India, served for a year in the Bursar's office on the College accounts, qualified for a course which Canon Platten designed for her and rapidly became Saltley's first Headmistress.

After the Governors' decision in May 1966, seven women, most of them married, were admitted to the one-year Post Graduate course for the coming September and nine to the first year of the three-year course ; these 'nine' single girls had an unenviable task since there were at that time year-lectures at which their presence (or absence) was especially noticeable amid so many men ; they proved to be a charming and gifted group and shone particularly during teaching practice ; it would have been difficult for them to have realised everyone's rather unreasonable expectations ; one, Gillian Day, became Vice President of the Student Union, the result perhaps as much as anything of the men students' desire to welcome them into the community.

The academic year, 1966/67, was spent interviewing both staff and students and, although it did not at first prove easy to attract well qualified women staff in some departments of the College work, six were appointed to the staff. These included Anne Brereton to be Dean of Women Students and it was indicative of her dedication to the College and the warm humanity with which she presided over the women students that the Governors appointed her to be the College's last Vice Principal ten years later. Pat Dixon, one of the first to be appointed, remained till the end and contributed tirelessly to the internal life of the community. Pat Brookfield, a dynamic teacher of history, became Secretary of the Committee to save the College in its final appeals and it was not through lack of energy on her part that the efforts were unsuccessful.

117

It took some time before the education world believed that St. Peter's had taken so irrevocable a step and during the first year student applications rolled in slowly and in paper qualifications they were disappointing ; there was some comfort to be gained from the fact that few of them transferred to Universities in the traditional general post after 'A' Level results were known. In subsequent years there was no flood of first preference applications, but the level of qualifications gradually improved and passed that of the men ; in one year only, 1971, did the number of women entrants actually exceed that of the men on the three year course. The geographical pattern of entry closely resembled that of the men and the strong contingent of students which arrived every year from between Tyne and Trent was maintained. In academic work the women certainly brought added numbers, although not always strength, to the English, History and Religious Studies Departments and to the Art Department now housed in its new studios above the Gymnasium. But there were also a number of mature women day students who, besides adding quality to academic work, were to play a lively role in the cultural and religious life of the College. The College did not accept women applicants for the main Physical Education course, although it was possible for them to offer P.E. on a subsidiary level. The Drama Department became popular and contained some most capable performers ; the wives of members of Staff found fewer opportunities than in the past to lend active support to the College theatre. The one-year postgraduate course had a remarkable expansion during this period from 13 in 1965 to 90 in 1971, 48 of whom were women. Many of these were highly qualified academically and offered themselves in shortage teaching subjects, like modern languages, mathematics and science, although they often lacked the confidence in front of classes of children enjoyed by their "three-year course" sisters.

One effect of the increased size of the College intake from 1965 was that more students whose homes were outside the West Midlands had to live (in digs or flats) off the campus. The policy agreed with the students was that all of these would be allotted a room in College during their first year and women students during their second year as well. Otherwise only those who held some student office contributing towards the running of the community life could be offered rooms in College. In addition the best accommodation in College in the Lyttleton and Adderley Blocks was reserved for women residents after 1967. Men students accepted cheerfully enough this privileged status that was given to the women, although men living out of College probably often made what some may have thought unreasonable demands of their girl friends for the use of their rooms in College and even on occasion, washing and bathing facilities.

The first large contingent of women students arrived in September 1967 ; the only demonstrations of male chauvinism came from some of the sports clubs, and these were short-lived and conducted with good humour. After the first year, women staff and students were accepted in Senior and Junior Common Rooms as if they had always been there. There were some grounds for disappointment ; girls made little contribution to St. Peter's long sporting traditions ; and the fruitful association which was enjoyed with Anstey College continued for mixed athletic matches. The girls played little direct part in the politics of the student union, although they may have exercised more influence upon student opinion than was apparent. There were notable exceptions, including Barbara Courts (Mrs. Kockelbergh) who courageously accepted the office of President of the Union in the middle of the Lent Term, 1973, when its incumbent suddenly resigned. There was both surprise and disappointment that few of the girl residents were prepared to give active support to the College chapel which continued to depend largely on the loyalty of a few men. At no time did the College contain as many as 40% women students, since the men's P.E. and Handicraft courses dominated the intake. It would have been unreasonable therefore to expect the women students to exercise a predominant influence upon the 'mores' or the morals of the College ; there is little evidence that they attempted to do so. Indeed it is possible that with the admission of women students it became more difficult to maintain the exacting standards that had existed in the forties and fifties in punctuality, attendance and dress. On the other hand, the girls who came to St. Peter's did not enjoy some of the home comforts to be found in newer establishments, and they had to learn to become teachers in a difficult environment ; but most of them stuck to the task with splendid vitality and good humour ; they rapidly absorbed from the men the traditions associated with life at Saltley and, by and large, became as proud of the College as most of their predecessors.

Chapter 20

The Robbins Committee Report, published in October 1963, had recommended that the colleges of education should be linked to Universities through Schools of Education, that Universities should award a Bachelor of Education degree for suitable college of education students after a four year "concurrent" course, that is to say embracing both degree and professional teaching qualification, and that the colleges should be administratively as well as academically linked to the Universities. Six years later, in July 1969, the first half dozen Saltley students achieved a B.Ed. Degree. The intervening years were engrossed in an absorbing struggle to achieve this result. By 1976, the B.Ed. was operating as a four-year Honours Degree course in Birmingham University in a way which offered to the Colleges almost all they would have asked for in 1963. In 1975, however, it was agreed to operate a three-year B.Ed. degree course and planning had to begin all over again. At all points St. Peter's staff were heavily engaged.

British Universities, especially Oxbridge and the 19th century group of 'Red Brick' Universities, of which Birmingham was one, cherished their academic freedom to award degrees without any interference by non-academic bodies, particularly government, central or local. There must have been lively suspicion in more than one University Senate that they were going to be required to establish a new degree they did not want, for students who were external to their authority, and who had been taught by staff they had not appointed. The new 20th century Universities saw possibilities for development out of a closer association with colleges of education and, since they themselves had sprung out of state initiative, they were less anxious about dictation from above, and quickly indicated that they would be pleased to establish the new degree. The older Universities, although subject to strong local pressures, were slow to commit themselves.

It was not a good omen that the Vice Chancellor of Birmingham had long ceased to show any public interest in the activities of the Institute of Education or to attend the meetings of its Delegacy. Early in 1964 Professor Jeffreys announced his intention to retire as Director of the Institute at the end of the academic year and made no secret of the fact that he believed that some other person might be more successful than himself in fostering good relationships with the University hierarchy at this most important time. His departure was much regretted at St. Peter's, where he had recently become a Governor. No successor was made to Professor Jeffreys until Professor Hilliard arrived more than three years later to occupy the post of Warden of the Colleges Division of the new School of Education. In the meantime Professor Peel, distinguished educational psychologist, agreed to accept the role of "acting" Director and he worked hard to build up an effective link between the University and the Colleges.

In November, 1963, the Delegacy established a Working Party to "consider the implications of the Robbins Report . . . and to submit a report in the first instance to the Delegacy "; but Professor Jeffreys warned the meeting that "it would be better to wait until the situation had crystallised before putting forward any recommendations to the University Senate". Canon Platten was one of the two College Principals placed on this Working Party. In March 1964 Professor Jeffreys reported to the Delegacy that the University Senate had been required to make known its views about Robbins to the University Grants Committee, but that these were still under discussion by the Faculty Boards and Senate itself. Nine months later Professor Peel informed the Delegacy that, although the Senate had received a copy of the Delegacy's Working Party report, it had not been prepared to consider it until the Secretary of State had declared his intentions. This was done eight days later in a carefully guarded statement :

"The Government . . . are glad to know that most Universities have expressed their readiness to consider making degrees available to suitable students, subject to appropriate arrangements for the safeguard of standards, and they hope that the universities will now proceed to work out with the colleges the form which such courses should take . . . "

University administrators doubtless took note of the absence from the Government statement of any promise of financial aid which might accrue from participation with the colleges, especially as the Secretary of State had firmly closed the door against the Robbins suggestion that the Colleges should be brought within the financial orbit of the Universities.

In March, 1965, it was announced at the Delegacy that the Senate had in February established a Joint Board of Studies "to consider and report on the proposal to establish the degree of B.Ed." and that, ominously, only two representatives from the Institute of Education were to be members, as against ten representatives of the Faculties of Arts, Science and Commerce ; in addition two College Principals were to be co-opted, one of whom would be Canon Platten.

In the meantime the colleges of the Birmingham Institute had become restless at the lack of decision and action and pointed out the advantage that some other colleges enjoyed in recruitment, because they had quickly been able to advertise degrees, and the likely consequences of this procrastination for the teaching profession within the West Midlands conurbation. Colleges were in the middle of departmental developments and new appointments, and the most tempting bait to be able to offer new members of staff was the opportunity to share in the degree work. There was some advantage to St. Peter's in having its Principal established on the Joint Board, since he was able to gauge progress ; one small consequence was that he was able, early in 1965, to insert into the College prospectus an amendment slip which stated :

"It is expected that a four-year course for a B.Ed. degree of Birmingham University will be instituted, and will be available for suitably qualified candidates entering Training Colleges in September, 1965. The degree will be of the standard of a General Honours two subject degree . . . ."

"Applicants who are interested are invited to write to the Principal for any further information which may be available."

In reality the colleges were now, eighteen months after the publication of the Robbins report, only at the beginning of a long and hard journey before success was achieved. The Working Party had already revealed some of the problems, and there were others remaining to be exposed. There was general agreement that for the first two years certificate and degree students should pursue the same course, which would have predominantly professional interests. Beyond that there was much lack of confidence in the colleges. The Joint Board established that during the third year a prospective graduate would need to fulfil the requirements of the Certificate, which included an extended period of final teaching practice, and also at an appropriate time to take qualifying examinations in Education and his Principal Subject to be marked by University staff to determine entry into the fourth year. In fact, of Saltley's first batch of B.Ed. candidates, out of 24 qualified persons at the end of their second year in July 1967, only six proceeded into the fourth year in September

1968. During the fourth year the student would receive three day's teaching a week in the University before his final ordeal by examination.

There were a number of anxieties for the colleges, some of which were made public at the Delegacy in December, 1965, by Saltley's Vice Principal representing college staffs and by Dr. Cornwell, speaking for his own college at Walsall. Would the staffs of the colleges be able to participate in teaching their own students or others in the more advanced work? Would the university insist upon laying down detailed syllabuses for the earlier years of the degree, which must inevitably affect certificate work especially in the smaller colleges, where it would be necessary usually to teach degree and certificate students together with the same syllabus? Would the University be prepared to admit students to the degree course after two years work on the certificate course on college recommendation, even though students did not possess the faculty requirements? Above all, would the University be prepared to recognise for the Principal Subject part of the degree those subjects which were taught in secondary schools like Handicraft, Drama and Home Economics, but which were not taught in the University? The first two of these subjects were of much importance to St. Peter's, especially Handicraft which comprised a significant proportion of the annual student in-take and in which there were far too few well-qualified candidates. The answers to these questions emerged only slowly and were not always favourable.

Regulations for the degree were approved by the Senate in February 1966, and these enacted that Boards of Studies should be instituted for each subject of the grouped degree and each Board should have five representatives appointed by the University Department concerned and five by the colleges, their deliberations being serviced by the administrative staff of the Education Department. These boards were to determine the syllabuses and lay down the detailed arrangements. In the matter of decision making, communication between the colleges now became most urgent. There were two Principals on the Joint Board of Studies and five collegiate representatives on the subject boards. But there were eleven colleges engaged ; no arrangements were made for the college representation to circulate regularly and fairly ; the Certificate Boards of Studies could not discuss B.Ed. matters ; the colleges needed therefore to organise costly and time-consuming meetings of their own and college departments realised for the first time how little they knew of each others' doings. This ignorance was nothing, however, compared to that of the University Departments, even the Education Department, about the work and life of the Colleges of Education. This ignorance explains the deep suspicion the University staff felt about the academic standards of the colleges ; it was understandable although not justified. All the colleges, like the University itself, had a wide range of students ; the best ones were very good. Some university staff were most helpful and cooperative and the colleges owed much to their goodwill ; others were obstructive and difficult from the beginning. But there were difficulties in most of the Boards of Studies, which were only slowly overcome. The University

English Department, daunted by the large numbers of potential candidates, insisted that the English course must have a substantial element of linguistics despite college protests ; on the other hand the University History Department accepted much against their will a particularly liberal range of college courses and examination papers in the 3rd and 4th years. Drama was not accepted as examinable by the University Drama Professor and the Maths Department clung tenaciously to the reasonable but quite impracticable proposal that all B.Ed. maths should be concentrated in one college. In Physical Education there were deep divisions of opinion between the college and University representatives and at first the University P.E. Department refused to accept the St. Peter's submission at all ; this would have been a most serious and unfortunate event and Canon Platten requested that the University P.E. department should make a second visit to Saltley at which he invited them to spell out their requirements ; with the assistance of the college science department and the purchase of new scientific equipment, the University was persuaded to reverse its ban ; one consequence was that there was a sharper difference here between degree and certificate courses than in any other subject.

In July 1966, when the first group of students were about to be registered, the University received the news that the government would not make extra funds available through the U.G.C. for a B.Ed. Honours degree and therefore fourth year teaching in the University would have to be abandoned. Senate decreed that Boards of Studies would proceed under new regulations to work out an Ordinary degree taught entirely within the colleges ; the University Departments would share in the process of examination. There was at the time much disappointment, but in practice this reduced a little of the pressure on the colleges and enabled the University/College enterprise actually to get under way. Slowly during the next ten years, the University modified its attitudes and a more satisfactory relationship was built up — four Principals were admitted to the Joint Board ; Letters of Credit were permitted and then Honours degrees, taught entirely within the colleges.

In July 1965, it was announced that the Senate had agreed to the implementation of another Robbins' recommendation by the formation of a School of Education. This was to be governed by its own Board directly under the Senate, which would take authority for all education activities — research, postgraduate certificates, responsibilities hitherto borne by the Institute ; it would be organised into four divisions, each headed by a Professor or, in the case of the Colleges division, a Warden with professorial status. Professor Burroughs came to Saltley one day to explain this development to the Staff. It did seem at the time that the University had missed a golden opportunity to create a Faculty of Education with sole responsibility for the B.Ed. degree ; by this means it might have been possible to break away from the idea of a "joint-subject" degree and establish in the colleges a genuine professional graduate qualification, which is what the St. Peter's staff had always hoped for.

123

The creation of the Board of the School of Education had serious political implications, which did not directly affect St. Peter's. It meant that the academic control of work in certificates as well as degree and in-service courses was the immediate responsibility of the University — at a time when the government had decided that administrative and financial arrangements would NOT be handled by the University. All colleges had as it were two masters and the Delegacy, the point at which they officially met, had become powerless. The Delegacy would continue to exist, but as a :

"deliberative, consultative and advisory body, which would also have the function of planning the supply and, in broad terms, the training of teachers for the Area. Its recommendations would be passed to the Board of the School which could transmit such recommendations to the Senate."

(Professor Peel, Delegacy, March 1966).

Sir Lionel Russell, who rarely missed Delegacy meetings, expressed concern that the L.E.A.'s who were "important partners in the A.T.O." had not had an opportunity for earlier discussion. The affair demonstrated tensions which had first been evident in the McNair Report in 1944 and may well have contributed towards the abolition of the A.T.O.'s in 1976.

In the meantime Canon Platten, exasperated by the delays at Birmingham, had made an interesting contact with the new Aston University, once the College of Advanced Technology, two miles from Saltley towards the City. He had been invited by the Vice Chancellor, Sir Peter Venables, to make a social call and had been most impressed by the plans which he was shewn of the University's promised developments. In return Sir Peter came to Saltley for lunch and he said over coffee that he saw no difficulty in the way of Aston University validating a degree for Saltley students, or any other college which wished. This would be helped by the fact that Aston was shortly to establish a non-teaching professorship in education. It was clear that as far as Sir Peter was concerned there would be no objection to suitable students who offered craft as their Principal subject, nor would the absence of two 'A' Level passes necessarily debar candidates from the course. In February 1967, Canon Platten wrote to Sir Peter :

"Reverting to our informal conversations about a possible link between this College and the University of Aston Education Department, I am wondering whether the time has come when any further useful steps could be taken. We still make very heavy weather of the B.Ed. degree negotiations and I would dearly like to make a fresh start in what I am sure would prove a freer atmosphere. If this letter is quite premature please don't bother to reply but if there is any prospect of fresh developments in the near future, I would be most grateful to hear from you."

124

One consequence of the letter was that the Aston Pro-Vice Chancellor became a College Governor. Unfortunately the D.E.S. was adamant that it was not prepared to consider the creation of another A.T.O. in the West Midlands area, and it would have been unthinkable for one University to control the certificate work and another the degree. At the time it seemed that a good opportunity had been lost. Coming events cast shadows before them !

Chapter 21

The most dramatic and far-reaching aspect of the College expansion between 1964 and 1968 was the increase in staff. What had been a stable situation in the Fifties became highly volatile with colleagues with careers to make, remaining sometimes one or two years only before seizing some opportunity for rapid promotion from Lecturer to Senior Lecturer or Principal Lecturer. Such opportunities came thick and fast in colleges of education, so that there was not merely an increase of staff, but also a rapid rate of change. Between 1965 and 1969, there were 42 newcomers to the Saltley staff, although the total never exceeded 63. St. Peter's may have been more fortunate than many colleges, since it retained until 1967 most of the staff who were there in 1953 and they were able to provide an important element of adhesiveness in a situation that might have become fragmentary ; St. Peter's was fortunate, too, that a significant number of newcomers rapidly became firmly rooted in the College life and work.

It has been indicated earlier that there had been some tendency towards departmentalisation in College ; the expansion accelerated this process ; each subject taught as a Principal Subject qualified to become a Department, except Drama which remained under Philip Dunn firmly linked to English ; some Departments like French and Music had two full-time members only, plus part-timers and a French assistant. The largest Department became the Education Department ; John Hamnett, its Head, pressed vigorously for its expansion on lines similar to those in other colleges of the Institute and the Department steadily grew from the three who had done all the work in the Fifties.

The tradition at Saltley had always been that all staff contributed in the ways they were best fitted in the professional teaching of the College and were in a sense all lecturers in education. This tradition had done much to preserve the unity of purpose of the academic staff and had, indeed, assisted them to get to know each other well. Fortunately all members of staff continued to supervise teaching practice and this brought John Hamnett, who wisely kept its control in his own hands as long as he could, in contact with all colleagues and able to assert direct influence upon their professional practice and judgment. Departmentalism had both advantages and disadvantages. Within departments there was increasing demand for specialist expertise, which may not always have

125

operated to the benefit of the teacher in training. On the one hand a college could offer more variety in its courses, but it probably became more difficult to integrate the work and activities of the students into a coherent entity. This was evident when students complained of repetition in their lectures or of conflict of interest between academic and professional work. Almost inevitably and often unfairly, student grumbles concentrated on education studies ; many of the new colleagues were recruited from applicants who were fresh from taking second degree courses in University Education Departments and these reflected the different academic disciplines into which education had become divided — psychology, philosophy, sociology, history. John Hamnett avoided such divisions as far as possible, maintaining the professional rather than academic character of the course. At St. Peter's during this period fragmentation remained a threat and most of the Staff retained a lively desire to work in unison and as a college.

Canon Platten did his best to foster this. After much thought, the large room built by Principal Blofield and known to students after 1945 as the "New Common Room" was made into a Senior Common Room, its predecessor now being manifestly too small. A partition was placed across this room as has already been related and half of it was devoted to staff meals, especially the mid-day lunch. By this means it remained possible for staff to have a meal together under the presidency of the Principal and in mutual fellowship. Except for special occasions the staff thus abandoned High Table in the Dining Hall where an informal cafeteria arrangement was now in use for the students. Unfortunately the effect was partly reduced by new charges that were imposed by the D.E.S. so that many staff chose to make their own plans for mid-day lunch.

One requirement was the establishment of a new Academic Board to be approved by the Governors and its status to be written into the College Articles of Government. A small sub-committee recommended an Academic Board containing all Heads of Departments plus a small number of elected members. This caused lively controversy and some Staff favoured the retention of all academics on the Board. There was much to said in favour of this view, but the Weaver Committee, a D.E.S. Working Party on the Government of Colleges, recommended the smaller body ; eventually the sub-committee's proposals were adopted and the new Board was established. The first meeting was held in September 1967, at which E. T. Norris was appointed secretary and a complete set of minutes existed from then ; the only subsequent major change to its constitution was when students were admitted to its membership. An Academic Council of the whole staff was created to meet once a term. This was an advisory body and subsequent efforts to supply it with some teeth were never successful, although during the period when the fate of the College hung in the balance, its meetings became suddenly well attended.

The expansion of the staff enabled the College to develop in a number of new directions and blossom out in old ones. For example, the Post-graduate course had 13 students in September 1965 and 83 in 1969. To meet this, M. H. Berry, who had joined the Education Staff in 1962, was promoted to be a Principal Lecturer and made responsible for its administration, a job which called for an unusual amount of tact in handling sensitive graduates and busy colleagues. The French Department, which acquired a language laboratory in the new teaching block, was popular with the graduates, since in addition to a basic method course in French, the College was able by a judicious harvesting of its own tutorial resources and a successful search for suitable teaching practice opportunities, to provide method courses for the teaching of German, Spanish and Russian. The College was also well placed to provide places for a number of science graduates from Aston University, although a scheme to allow Aston University undergraduates to take a year's certificate course at Saltley within the four years allocated for the degree proved too complicated to operate. The Science Department showed itself adept at salvaging undergraduates who had failed their science finals by providing them a one-year course, working with the graduates but satisfying the three-year certificate regulations and becoming after all useful school teachers. It was decided to appoint a tutor to conduct a Subsidiary Economics course for three-year students and the College was fortunate to acquire Roger Hyde, a young schoolmaster who fitted into the History Department and was able to conduct postgraduate method courses in modern degree subjects like politics, applications for which began to arrive at College in some profusion. The Headship of the History Department was taken over by J. K. Taylor, when the Vice Principal received responsibility for student admissions, itself a time-consuming job. To replace J. K. Taylor as Tutor-Librarian, the College was able to employ a fully professionally qualified Librarian with paid staff in support.

The Education Department was enabled to develop its third-year extra-curricular activity courses to a satisfying extent; for example courses giving practical guidance in dealing with backward children, where Cliff Rowley. who arrived in 1965, was soon recognised as an experienced teacher of unusual talent. Both this course and the Youth Service Course were examples of the way the College could react to the urgent problems of its environment, which was to become an important element during its last ten years. Geoffrey Brown who joined the Education Department in 1966 was deputed to run the Youth Service course. The course formed a Youth Council which published a regular News Letter ; No. 3 of the series being worthy of quotation :

"... We are not yet two years old but we are already established as an important part of College life and as our reputation grows so requests for our help from all over the city will become increasingly numerous ... "
(G. Brown).

"... it is ... my opinion ... (that) Mr. Brown's Youth Service Course could be the most exciting and useful section of the Education course as a whole ... "
(Ian Wainwright — Secretary of the Student Union).

"The Double Zero Club.

The club was founded in 1965 to cater for the needs of those young people rejected by other clubs in Birmingham. By 1967 it had taken over the whole of St. Basil's Church, Deritend . . . On paying my first visit I was worried about meeting so many 'rockers' gathered together in one place . . . I left my scooter parked half a mile away and walked to the club, but I need not have worried because apart from a sort of bored curiosity I was ignored . . . The situation was difficult, but I feel the rewards were proportionately greater ; and I have learned more about myself and young people than in a more formal situation . . . " (Derek G. Metters).

Efforts were made to obtain the use of Norton Hall, lying unused, some seven minutes walk from the College with the Principal as one of its Trustees, first as a supplementary teaching block and later as a local centre for youth work. Unfortunately the other Trustees and the Charity Commissioners would not agree and it was not until the Seventies that the College was able to share in the control of a local youth club.

Field courses now became a permanent feature of most college departments. Hitherto the Biology Course had included a fortnight usually in collaboration with the course at Dudley College at one of the established Field Centres. Pat Bailey had established Geography field courses and these were developed further by his successor, Bob Prosser. Now a week was set aside in May for second-year students from other Departments to go off with tutors for day trips or planned programmes of historical investigation or simply as opportunities for writing and reading and discourse ; the English students would go off with Philip and Ida Dunn and what other tutors could be spared to the Lake District to recapture the inspiration of their beloved Wordsworth :

> "The sounding cataract
> Haunted me like a passion ; the tall rock,
> The mountain, and the deep and gloomy wood,
> Their colours and their forms, were then to me
> An appetite . . . "

Many tutors, including the R.K. Department, fresh from a week at Wydale Hall in North Yorkshire, felt these jaunts to be the most worthwhile element in the three-year course. P.E. students attended a well-known centre like Capel Curig, but they were required in addition to undertake an adventure journey from which they returned full of strange tales. It was indeed remarkable how well the P.E. course maintained its popularity during these years ; there was never difficulty in filling the course and the College owed some debt to the P.E. Department for exceeding its quota on occasions when it was proving hard to reach the total numbers required. While some of these P.E. lads were below average in paper qualifications, one should beware of the image of muscular athleticism, since the P.E. course held its own with other departments, except English, when it came to the award of B.Ed. degrees. Saltley P.E. students and teachers seemed to have no difficulty in obtaining jobs

128

and deserved the splendid reputation that they enjoyed in the West Midlands ; it was therefore particularly galling that the D.E.S. continued to deny the course the public status that the Principal felt it merited :

"The Secretary of State, D.E.S.   14th March, 1968.
You may have heard in one way or another that I am retiring at the end of the present academic year . . . Before I go I want to make one last plea for the inclusion of this College in the list of those providing Specialist courses for Physical Education (Men) in Secondary schools, in Part 'C' of the Compendium of Teacher Training Courses. This continues in fact to be our most popular subject for men students. . . We feel that in view of the long history and tradition of this course in our College we ought to be placed on an equality with those others and given a chance of attracting some of the better students . . . "

He received a reply, friendly as ever, with a promise to examine the situation again, but no further encouragement.

It would not be appropriate here to detail all those staff who came or departed in these years, although two of those who made outstanding contributions during the last ten years were Old Salts, John Edge and Harry Jones appointed in 1967 to teach Mathematics and Music respectively. John Tarrant became Chaplain in 1965 and stayed for five years, during which time he married. He and his wife threw themselves into the life of the community ; they took trouble to get to know as many students as possible and students and staff readily went to them with their problems. Since the tasks confronting a chaplain did not grow easier as students rejected values traditionally upheld, John Tarrant would have preferred a situation in which he was free of academic and tutorial responsibilities.

In 1965 Tom Fowler retired after 31 years on the staff as Art Tutor ; his influence as the senior member of the staff since the retirement of W. Burrow had been profound, if exercised gently, and his departure was a warning to all that the post-war order was bound to change. At the first meeting of September 1967 Canon Platten informed his colleagues that he intended to retire at the end of the academic year. In some ways it seemed unnecessary since he was fit and tough and as able to cope with the problems of the day as he had ever been. But he no longer retained the relish that dominated his activities in 1947; in November 1967 he wrote to Harvey, himself shortly to retire :

"Dear Harvey,
I enclose a copy of the reply which was sent to the Department's College Letter No. 16/7 . . . these are suggestions put forward by my colleagues on the Academic Board. They do not have my own wholehearted support because I think that the number of students on this site is already too great and that an increase of a further 100 will make conditions unbearable ; but this view is not shared by the majority of the staff, and as I am leaving at the end of the academic year I do not wish to contest their point of view. I have to admit

129

South Block.

that after years of experience of a college as a genuine community, with some Christian foundation, I find myself quite unable to accept the notion of a college as a sort of mass-production factory, in which our real purposes as a church college become lost. However, in this view I am obviously swimming against the stream of most current opinion which seems to believe that everything must get bigger and bigger."

Most of what has so far been written in this book is a testament to the idealism and untiring, selfless energy of Tom Platten. His Principalship deserved wider publicity. The respect of other Principals and figures at the University was unbounded, and the affection of his colleagues and students at St. Peter's very deep.

Two other colleagues left the Saltley scene at the same time. The influence of Edwin Norris over the professional achievement of Saltley in these post-war years was comparable with that of James Chance and Jack Cornwell and his national status as a teacher of mathematics was high. While his general efforts were unflagging, in recent years much of his interests had gone into the development of in-service courses at Saltley for secondary or junior teachers, lasting for a year or sometimes a term. These were most popular and successful, the limiting factor being the meanness and short-sightedness of local education authorities in allowing secondment at a time when they were all screaming for mathematics teachers. The Rev. John Bateman had been a resident tutor for 12 years ; no one quite knew why he decided to retire when he did and the College lost a real personality and a clergyman who did not spare himself when it was possible to perform some act of kindness for colleague or student.

The administrative explosion was almost as devastating as the academic. In 1953 two most competent ladies assisted the Bursar, all gathered in the same general office, next door to the Principal ; fifteen years later there was a whole corridor devoted to administration, including the old Senior Common Room which had been partitioned into Offices for the Bursar and the Vice Principal, leaving an area for the reception of visitors, tastefully furnished and decorated with prints of old Birmingham. In 1968 a Deputy Bursar was appointed, J. E. Blanthorn, who was to become Chief Administrative Officer at the Church College at Canterbury ; among other qualities which made him a splendid colleague was that he was a fine badminton player. The supporting staff of lady secretaries, typists, telephonists would have astonished Pat Harrod and Pauline Nash of the Fifties, but with rare exceptions they brought a similar dedication and acquired an affection for the College unusual, one supposes, in administrative places. The Porter's house was built in 1964 and its first occupant should have been Harry Taylor ; unhappily he died suddenly from a heart attack, alone, but for the presence of his lovely alsatian dog, Solo. His successor, Charles Taylor, (but unrelated), also died within a year quite unexpectedly. After one or two unsatisfactory appointments, A. Dent, technical assistant in the Craft Department, was appointed Head Porter and he has occupied the Porter's house since.

Commander Heathcote commenced a policy which worked well of forming a team of assistants under the Head Porter who proved a splendid leader, cheerful, firm but unflappable ; some of these were pensioners who were responsible for security and the post; mostly they were slow to understand the strange ways of students and staff, but they were rarely ruffled and some even mastered the small telephone exchange ; others were handymen of much skill and able to cope with many of the repair jobs about College ; of these, Howard Penrice had been an employee of Wall's, the College heating engineers, and he had worked at Saltley, off and on, for over 50 years.

Chapter 22

Jeremy Treglown (1964-67, Editor of "The Salt", 1967) wrote in reply to the Author's request for impressions of College life :

"The images that come back most vividly of Saltley tend to be something to do with a combination of solid, paternal traditionalism with innocent energy and enthusiasm. It was a mixture even my arrival prepared me for. My bags and cardboard boxes full of books were all buoyantly manhandled out of the car by a hearty, talkative, slightly balding porter in sweater and flannels who later introduced himself as the President of the Students' Union. And the very survival of these neo-Gothic Oxbridge buildings, with all their solemn unworldly claims, in amongst the railway lines and gas works and slums, itself seemed a similarly incongruous but admirable gesture which as students we all found ourselves acting out year by year in various ways, especially on teaching practice in the Inner Ring schools — pink faced eighteen year olds in college blazers, fresh from 'A' Level, selling the New Maths as fervently as Victorian missionaries with the Gospel.

"Of course, any kind of idealistic enthusiasm seemed quixotic in the satiric Sixties, and my own group did its mildly cynical bit towards sending the whole thing up in a couple of revues, as well as less ambitiously in our practical jokes. Even those mostly had a pre-war, jolly-japes kind of niceness about them, though — someone planted plastic flowers in the Principal's garden one winter ; and there was an unsuccessful attempt to glue up the clapper of the chapel bell with Araldite . . . .

"Saltley students were frank in their reactions but tolerant too, and it was in that encouraging but not uncritical environment that I rather belatedly discovered two things : that activity almost always produces results while inactivity never does : and that while some results are better than others, any result is on the whole likely to be more satisfying than none . . .

"Among the things I remember very gratefully about some of the tutors in the fields I worked in . . . are a love of the subjects them-

132

selves, respect for traditional scholarship, and a sense of the extension of these things in the creative work of writers and other thinkers and artists. These attitudes weren't all shared by everyone, of course, and there were inevitably many times when the college (like any institution) seemed dull and restricting . . . When I first met Canon Platten he remarked that the college was something of an oasis. He was talking about the campus, but he was right in many other ways as well.''

To say that the last four years of Canon Platten's Principalship were less happy than earlier years implies no particular criticism of any individuals, but rather that the student malaise, complicated by lodgings and overcrowding, was making its impact. On the other hand they were in terms of achievement years of highly succeessful activity and it is improbable that St. Peter's image in the external world ever appeared brighter.

In 1964/65 the Church Colleges Council for Education conducted a mini-inspection of its colleges by a Working Party under the chairmanship of the Bishop of Salisbury to enquire into their effectiveness in communicating the Christian faith ; four clergy were detailed to come to Saltley during the last week of February 1965 ; only three turned up and their visit was a brief one, making too little impact in general upon either the staff or students. The printed report when it was received might have been more useful if it had been rather more contentious and a little less fair. The Working Party had devoted much attention to the new Church College at Canterbury, where they were much impressed by a Contemporary Studies course ; in turn, Saltley began its own course, at first a series of general lectures given by members of staff under the chairmanship of the Principal followed by general discussion, but not, at first, part of the established syllabus of the College. Canon Platten was unimpressed by the Report :

"Dear Harvey,

. . . It is better at analysing our present difficulties than making positive suggestions, but I cannot myself offer the positive contribution which ought to be made. The fundamental trouble does not spring from inadequate syllabuses or mistaken methods but from the general ethos of the day."

Canon Fenton Morley, Vicar of Leeds, who led the visiting team at Saltley, informed Canon Platten that he was satisfied that students were presented with the main elements of the Christian challenge through the basic Religious Education course which all were expected to undertake ; how they responded to that challenge was, of course, their affair. A copy of the Report was distributed to each member of the Governors, and it was discussed at a special meeting one Saturday in June 1966. Apart from the Chairman, only one clerical Governor was present, but it was acknowledged that the dioceses had little idea of the problems that colleges faced or the ways in which they responded to them. The Chairman promised that the Birmingham diocese would endeavour to establish closer communications with the College.

133

The College Chapel was able to maintain itself at the same level of interest as in recent years, there being usually a nucleus of dedicated and involved students to form an enthusiastic committee to support the Chaplain. Occasionally, the Chapel had its successes, as, for example, that Christmas Carol Service when, by dint of removing the altar table, it was possible to crowd in a congregation of between 400 and 500. In 1965/66 a weekly corporate service was held on Friday mornings at midday; attendances was not compulsory but all lectures were cancelled, and for a time these were well supported. There were visiting speakers, but the most popular were members of staff and students, one of whom, Brother Jonathan, made a deep impression. In the end, the novelty wore off and attendances declined and members of staff began to ask whether the College could "afford" to abandon its work with so little effect.

Probably student reluctance to attend College Chapel sprang in many cases from genuine perplexity about moral issues and an aggressive honesty relating to themselves and religion. Chaplain's conferences discussing their difficulties reported the constant recurrence of the topics : Who are we ? What is society ? the refusal to accept any authority external to themselves ; the danger that student and staff positions were becoming entrenched ; the student preoccupation with concessions to be won.

The tensions were present at Saltley but conflict, if any, was muted. This was due partly to the deep respect and affection the students had for the Principal and also to a series of fine Student Union leaders who saw themselves as trouble-shooters rather than revolutionaries. One of these, whose period of office as President of the Union coincided with the last year of Canon Platten, was Pete Moore. He came from Southport like Norman Francis in the Fifties and he had attracted the attention of the students when he had stood as the Liberal candidate in a mock election and had narrowly defeated both the Conservatives and Socialists ; the election was taken seriously and was hard fought, unlike a similar occasion in the Fifties, sponsored by the Vice Principal, which had ended in something like a student rag and had attracted the attention of the local press, to the anger of the Principal. Pete Moore was thus a popular choice and a determined one. He was especially keen to maintain old traditions and a good relationship between students and staff. He went to much trouble to arrange a Christmas Ball which would be acceptable both to the old timers and the jivers and, when only one or two staff turned up, he published an angry letter in the following issue of the "Saltette" — with every justification. He strove hard to ensure a disciplined but lively student community, and probably incurred unpopularity in some student quarters as a consequence. He worked so hard at the job and became almost a student welfare officer, in addition to his other functions, that he had to abandon his own ambition to take the B.Ed. for which he was well qualified. He thus established precedents for the student presidency which became within a year or two so exacting that few students could be persuaded to offer themselves for the honour.

The areas of disagreement concerned residential life. Canon Platten regretted the passing of the opportunities that existed in the Fifties for him to meet the Union Committee and therefore during the Sixties the practice was developed for informal meetings after supper once a month between members of the S.U. Council and all the residential staff. The object was to discuss matters of residential interest; eventually the students prepared an agenda and minuted any agreements that were concluded. It was difficult to avoid discussion of more general issues and sometimes non-resident tutors complained that matters were discussed and decided which concerned them. But usually debate was focussed on the residential rules and their interpretation and the student union desire, under severe pressure from the main body, to relax these. Meetings could be long, repetitive and argumentative and more than once broke up in confusion. Eventually a painful compromise would be hammered out. The most controversial subject was the "visiting hours", both on workdays and week-ends; as the years went on these became ever later as the Principal agreed to an extra half hour here or there; simultaneously, the College became noisier at night and students more reluctant to rise in the morning. Almost as contentious were the times for opening the Bar, which were extended gradually, and the programme of dances.

These became more frequent and spread to mid-week when a Dancing Club was formed with the laudable intention of teaching learners how to dance; this soon became a regular dance fixture. Perhaps there was disquiet about the character of the dances as much as their frequency since this was the middle of the 'beat' age. The Entertainment Committee reported in "The Salt" in 1966:

"Bigger and better bands and groups are being booked due to the increase in numbers in College and such names at The Zombies, The Move and The Mighty Avengers have appeared during the year . . ."
(J.M.).

There was still at that time a College Dance Band which kept pace with the times:

" . . . The Band played a much more active part in College dances, being featured on numerous occasions with visiting "rock-groups." This catered for everyone's taste in dancing."

The Editorial for that year might sound complacent, although its sentiments were to be applauded:

"If the expansion envisaged is to be at all satisfactory in providing for the social, educational and individual welfare of the teacher in training, it is important that the liaison between all its members, which has always been a valued element of the Saltley tradition, should be preserved in the college. The revision of the rules governing behaviour in the college and the introduction of extended visiting hours and Bar facilities, which have taken place this year, are examples of how this contact can be achieved in the future."

135

There were other examples of such contact. In 1961 a printed termly College Calendar was started, which the Student Union agreed to back to the extent of £5 per issue. The Calendar was to be continued till the College closure. It necessitated a termly meeting between the Vice Principal and Student Officers, so that the academic, sporting and social programmes could be agreed for the following term ; this had many advantages, since it obliged everyone, tutors and secretaries alike, to plan ahead and it gave publicity to coming events; it also provided the Vice Principal with an opportunity to discuss the timing and propriety of the social events that were proposed. Saltbuild was another venture which encouraged staff-student contact, and which, despite many vicissitudes, persisted throughout the Sixties and Seventies. After £2,500 had been raised as a contribution towards college building, as related in an earlier chapter, it was decided that a fund-raising committee should continue its existence in a more leisurely way and under guidance from the Chaplain, John Tarrant, it divided its receipts between the College Foundation Account and projects which appealed to the students, like the provision of a wide screen for the Film Society. A good many staff served on the committee over the years and contributed to its efforts ; for example running Edwardian Evenings and Wine and Cheese parties ; for several years jumble sales proved a most lucrative source of funds. Jack Grayson and Derek West from the creative arts departments assisted the students to open up some of the College cellars for social functions, a project of somewhat doubtful health value. The committee even joined the Co-op in order to get a dividend.

These years were outstanding for all sports and included new activities like badminton and fencing, in which E. P. K. Hudson was on the verge of national recognition and in two successive years the club organised open tournaments at Saltley. At the beginning of this period the Soccer Club was in the ascendancy. In 1966 two members of the club, John Cocking and John Mason, were summoned to the amateur international "squad" and John Mason was chosen to play for England against Holland ; many thought that John Cocking equally deserved the honour. But in 1967 the Rugger Club attracted the attention with its remarkable record :

		P.	W.	L.	Points For	Points Against
1st XV	....	25	25	0	641	80
2nd XV	....	19	18	1	613	63

The following year the record was not quite so good, but the College had regularly turned out three XV's. The secret behind these results was largely the high team spirit which was engendered, but it needs to be added that this was the period when the Corless brothers, Barrie and Trevor, were at College. Barrie Corless was Saltley's only International Rugger Cap and his brother obtained an International Trial. Barrie played for England against Australia in 1975 and again in all the home international matches in 1977 and 1978 ; he turned out again to play for a College team in their last match at Stechford in March 1977.

136

The greatest triumphs, however, were reserved for the dramatists. In 1965 Chris Martin's dramatized anthology of First World War poetry reached the Final of the "Sunday Times" National Union of Students Drama Festival at Bradford, the only College of Education represented that year. It was clear to those at St. Peter's, who saw the earlier performances that this was a production of unusual merit, and it was particularly well received by the university audiences. Unfortunately the adjudicators, who included Harold Hobson and John Russell Brown, said that they found it too openly emotional and that the agonies of Wilfred Owen and Siegfried Sassoon were "better shared on the page than on the stage"; Jeremy Treglown, who himself played a leading role, wrote:

"It's hard to tell whether or not I would agree with them now, but at the time I was moved by the other actors' performances and I vividly remember watching the first moments from the wings — rifles and helmets silhouetted against the smoky red cyclorama, Holst's 'Planets' suite booming over the speakers and David Town in full kit crawling on his stomach inch by inch to the centre of the stage."

The following year Jeremy Treglown's Revue, "Six over the Severn", was not entered for the Competition but its performance was paid for by the "Sunday Times" as the final item in the entertainment at Cardiff and then it moved to Bradford where it was performed at the University in aid of War on Want. Its author and producer wrote:

"Few things have given us more hilarity and excitement than helping Gordon Creese pile "Six over the Severn" into its van, setting it up in Cardiff and performing it there in front of a packed audience which laughed so much that by the end some scenes could hardly be heard . . . We all felt so famous that it's astonishing that we didn't turn into wandering players on the spot — but however respectable and predictable our lives went on to become despite that occasional fantasy, it's a good memory to have."

The official farewell to Canon Platten was held on 28th June 1968 and most fittingly coincided with the annual St. Peter's Day celebrations. The Festival Service was held during the morning and followed the traditional pattern of these services: "Now thank we all our God"; the festival lessons of St. Peter, read by the President of the Students' Union and by the Vice Principal; the Vaughan Williams anthem, "Let us now praise famous men"; an address by Dr. Wilson, Bishop of Birmingham; finally, the hymn, "Lord of all hopefulness", ending with the words:

. . . and give us, we pray,
Your peace in our hearts, Lord, at the end of the day.

In the afternoon, there was a public meeting, a nostalgic affair; at Canon Platten's request the invited spokesman was Professor Jeffreys, returned from retirement; to open the new teaching block came Canon Platten's first Chairman, Michael Parker, now Bishop of Bradford; the many guests included Principals and representatives of the University; R. J. Harvey had now retired, but his successor, Canon J. S. Robertson, made his first official visit to Saltley. During the proceedings there was a violent thunderstorm which prevented the gathering from moving across the field to the new block ; instead the Bishop of Bradford, having received the golden key from the architect, Maurice Hobbiss, performed a magical operation of opening from the College Hall. The Chairman of the Governors presented to the S.U. President the portrait of the Principal which the Governors had commissioned from Mr. Moody of Malvern in May 1965.

During the following week the students and the staff and the Old Students' Association made their less formal farewells to Canon and Mrs. Platten and this provided an opportunity for the return of many old members of staff. It also provided the students with a last hearing of the Norfolk stories which had delighted so many Christmas dinners. Canon Platten claimed that as long as there was only a two-year course, no one except his colleagues, need ever listen to the same story twice, but that the advent of the three-year course upset his arrangements. In fact, no one objected to hearing as often as he liked to tell it, the story of the farmer who fed his mare with a pint of "tarpentine" as a remedy for the botts or the farmer who took his lantern to go courting.

---

5   SALTLEY FACES UP TO CHANGE (1968-73)

Chapter 23

In February 1968, the Governors appointed the Rev. Charles Buckmaster as the new Principal. Four of the five Diocesan Bishops who were Governors were present to lend the weight of their support to the newcomer and also Sir Lionel Russell, due to retire at the same time as Tom Platten, made his penultimate appearance ; by special invitation R. J. Harvey, representing the Council of Church Training Colleges, assisted in making the new appointment ; it was also his last appearance at Saltley. During the ten following years Principal Buckmaster would doubtless have valued the united strength which these eminent men could have brought to the aid of the College and its Principal.

The new Principal was a graduate of Durham University and was well known in the Church Colleges ; he had been Chaplain and Head of Religious Studies at Ripon College and Vice Principal at Bishop Lonsdale College, Derby, Saltley's pre-World War I sister college. Tom Platten had come from the stable Edwardian background of East Anglia and Charles Buckmaster from the turbulent Twenties and Thirties in London. It was much to be expected that he would approach his responsibilities differently from his predecessor and bring to his office new ideas about the role of a College. Especially, he was concerned that Saltley should be apprised of the accelerated pace of change and prepared to adapt itself positively to the new demands that would be made upon it. Although the Principal was to prove that, like his predecessor, he was an able administrator, he insisted that structured institutions were in danger of becoming hardened like arteries and that they must not be allowed to obstruct healthy life, the purposes of which were creative ; in education this was of primary importance. Thus the function of a college was to serve the needs of its students and of the teaching profession ; and the function of the Church, of which the College was a part, was to serve and to care for the whole community. His first article in "The Salt", 1969, expounded some of these ideas :

> ". . . the Principal has become the co-ordinator of a joint enterprise . . . Most students now in college will still have a decade of their teaching career to serve when the year 2000 comes round. Will they then still appreciate the pattern of education they received in the Seventies? Will they still live by a faith or a philosophy of life they have come to understand in these their student years ? These are fundamental questions which may need radical answers . . . the answers will only be achieved by Principal, staff and students together, for all have now become the guardians and the innovators for the next decade . . . How effectively we are able to meet this challenge, find and put into operation the answers, time alone will tell, for Time, as Francis Bacon said, is the greatest innovator . . . I am proud to be Principal during these times of change and reappraisal."

There was plenty at Saltley in 1968 to justify the Principal's call to meet the challenge of change. In 1967 the number of students was 582, in 1968 it was 662 and it was earnestly hoped to raise the figure to 750 within the next two years ; 7 new members of the academic staff arrived at the same time as the Principal and another 9 were to come in 1970 ; the Latey Commission had recommended in July, 1967, the lowering of the Age of Majority from 21 to 18 and Principals were required to adjust themselves to the idea that there was no longer for them any meaning in the phrase 'in loco parentis' ; a large national storm was brewing up about the training of teachers and the supposed inadequacy of Colleges of Education ; there was a new economic crisis overtaking the Labour Government and within six years this was to engulf the whole nation ; locally, a large body of immigrants from Asia and the West Indies changed the character of the College's immediate environment at a time when large industrial plants like Morris Commercial were falling idle and inducing depression.

The new Principal first met his staff at a meeting of the Academic Council in September 1968. He told them that in his view the essence of a Church college lay in its concern for individual personality and whether it be among the staff or students this was what chiefly distinguished it from its secular contemporaries. He then listened carefully as three of his new senior colleagues accepted his invitation to enlarge upon matters of College policy which seemed to them most urgently to need attention : John Hamnett called for closer links with the schools used by the College for teaching practice ; Philip Dunn for curriculum reform which would enable the students' courses to have a much stronger professional bias ; and Jack Osborne for improved recreational resources for the students, if possible centred upon a Sports Hall. Principal Buckmaster promised to give prompt attention to all these matters.

The Editor of "The Salt" wrote in 1969 : "The new Principal has begun to revolutionize many aspects of college life, and at the same time has maintained the strong links with our traditional past." In fact, revolutions take longer than this to establish themselves and the remaining chapters of this Section will be concerned with the successful revolutionary process during the following five years, 1968-73, before further dramatic changes finally engulfed the College.

Chapter 24

The curriculum changes which Philip Dunn had proposed inaugurated a prolonged debate first in the College and then throughout the A.T.O. area. It culminated in sweeping changes in the three-year certificate course which, it was hoped, would answer sympathetically some of the young students' criticisms of deficiencies in their college course. Much of the credit for these changes must be given to Professor Hilliard, the new Warden of the Colleges Division of the School of Education and all the colleges made their contributions. But the St. Peter's proposal to abolish academic subsidiary subject courses and replace them by a Contemporary Studies course, compulsory for all, but containing opportunities within for the development of some specialist expertise, precipitated the subsequent widespread debate.

It was stated in an earlier chapter that Contemporary Studies had originated in a series of lectures for first year students to which most Departments had contributed, and which were designed for general interest and to enhance social awareness rather than to fill a part of the examinable course. After the report on the "Communication of Christian Faith" had praised such a course at Canterbury a committee under the guidance of the Religious Education Department was instructed by the Academic Board to devise how such a course could be developed and brought under the existing regulations at Saltley. The Report of this committee was published in January 1969, and it received the strong support of Principal Buckmaster. A vote in the Academic Board "that all certificate students should take the Contemporary Studies Course as their Subsidiary Subject" was carried by "16 votes to 2 with 2 abstentions." At the same time, "Basic Courses" were to be abolished and the professional courses completely reviewed. This simple statement hardly indicates the liveliness of the discussion.

The Rev. Peter Street who had joined the R. E. Department in 1966 was made the director of the new course, an ideal person to be put in charge of studies requiring detailed integration and co-operation between departments, because he was universally liked both by his colleagues and the students. He worked particularly hard to construct a workable arrangement and succeeded in generating much enthusiasm for the project. It was now a matter of waiting to see how the University would react. The School of Education finally decided to drop subsidiary courses, and to allow Colleges instead to extend that section of the work which was devoted to "professional" studies — "to be studied in the context of the principles of the curriculum and the teacher's part in the learning process". The College Academic Board, after a tense debate, reversed its earlier decision and abandoned Contemporary Studies much to the disappointment of Peter Street.

It was necessary now to create a structure to handle the new professional courses and, prompted by the Principal, committees were formed cutting across departmental organisation to develop courses suitable for the different teaching-age groups — Primary, Middle and Secondary ; for the Middle and Secondary teachers, the Committee proposed a number of integrated courses, such as Creative Studies or Environmental Studies or Humanities, and "second teaching areas" like Mathematics, French, Science and Technical Drawing. All these courses and the academic Principal Subject courses were now expected to operate school teaching method courses, so that it would no longer be possible for a student to say at the end of his course, "You have taught me History, but you have not shown me **how** to teach History". For Primary Teachers, Gerry Paget was able with co-operation from different parts of the College to develop a 'first-school course' in depth and lasting three years especially after the arrival of Norma Anderson to assist with the training of Infant Teachers.

141

Of course, other colleges were also adapting their own courses in similar directions, but the point of this chapter is to emphasise that under the new Principal Saltley energetically set about the examination of the usefulness of the courses it offered. There was much gained ; students received far more direct preparation for teaching practice and their professional careers ; the new arrangements offered boundless opportunity for closer contacts between the college tutor and the teacher in his class-room ; by throwing staff together in interdepartmental groupings and bringing students with different skills and interests in new ventures into working co-operation, the professional courses helped to maintain the idea that the College operated with a unified purpose and was not just a collection of departments. But it was not all gain ; some schools were reluctant to accept students trained in unfamiliar subjects like "creative studies" and "humanities" which did not appear on their own curriculum ; it was quickly learned that a highly mobile college staff could leave gaps difficult to fill and integrated studies depending on team work suffered more than established disciplines in rapidly changing situations ; above all, the disappearance of "basic R.K." and the decision not to go ahead with Contemporary Studies created a problem, serious for a Church College, of how to undertake an element of religious knowledge for all students beyond the Primary School age range except, of course, the dwindling numbers of religious specialists.

The School of Education instituted one important change in its examination practices at this time, which, although it was progressive and sensible, involved complications which should have been foreseen. The assessment of final teaching practice was reduced to a choice of three marks — credit, pass and failure. Previously a mark of D had represented a "weak pass" and this mark served a useful purpose in that it gave warning to the teaching profession that a recruit with such a mark would need careful guidance and support in his early years as a teacher. It was now necessary for colleges to come off the fence and declare clearly whether a student was suitable or not. This was far from easy in individual cases where there was pressure on the College to be both fair and just and this may explain why some students qualified when they would have profited from longer apprenticeship.

Another important new direction for the Certificate course was the introduction of a "modular" structure into the Education course ; the modules themselves were carefully devised so that they would involve a child and school-based approach rather than appear to follow so-called education disciplines ; it thus became easier for a student to understand the pattern of the whole course. The third year Youth Service option was helped by the establishment of the Naseby Youth and Community Centre, of which the Principal was made a Governor. In this and in other ways the Education department strove to adapt the Education course towards the deteriorating scene in Birmingham's "inner ring" ; David Hill and Cliff Rowley made strong contributions in the field of compensatory education and attention has already been drawn towards the work of the Youth Course and the Youth Council, both of which continued to be developed. The commencement of an Infant Course provided the opportunity for the commencement of a St. Peter's Playgroup and in 1970 a group of staff and students took over the gloomy room next door to the Music Department for this purpose ; they painted the room in bright colours and advertised in local cafes and shops and the welfare centre their intention to establish the Group. Thereafter every Wednesday afternoon in term time groups of local under-five-year-olds, often accompanied by their mothers and of varied backgrounds — English, Irish, Asian, West Indian — assembled under the guidance of Norma Anderson and an appropriate group of students.

Gradually after 1970 the number of students at St. Peter's of West Indian or Asiatic origin increased, especially when they could be recruited straight from Midland schools. Earlier, mature immigrants, often already with teaching experience, had applied to the College, especially for admission to the one-year postgraduate course, but many of these encountered language difficulties and during teaching practice disciplinary problems arising from the different pedagogical philosophy prevalent in English schools from that in their previous background. The three-year students bred, if not born, in England, remained a small minority of the total, but even so there was plenty of evidence of the severe cultural conflict which some of them suffered between their home-life and student-life.

The changes related in this chapter to the professional and academic studies in the College give welcome evidence that it was capable of adapting itself to a new age, and that the professional needs of student-teachers remained a paramount consideration. They brought the College close to schools and teachers closer to the College. The efforts to integrate the work of different parts of the College were not always successful, but stimulated much thought and activity. Scarcely had these new courses established themselves firmly than the James Report and its subsequent developments set St. Peter's and other colleges the task of planning their courses afresh from the beginning. It seemed a pity that the changes worked out in the colleges during the early Seventies did not have the opportunity to take root in stable conditions.

Chapter 25

The four years between 1968 and 1972 saw the departure of a number of those whose influence and responsibility was most likely to provide strength and stability in the changing scene and whose retirement might leave the College most vulnerable. The first of these was the Chairman of the Governors, the Bishop of Birmingham, Leonard Wilson. This most distinguished man presided over the College from the elevation of Michael Parker to be Bishop of Bradford in 1961 until he retired in June 1969. During this period the College had passed through the phases of its expansion and the Vice Principal was able to announce at the luncheon given by the Governors as a tribute to Bishop Wilson that all the buildings so far projected had been completed and that every penny of debt had been paid off. Bishop Wilson had regarded his Chairmanship in the light of a watching brief and did not appear to wish to influence policy in any specific direction. But he attended meetings with regularity and his interest grew with time ; he opened all Governors' meetings with the collect for Whit-Sunday : "Grant us by the same Spirit to have a right judgment in all things, and evermore to rejoice in His holy comfort . . ." His addresses in the College Chapel were superb and brought guidance and comfort to many beside the author of this book. But he became most lively and interested when he was among the students, being equally at home relating his war-time experiences in Changri Jail in Singapore to the S.C.R., helping Mrs. Wilson to choose the Beauty Queen at a May Ball, or telling Geordie "folk" stories to the rather inebriated College during a Christmas smoking concert. The College was fortunate indeed that his successor to the See of Birmingham agreed to continue Leonard Wilson's chairmanship. Laurence Brown became Chairman in March 1970, having already, when suffragan Bishop of Warrington, had close experience of college of education problems as Chairman of St. Katherine's, Liverpool.

The retirement of John Hamnett in 1971 was a severe blow since he stood at the end of thirty-five years direct tradition in the educational thinking and practice of the college through James Chance and Jack Cornwell. He was well known and immensely popular in Birmingham schools ; his friendly and jovial manner cloaked a firm purpose and high principles and he didn't suffer incompetence gladly. Bill Powrie wrote of him in 1971 :

"He it was who planned and organised all the courses, allocated the groups, worked out the . . . timetables, dealt with assessment and arranged all the teaching practice, when he wasn't running the F.T.C. and Postgraduate Certificate courses. And he took an equal share in the teaching load. But he managed to be up with and even ahead of major changes . . . With the rapid expansion of the College . . . and the movement away from formal lectures, there has grown up under J.H.H. a new structure to which the whole Department, students included, has been able frankly and freely and with a minimum of restriction to contribute . . ." ("The Salt", 1971).

It would have been difficult indeed to step into the shoes of this prince of lecturers ; the College looked to the world outside and David Fontana from the City of Leeds and Carnegie College was appointed. He stayed only two years before accepting a University post, and perhaps did not feel wholly at ease in the more confined circumstances of St. Peter's.

During 1969 it was decided that English and Drama, which had long been available as separate certificate subjects, should become distinct Departments. Since Philip Dunn would be heavily involved with the reorganisation of professional courses in addition to being in charge of English, which with women students could claim to be the largest depart-ment in college and certainly had most B.Ed. work, he agreed to end his long connection with Drama work. For more than twenty years he had supervised the activities of the Dramatic Society and had thus influenced decisively one of the main activities by which the College presented its image to the world outside. John Pick, Senior Lecturer in Drama from Nottingham College of Education, was appointed as the new departmental head and at once impressed by the force and new directions of the ideas he was eager to develop at St. Peter's. The drama courses flourished ; he was, however, less concerned to maintain the same traditions of public stage or arena performances which had been a feature of Saltley life since the War.

In 1972 three of the senior heads of department retired at the same time, Philip Dunn, Jack Osborne and Dick McDonogh, who had obtained a post in Australia ; all three had played a leading role in the academic, professional and social life of the College and had firmly grafted their ideas and personalities on to its development. It was fortunate that these vacancies were filled so successfully, since there were already rumours of drastic changes in the offing. Douglas Courts, who had been a colleague of the Principal's at Derby and was already in the English Department at St. Peter's, became its head ; John Kitchen, a kindred spirit to McDonogh, came from Dudley to take charge of Science. Jack Osborne was one of the Saltley figures who had dominated its life since the war and his influence on students was immense. He was strongly devoted to the College where he had himself been a student and to the P.E. course which he had run for so long. He deplored injustice and supported the freedom of others to speak their mind. He served for a time on the executive committee of the A.T.C.D.E. His retirement was complicated by the fact Steve Allatt had decided to move back into school-teaching and that Colin and Rita Jones were shortly to move away north, Colin to a University post. His successor would therefore be faced by much reconstruction. This was Clive Bond, a senior member of the Loughborough staff, who was well equipped to attempt this task. During his four years at Saltley, he achieved a national reputation in the field of experimental scientific work in P.E. and there could have been no surprise when he moved to Leeds as Director of Carnegie School of Physical Education.

Thus by September 1972 there was a new Principal in the Chair and new heads of department in nearly all the important areas of college work, including Mathematics over which Raymond Heritage had presided since 1968; the St. Peter's Academic Board was poised and ready to adapt itself to whatever new ventures in teacher training should be required of it. The staff was younger, full of ideas and had been injected with experience and expertise from other institutions.

One other important change in staff needs to be recorded here, the retirement from the administrative staff of Commander W. H. Heathcote and the appointment of Brian Strand, in 1972. Tribute was made in an earlier chapter to Heathcote's administrative and financial artistry and it is hard to imagine how the expansion of the college could have come about without him. His reputation at the D.E.S. must have been high indeed for St. Peter's to have been selected as one of the colleges for experimentation with a direct cash grant scheme — a subject for another chapter. Saltley was lucky indeed to have the loyalty and services in retirement of this distinguished naval officer.

Brian Strand was appointed as Chief Administrative Officer and the post of Bursar went to the chief accountant. Strand came from the University of Salford and was well versed in administration in Higher Education. He prized the opportunity which St. Peter's offered him to share closely in the life of the community. When a job needed to be done, he readily took his jacket off and got on with it ; the students much appreciated his interest in athletics and his services in the College Bar on a Saturday evening. But Brian Strand wisely adopted the same accountancy techniques as his predecessor and was equally successful in accumulating funds to support the Governors' Foundation Account.

One of the issues about which Principal Buckmaster felt strongly was that of providing for his staff suitable opportunities for secondment in order to pursue projects for further study or experience. This was difficult in a small college like St. Peter's, especially in the subject departments where there were only two or three tutors. When in 1969 the D.E.S. pronounced that fully salaried staff, who were absent on study leave, must count within the total permissible salary bill under the agreed staff/student ratio, the Principal pointed out to Canon Robertson that this placed Church colleges at an unfair disadvantage compared with L.E.A. colleges, where "provision can be made for a temporary lecturer to take over from some other post in the authority and the matter be adjusted on the authority's internal accounting system." The Principal's protest was accepted and from this time there was each year a small number of staff engaged on study leave, to their own personal advancement and the benefit of the College. It meant, too, that there was a welcome stream of new faces in the Senior Common Room. These included during 1969/70 Wilbur J. Switzer from San Diego, California, in exchange with Robert Prosser teaching geography in a large higher education institution in San Diego. Jim Switzer proved to be a most friendly and hard-working colleague.

Chapter 26

He would have been a bold man who dared to forecast in 1968 that St. Peter's had still to design and create its most imposing and costly building or that it would be accompanied by few of the financial problems which bedevilled the earlier ventures, despite the fact that Harold Wilson's first Labour Government was just recovering from a severe balance of payments crisis. In June 1968, a letter was received from the D.E.S. stating that, although the estimate for 1973/74 for 110,000 places in Colleges of Education would be exceeded years in advance,

"Nevertheless there is a continuing need for some further expansion, particularly in areas of growing population, and the Secretary of State has accordingly approved, in principle, a limited number of proposals

146

The Quad, 1950.

and further consultation . . . will now be initiated . . . College authorities are accordingly invited to submit as soon as possible, proposals for the improvement of buildings and facilities and the replacement of obsolescent accommodation . . . "

It is curious how late the idea persisted that Colleges of Education were still on the verge of further expansion ; in March 1969, the A.T.C.D.E. pursued an enquiry from College Principals on the "size and development of Colleges" which caused Canon Robertson at Church House to write to the new Principal :

"I have just read this morning of the proposed increases in Higher Education by 1982 and if the 50% increase envisaged in Colleges of Education by then is planned for, we shall have a great deal of thinking to do together."

Canon Platten warned the Governors about the D.E.S. letter at his last meeting with them and not surprisingly they gave it a somewhat tepid reception ; despite this, he wrote to the D.E.S. in July, having first corresponded with his successor on the matter :

"It is desired to submit the following proposals for the improvement of buildings and facilities . . . The most urgent need is for the provision of further study rooms and other facilties for day and lodging students . . . we think that the need would be suitably met by converting to this use the present accommodation for the Music and Drama departments in College and building a new Music and Drama block, . . . in place of the somewhat makeshift arrangements which now exist . . . The next priority would be the improvement of physical recreation facilities, as already proposed in my letter of May 20th."

This was for the construction of a Sports Hall for which Jack Osborne had been pressing insistently. Principal Buckmaster rapidly consolidated the ground so far gained. He placed the development proposals as the first item on the agenda at his first Governors' meeting in October 1968, and with the Governors' blessing wrote at once to the Secretary of State to remind him of Canon Platten's letter. The Principal conjectured that "the whole scheme outlined would be in the region of £80,000 of which the College would, of course, be responsible for 20%." To encourage the D.E.S. the Principal added,

"I understand that this area of Birmingham is due for re-development in about 10 years time. As far as I can see, the arrival of the motorways link road about one mile from College, will make it a most desirable area from the point of re-developed residence. This will enhance the value of the College site as the environment in which it is situated improves, and at the same time help a College in an urban area where access is easy and a very wide selection of schools available for School Practice."

The Principal's letter almost crossed in the post with one from the D.E.S. which showed how enthusiastic they had become about "major building programmes for colleges" ; a new system was to be created

148

making three new lists, so that Colleges might commence in the Third Division ("the preliminary list") and, after passing through the Second Division ("the design list"), eventually reach the Premier Division ("the starts programme"). To attain to the "preliminary list" Colleges' schemes "will be included when the Department is satisfied that it meets a specific need within five years and hence justifies preliminary work." Principal Buckmaster assisted by the College Architect and Commander Heathcote proceeded to marshal the necessary evidence to meet this clause. The D.E.S. had produced in 1967 a pamphlet in which they specified permissible areas of accommodation, so that figures for a College of 700 students and 70 staff could be set against the actual figures of accommodation available at Saltley. The results were interesting; they revealed that in teaching accommodation the College was reasonably well placed ; there was, of course, a serious shortage of residential accommodation but the D.E.S. had no intention of supplying money under this head ; the expected gap between the permissible and the actual in communal accommodation for non-residential areas of College activity was 8,500 square feet although it should be remembered that day students and lodgers imposed themselves ruthlessly upon the residents, so that the over-crowding was never quite so bad as it appeared. But the investigation revealed also a gap of 2,600 square feet in desirable library accommodation ; this should not have come as entirely unexpected, since that opened by Lord Cobham in 1962 had been built for a College of 300 students, mostly resident. This was a most suitable object upon which a major project might be focussed and it appealed both to the D.E.S. and the College Principal ; this would not, of itself, provide direct help to the communal accommodation, but Principal Buckmaster had other plans in this direction and there was always the possibility that the D.E.S. might be encouraged to think of a second phase.

The new proposal attracted a visit from N. E. Worcester, the Territorial Officer from the D.E.S., on 30th October 1969 and he was asked to consider a new building for a library of 7,590 square feet, the moving of the education departments to the existing Library block and some reallocation of other rooms to make more space for student common rooms. This proposal he took away with him for further consideration and a few days later it was presented to the Governors who established a sub-committee to review it.

In the meantime the College received a visit from H. A. Harding, top civil servant in charge of teacher training at the D.E.S. He was to achieve the reputation within a few short years of a 20th century Thomas Cromwell, but this visit which included other midlands colleges seems to have been no more than exploratory, although what he was exploring he kept to himself. It was a pity that the visit had to be made on a murky November afternoon when Saltley looked its worst and, although he gave his blessing to a Library project, it is hard to believe that he had undertaken much preparatory work about the institution he was visiting, since he recommended that St. Peter's should take more women students and commence a

149

nursery teachers course — which would appear to conflict with the logic of the College's history and the actual realities of what went on there. For the rest he asked a group of staff to suggest what errors the D.E.S. had been guilty of, but hurried away before they could assemble their answer and rejected out of hand the requests of a group of students for the provision of a "student union block" and the abolition of the parental means test on the assessment of grants.

In February, 1970, the Principal was able to report to the Building Committee

"that the D.E.S. considered the provision of adequate library space to be a high priority in the allocation of finance and that, in their view, the provision of additional communal accommodation for students. . . . was a much lower priority.

"They pointed out, however, that 'whereas a College of this size should have a library space of just under 9,000 square feet the proposals provided for one of only 7,590 sq. ft.' "

It is tempting to wonder what Canon Platten's reaction might have been to this extraordinary reply by the D.E.S. in the light of his own experiences during the Fifties. The Building Committee hastily revised its plans and decided that one more of the hard tennis courts would have to go in favour of a larger two storey block, adjacent to the new teaching block.

Bruce McGowan, then Headmaster of Solihull School and Birmingham Diocesan representative Governor, had been made chairman of the Building Committee and he skilfully steered the new proposal into calm waters at the Governors' Meeting in March and it was resolved formally to apply to the D.E.S. for its implementation. Permission to join the "Preliminary" list was given in May, 1971; the estimated cost of the building was then £100,000 and the College's share £20,000; it was estimated that if the five dioceses each contributed £50 a year for five years, and each student £1 for three years, enough could be raised to cover this when added to the Bursar's contribution.

In September, 1971, there was a further ironic twist when the D.E.S., now in the hands of Margaret Thatcher, cheerfully discovered that "there is always an outside chance that the money for Phase 1 could be increased to cover the whole job, i.e. Phase 2 in addition . . . Obviously this is a pretty remote chance but it is useful to know that there would be no snags on your side should the opportunity arise."

In other words money might be available for a more ambitious venture which would bring all of St. Peter's up to the latest specifications. A wink is as good as a nod ! By the following February, the project now allowed for a ground floor/basement area devoted to an Education Resources centre and the Governors contribution had risen to £28,000 ; in June, the Education Department had been promoted to the top floor and the Governors' contribution to £32,000, to be raised in November to

£37,885. There were no snags ; in November, 1972, the College achieved the Starts List for 1973/74. In March 1973 the Principal was able to write to the Chairman :

' . . . you will be glad to know that agreement has been reached on the telephone with the D.E.S. for the New Library Building. The agreed cost is . . . £214,120. The Governors' portion of this is approximately £43,000. The Governors already have in their funds a reserve of £20,000, a profit last year of £12,000 and by the end of the current financial year an additional £10,000. This means that the Governors virtually hold sufficient money to cover their contribution to the actual building. There will be, however, additional expenditure of not less than £30,000 . . . This will entail the Governors in an additional expenditure of about £6,000 which will be raised by conferences etc. during 1973.

"It is hoped that the building will start within a fortnight and we should be using it in September, 1974."

Lest any reader should suppose that the D.E.S. was acting with cavalier generosity with public funds, he will be pleased to learn that there was no agreement to instal double glazing until a special noise measurement test had been undertaken to establish the decibels created by Bridge Road traffic throughout the day. The building was completed for occupation within the time forecast, but by then the College was deeply anxious about its future and the meeting held by the Governors in October 1974 in the new Library itself was to discuss a possible move to Carlisle. As it had grown it had seemed something of an assurance about the future for both staff and students and when one of the Governors had suggested that it was improvident to continue with this venture, all had been agreed that it must go on. There had been some hope that some V.I.P. would officiate at a ceremonial opening, but by 1974 such an event was no longer appropriate.

It was (and is) a fine building, well designed and most pleasantly furnished in a modern style. It gave the College space and elegance which it had lacked and contributed richly to its assets in a competitive world. The Library was a success from the beginning and was increasingly used by students, notably B.Ed. degree candidates, who found the facilities and atmosphere for study admirable. The Resources Centre could be equipped only slowly and many of the staff, who had not before enjoyed this amenity, needed to be educated in its full use. Peter Baker from the English Department was placed in charge and he was able in the short time available to make it one of the focal areas of College teaching.

During this period the erection of a Sports Hall remained an important objective, but made little progress. The provision of a site was the first obstacle and the Vice Principal's garden, which had been suggested as suitable, was hardly large enough. A rough plan existed to construct a ramp or bridge from the bank of the cutting and over the main railway line, but no one developed it further. Eventually the Principal conceived the idea of building a Sports Hall on the site opposite the College on the other side of Bridge Road as a joint venture between the Governors and the City (possibly without involving the D.E.S.) :

To the City Engineer and Surveyor, June 1972.

Enclosed you will find a proposal for a Sports Hall Complex which it is suggested could be built by the College opposite its present site in Bridge Road, Saltley . . . it would be my intention to allow the College P.E. course to use the Hall for their own instruction and training, and to encourage them to give it supervision to be used as a community Sports Hall allowing properly structured groups from the area to use it at the evenings, week-ends and during holiday periods. It is hoped it would be used 52 weeks a year and seven days a week on this basis . . . You will appreciate that this area of the city is very poorly equipped with this kind of facility . . . and I would see it as a real encouragement to the young people of the district . . . ''

The Principal succeeded in interesting Denis Howell, the Saltley M.P. in the venture and he thought that it might well be possible to gain the financial support of City business men. Unfortunately the site chosen was one available for house-building and the Governors considered the rent demanded by the City as exorbitant and the idea was dropped. Instead the Roman Catholics built a nursery school there.

It had also been hoped that the sporting facilities at Stechford might be improved and the Bursar enquired whether it would be possible to purchase an additional piece of land there, till that time used as allotments. Not merely was it not possible, but the City Council had decided to build houses thereupon ; this seemed unjust to the Governors since the College field had been designated by the authority as public open space. It was decided therefore to apply for planning permission for building, with the intention that if and when this were granted, the College would be able to buy land in the green belt for a new sports ground. Eventually after several years of argument, planning permission was granted for half the site, but too late to take the action proposed.

Meanwhile a number of important adjustments were made to the existing College buildings to improve communal facilities ; all of these were paid for from yearly maintenance accounts or by other means and they were not a drain away from the major building project. Some, like changing the boilers to light-oil fuel, and ultimately, to gas burning, or like the provision of wash-basins in all study bedrooms, involved a carefully prepared programme lasting several years. Others, like the establishment of an S.P.C.K. Bookshop in the Flat on Lower South or a branch of Lloyd's Bank in the main corridor or new floors in the Dining Hall and Assembly Hall or a Launderette, were completed in one summer vacation. Two of the most significant changes affected the South Block ; the Lower South study bedrooms were converted into a day-time study area for non-resident students ; many of the internal curtain walls were dismantled and the space fitted out with tables, chairs and reading lamps and pleasantly decorated ; another part of the area was equipped with lockers. On the whole this area was well used and appreciated by the lodgers and day students, especially those who had no close associate among the residents. The other change concerned the fine room immediately below, which, once a library, had been the main student common room since the building of the Burrow English block. At its far end was a tutorial resident flat, but when John Tarrant left in 1970, it was decided to incorporate this within the J.C.R. so that a fully equipped bar could be established there. This required some ingenuity since there was a problem of levels and also a large brick chimney-pillar between the two and this could not be pulled down. The job was done successfully at a cost of £4,800 and with the assistance of one of the big brewery companies a splendid bar was erected. This change significantly swung the focus of College life, at least after 9 p.m., towards South Block and would probably be regarded by most of the later Saltley students as a key improvement. The J.C.R. itself gradually assumed the appearance of a dismal and characterless pub, especially after students insisted, against the earlier wishes of the S.U. Council, upon the installation of a juke-box and darts board, but the canned-football machine had to have a home elsewhere. On Saturday nights it was enlivened further by the students' purchase of disco equipment. When the new library was opened in 1974, history completed its cycle by the return to the students of the ground floor of the East wing of Old Quad, which had belonged to them after the war and was then known as the Old Common Room and housed billiards and table tennis tables ; now the Student Union established a Television Room and a Union Office.

One of the frequent problems at Saltley — and at other colleges all over the country — was that of security against theft and vandalism. There were occasions when the student union established their own security patrols but when wheel hubs and eventually complete cars vanished, the problem was getting out of hand ; one member of staff discovered his car outside the gates of Cardiff City gaol. Principal Buckmaster proposed the construction of an inner perimeter road which would enable all entries at night to be locked except one which could be guarded ; this was a more difficult enterprise than might be supposed, including the need to demolish the Vice Principal's pantry and coalhouse, and it could be undertaken only as a minor project when money allowed ; in fact it was completed in two stages to the general public benefit.

During 1970, a small Church School due to lose its pupils was discovered near Appleby quite literally at the foot of the Pennines and the College took out a five-year lease and established its own Field Centre. Much skilled work in plumbing and redecoration was needed before it could be used effectively and some of this was undertaken voluntarily by members of staff and students during vacations. Thereafter most of the college courses which encouraged outdoor field work were expected to use the centre and it was available for school or private groups at other times for a small charge. Since some of the new integrated courses were eager to seize this opportunity, many students from different college activities were able to enjoy a change of environment from Saltley.

This chapter concludes at a point at which perhaps it should have started. Principal Buckmaster, after consultation with the Chaplain and with the Chapel Committee, determined upon a simple but radical change in the Chapel. The old choir pews were removed and a heavy curtain hung between the choir and the nave ; a door was made from the chancel to the outside world so that for safety's sake, there now existed an alternative exit. The choir thus became a worship area, which could be curtained off from the rest of the building although normally the curtain was not drawn. The intention was that college academic and social life could be brought into the body of the chapel (under certain restraints) so that the sharp distinction between the religious life and other sorts of activity might be reduced. Some tutors used the chapel for lectures and for display purposes and a few examinations were held there ; but it did not become popular for academic purposes despite its superb acoustics. It was, popular, however, with musicians and the chapel became the centre of the series of choral society performances and celebrity concerts, which were one of the joys of St. Peter's in its later years.

This section would be incomplete without an account of a remarkable piece of skill and dedication which took a number of years to achieve — the rebuilding of the College organ, a genuine piece of self-help, bringing together staff and students of the Music and Craft and Design departments in a project demanding expertise, craftsmanship and patience of a high order under the general direction of Wally Wragg. The total cost of the venture reached some £2,300 spread over four years, although the cost for a professional rebuild would have been nearer £20,000 at the time.

There had been an organ with a hand pump on the gallery before the War and in 1951, as a part of the war memorial, a local craftsman, Martin Williamson, was commissioned to build a new organ. This instrument consisted of new pipework and electric action, although some of the older instrument was probably included. For some years during the late 60's the organ had been temperamental and Wragg was asked to make an inspection ; he reported :

"Owing to the age of this instrument, the type of electric action employed is obsolete, therefore a thorough and reliable renovation is virtually impossible, and I see no really satisfactory solution other than a complete rebuild."

The Principal decided to follow Wragg's advice and the work proceeded. A music student, Michael Thompson, with professional experience in organ building, assisted with the original planning and was responsible for the technical work concerned with the circuitry ; a new console, pedalboard, oak case-work and walnut console fitments were fashioned in the workshop by Craft students ; secondhand and new pipes were obtained to give much needed tonal variations and eventually the

154

instrument was assembled, the console being placed in the choir while the pipes remained on the gallery. The Williamson memorial case-work and inscription were preserved but suitably modified to encase the new instrument. Professional organists and organ builders have declared the organ to be a masterpiece, one local expert being of the opinion that this was "the best amateur-built organ he had ever seen".

Chapter 27

In 1968 when St. Peter's changed Principals, staff/students relations had reached a dangerously high temperature in many institutions of higher education and it could not be expected that colleges of education, voluntary or not, would be sheltered from disturbances. Conflict was concentrated upon issues of control and participation in decision making, although behind this lay some cultural confusion springing from a tendency of many young people to reject the authority associated with traditional thought and institutions. One must, however, be especially careful in one's generalisation about staff and student attitudes towards each other ; on the one hand an increasing number of staff sympathised with students on some issues, if not on all ; on the other hand, many students were largely indifferent to student power politics and even the most apparently avant-garde were usually prepared at least to examine the arguments of the traditionalists.

In 1950 the authority and the responsibility for the exercise of control and discipline in a training college lay with the Principal, subject only to the approval of his Governors and the co-operation of his staff, of whom the most important in this context was the Vice Principal. It was essentially a personal affair and there were liberal and popular regimes, as there were also some harsh and unpopular. By the end of the Sixties, other external bodies were laying down principles upon which the college authorities were expected to act. The most demanding of these was the National Union of Students, acting nationally and regionally, which bombarded college Student Union officials with literature containing codes of discipline, model constitutions, pamphlets on "student participation", and "further advice and information on negotiating amendments on Instruments and Articles of Government", beside promoting campaigns on specific issues like visiting hours and intervening, on student request, in disputes.

The staff association, the A.T.C.D.E., joined in with its own advice ; in 1961, there was a statement agreed with the N.U.S. of "fundamental principles which should underlie college life" and again in 1964 a further one on "College Regulations on Residence"; this was spelt out in more detail in January 1968, the document ending with :

"We recommend students' unions, principals, and boards of governors, to initiate discussions early with a view to bringing their regulations into line with the recommendations and observations made in this joint statement."

In December 1969, the A.T.C.D.E. brought out its "Notes of Guidance on the Responsibilities of a Resident Tutor in a College of Education", which annunciated these responsibilities in some detail and restated the important principle that :

"...A student's room is his home during term-time, his privacy should be respected, and he should have the right to be present if his room is to be inspected..."

In 1973, the A.T.C.D.E. published a loose-leaf folder entitled "Handbook for Principals of Colleges of Education", a sort of do-it-yourself compendium of knowledge for Principals, most usefully arranged and up-to-date. One wonders what significance Principal Cooper, or for that matter, Principal Platten would have attached to the folder.

The D.E.S. too claimed to exercise some control over collegiate life. Following the report of a Departmental Committee, the Weaver Report on the "Government of Colleges of Education", an Education Act 1968 required colleges to amend their Instruments of Government and by a letter of September 1969 suggested student membership of Governing Bodies and Academic Boards, provisions for consultative committees and new disciplinary machinery. The D.E.S. took pains to ensure that Principals were aware of the changed legal status of students subsequent to the Latey Report and that their powers no longer allowed them to discuss students' personal affairs, even health, with their parents.

One further element should be noticed that staff/student troubles made good news for the media, particularly the Press. Few Principals can have relished for their colleges the publicity gained by the London School of Economics during its period of conflict and the threat of publicity by Student Unions, a legitimate weapon after all, must have encouraged many Principals to seek compromise.

At St. Peter's the Student Union had moved into a new era with the arrival of Keith Sach (1967-70), another Southport President, charming, persuasive, determined ; he devoted a large amount of his time to Student Union affairs, he was an assiduous supporter of the N.U.S. and used his drive and talents to achieve the ends which the N.U.S. sought. Not all students, including some of his own Executive, approved of his leadership, but few could deny him the credit of being the architect of the new student order in the college.

Principal Buckmaster lost no time in getting to grips with these matters ; at his second meeting of the Academic Board in October the Board elected representatives to a committee to examine proposals for student participation in college affairs and by its nomination of Major Osborne, Peter Street and John Taylor it revealed its sympathies to be with the student aspirations. The Academic Council was less unanimous in its support, since some staff felt themselves to be deprived of participant rights in decision making and didn't see why students should be given preference. The Governors faced the issue of admitting students to their numbers at their meeting in March 1969 ; one Governor stated :

"that he had no confidence in the scheme and that in his view students would be unlikely to contribute anything. He considered the proposal would result in a weakening of the authority of the Board of Governors and suggested a Joint Consultative Committee."

The Chairman and the Principal both supported the idea, however, and it was agreed that the students should have two Governor representatives, the President and Vice President or Secretary. As a quid pro quo the students agreed at the following meeting to admit one Governors' representative as a member of the Student Union Council, from which time the Vice Principal became that representative.

It is reasonable that we should ask what impact, if any, resulted from the admission of students to the government of the college. At first the Governors were impressed by the student contribution but in later years, as their membership changed frequently, the finer points of the questions under discussion seemed to elude them and, when appealed to by the Chairman to state an opinion, they rarely seemed able to do so. There were exceptions, however; in March 1971, Union President, John Thompson, persuaded the Governors, in the face of opposition from the Principal, Commander Heathcote and Bruce McGowan, to send to the D.E.S. the resolution:

"The Governing Body of St. Peter's College, Saltley, requests the Secretary of State for Education and Science urgently to review the present system of parental contributions towards the support of recognised students enjoying higher education."

They were less successful in March 1973, when the Governors considered a request from the Student Union for the installation of a machine for the sale of contraceptives in college. There were a number of interesting aspects about this issue, which was at the time one of those being promoted by the N.U.S. Indeed it probably involved more a question of who controls the residential life of the college — the students or the Governors — than a sensitive moral problem. It seems to have been the only occasion during the post-war years that the Principal found it necessary to raise a general matter of internal residential life at a full Governors' meeting. The two students who had to open the debate needed plenty of courage since there were three Bishops present on this occasion; they received support from all the Head Teacher governors and others, but the odds were heavily against them and the request was "refused on a majority vote". The students accepted their defeat gracefully and made no further effort to repeat their request.

There were four student members of the Academic Board, but, after the first fine careless rapture in the days of Keith Sach and his contemporaries, interest among the students waned and they played little active part in the proceedings, rarely raising subjects for discussion except under Other Business. The students had elected an Academic Affairs Officer whose functions could have proved important and useful in the rapidly changing course structure, but general interest among students flagged and they rarely seemed to choose officers with the ability or determination to make the job successful. In April 1970, Sach raised confidentiality of college student records, which was another on-going issue with the N.U.S. As a result the Board agreed that students should scrutinise their record cards but the Principal emphasised that "it could only be in the interests of past, present and future students that the confidence established between the College and the Local Authorities should not be undermined". By and large, the students accepted this and it was all a storm in a tea-cup. It was beyond doubt useful to have students at Academic Board meetings since it was often desirable to obtain a quick student reaction to current problems and, when the Board made an unpopular decision, the failure of student representatives to register their dissent diverted public wrath from the Board to the students concerned.

The staff/student Participation Committee in due course came up with its recommendations for a new set of structures to handle internal and domestic affairs and matters of discipline. These were all to be put under the authority of joint staff/student committees, which would be under staff chairmanship but numerically balanced either equally or in student favour. Most attention was concentrated upon the Disciplinary Committee, which was required to form itself into a tribunal to conduct proper and appropriate judicial proceedings against an alleged offender ; its powers were restricted to £2 fine, although it could recommend suspension (rustication) to the Principal. The documentary basis for this was the D.E.S. letter of September 1969, which stated :

"The new concept is for a disciplinary committee to be set up with powers of decision and for that committee to be composed of equal numbers of staff and students . . . This new concept stems from the belief that in a self-governing academic community those who live and work within the community should as far as possible be responsible for its internal discipline. . . . "

This document did not make it obligatory for Governors to conform, but it would have been difficult for them not to have done with a rampant N.U.S. on their tracks. The Governors considered the proposals in March and again in June 1970. At the first of these meetings, Commander Heathcote, as Clerk, made a long statement in which he stated :

". . . that after reading all available documents concerning both discipline and the Union constitution it was clear that both far reaching and very important matters of principle were involved . . . the proposals removed the power and authority of the Principal as it is at present exercised."

The Governors appointed a powerful sub-committee of educators under the chairmanship of the Archdeacon of Stafford to go into the matter. Meanwhile a Working Party of Church Principals had made its own comments, which, while recognising that "there is general acceptance of the belief that . . . those who live and work within a community as far as possible be responsible for its internal discipline", also made it clear that :

"The authority of the Principal, whose views or decisions on disciplinary matters could now be over-ruled or by-passed by a committee of staff, students and in some cases governors, would undergo an alteration which would profoundly affect his role of leadership in the college."

In June the Archdeacon's report recommended a double-tier system with both a College Disciplinary Committee and a Governors' Disciplinary Committee and after a brief discussion it was agreed to amend the Instrument of Government accordingly.

Presumably other colleges throughout the country adjusted their practices similarly. At Saltley the Governors' Disciplinary Committee has never met, which, superficially at least, was a satisfactory state of affairs. The College Disciplinary Committee met on a number of occasions ; its proceedings were slow and cumbersome and those who had to put them into effect had no legal training. In all cases that it dealt with preliminary investigations had revealed that the accused persons accepted their liability ; this was fortunate since it would not have been practicable to expect college administrative staff, cleaners or porters, to appear to give evidence and to be cross-examined. The function of the tribunal was therefore to assess the nature and the gravity of the offence committed and the penalty to be exacted ; these were precisely the areas in which to expect disagreement, especially as the students were keenly on the look out to reject anything that might resemble old-fashioned morality, and there was no body of case-law to which one might refer. Despite these adverse comments, it would probably be true, however, that students disliked the embarrassment and publicity that the tribunals involved and often preferred to accept the escape clause which allowed the offence to be handled in confidence by the tutor concerned.

Another of the new democratic institutions proposed by the Participation Committee and approved by the Governors was known as the College Committee, which was to approve the rules applicable to residential life and to discuss urgent problems (except catering) as they cropped up. Once more the Vice Principal was in the Chair and the Committee brought together round the table representatives from the different residential quarters, day students, officers of the Union, the Principal and all residential tutors, the Senior Administrative Officer, Matron and Head Porter and a few other important persons like the Chaplain. This imposing group ought to have been more useful than it was ; it suffered from frequently changing membership and it never acquired among the students any real worth-while status. This was partly due to the fact that when students had complaints their immediate action was to approach a S.U. Officer or to have them raised in the S.U. Council ; they could then be raised with Brian Strand or the Principal whose doors were ever open. Still, the Committee spent some useful time debating washing machines and electric irons.

The College Rules were brief and after 1968 little attempt was made to enforce them by direct supervision ; although all students were told that they were expected to conform, some rules may well have been discreetly ignored from time to time. Control was exercised through an agreement that all students were required to sign before coming into residence :

"RESIDENT STUDENTS AGREEMENT   Academic Year 19

. . . . The College offers a collegiate life in which order and personal discipline are expected of each student together with a loyalty to the total community. It follows that students who break the terms of this agreement may be asked to find non-residential accommodation for themselves.

I Agree :

3. Not to allow any other persons to use my room in my absence without proper authority.

4. Not to allow any other person to 'kip down' in my room without permission of the College authorities, except in an emergency.

6. To accept and conform to the discipline of community life within the residence.

8. To allow the Principal or his authorized agent reasonable access to my room.

Signed.. "

It seems probable that a lawyer might have found much to criticise in this document abbreviated above, and certainly the phrase "kip down", although meaningful to students, was inelegant. But it was effective in reminding every one what sort of standards should be achieved and those, who admitted residential lapses, could be rebuked on grounds of breach of contract rather than on moral precepts to which they would have objected.

Two other joint staff/student committees which became increasingly important were the Catering Committee and the Management Committee of the Union Society, which ran the Bar. The Catering Committee comprised Brian Strand, a member of the academic staff, the Lady Caterer, and a group of students under the President. When the Direct Cash Grant system commenced (see next chapter), the President took over Chairmanship. This committee resolved its difficulties, as they arose, admirably, although the claim of one group of students that they could manage the catering much more economically if left to do it themselves could not be supported. The management committee of the Bar also operated successfully, if its expansion of business is any criterion. The Principal, in his capacity as licensee, retained the Chairmanship, although the Student Union executive insisted that the Bar management should be their affair ; they were in fact well represented on the Management committee, but

160

this did not prevent them occasionally sulking and neglecting to enforce proper discipline in the S.U. Common Room on the grounds that this was the province of the Bar management.

There was a prolonged difference of opinion between the Governors and the Student Union over the details of the Student Union constitution, which the Governors were required to approve. Commander Heathcote reported to the Governors in November 1970, that :

".... the draft constitution was now in the hands of Student Union officers who were examining a few points at the request of the Committee."

This was the same committee who had inspected the proposals for discipline. What these "points" were was not divulged, but it seems likely that one of these was the treatment to be handed out to what the Union called "scab" members who refused to pay an extra subvention to support the subscription paid directly from L.E.A. grant. Although the subject was raised at each Governors' meeting, it was two and a half years later in March 1973, that Bruce McGowan was able to report that the new draft of the constitution was in the hands of the sub-committee, but that "certain clauses were completely unacceptable and a considerable amount of work and negotiation would be necessary to reach any form of agreement." He proposed that the Governors "receive" the constitution rather than "approve" it. The Principal now rescued the situation from farce by obtaining a note from the D.E.S. that Governors' approval of Students' Union Constitution could be "limited to the aim and objects of the Union and would not be concerned with the procedures by which those aims and objects were pursued." The students now presented a brief document, for the most part innocuous, apart from its use of a new word, quorate, meaning 'establish a quorum' and garnered presumably from some N.U.S. usage ; the Governors approved and all was well.

Chapter 28

In December 1973, five years after coming to Saltley, Principal Buckmaster wrote to the Secretary of the Church of England Board of Education :

"I do not myself think that the implications of the new order are yet fully understood either by ourselves or by the Church at large . . . We can no longer provide the kind of residential community that was once considered to be essential. From the religious point of view our chapels no longer command allegiance of our student bodies and from the academic point of view, we are more and more facing changes which are outside our control. The British way in the past has always been to watch the evolving relationships with other institutions and proceed pragmatically from one situation to the next until finally we sit back in our new situation and evolve a theology and philosophy about it. I personally doubt whether this approach will work this time . . . "

In 1968, Miss Skinner, the Principal of Lincoln College of Education, had said much the same in her Presidential Address to the A.T.C.D.E. :

"I can only give the existential answer. We have got to make our communities as we proceed, constructing with what we have got, making it up as we go along." ("Education for Teaching", No. 72).

It is clear that, in the face of the sweeping changes noted in the previous chapters, the Principal and his staff needed to be flexible and adaptable if they were to hope to achieve that leavening that community life in a Church college gave during the Fifties and earlier. Many students saw college as the place for an alternative culture, created by themselves, spontaneous, depending upon instinctive responses :

". . . no longer a total community of like-minded people, but a series of independent units ; hostels in which they lived on their own terms ; lecture rooms and working areas in which they acquired sufficient credits to clear the intellectual hurdles of the three-year course ; the bar, the centre of social life ; discos, in which they escaped the reality of things in darkness and noise . . ."

(Principal Buckmaster, in a private letter).

One such unit was concerned about College chapel ; on week-day mornings this was largely, but never entirely, senior members of staff and committed day students, often with a strong sprinkling of mature persons and graduates ; the Sunday services, usually an 11 a.m. Holy Communion, were attended by a group, varying in size from year to year, of friendly and dedicated students, who did well to preserve their enthusiasm as long as they did in the face of general student apathy. The Chaplains strove manfully to close the cultural gap and each of them, John Tarrant, who left in 1970, Alan Bradbury 1970-72 and Peter Bellamy from 1973-78, introduced imaginative services and experimented in new forms of worship. Contacts were renewed with other Saltley congregations and with Queen's College in Selly Oak. They made good use of special expertise among both staff and students, and much hard work went into attempts to stimulate curiosity and interest in the principles underlying the Church Foundation.

The Chapel Committee did their best to promote support for the Chapel ; on one occasion, for example, they undertook to clean up the Student Common Room after someone else's party the night before ; they organised coffee parties and outings ; Holy Communion took place by candle-light in winter and in the Quad on Summer Sunday mornings ; but they must often have been disheartened by the apparent lack of success they achieved. It was a pity that they received little continuous support from the Christian Union, which flourished as one of the independent units the Principal probably had in mind when he wrote the passage quoted above.

As the role of the Principal, 'in loco parentis', disappeared and as the idea of the College as a community diminished, the numbers of students in distress for one reason or another grew. The College had long operated a personal tutorial system but the students complained that this was often ineffectual. One consequence was that student union officers found themselves acting as unpaid welfare officers and the burden for some of the Presidents, especially during periods of stress, like teaching practice, became heavy. It was natural therefore that they should turn to the professional counsellors either on the staff or outside for assistance ; at one time a counsellor from the University of Aston conducted a "surgery" at St. Peter's.

From 1968 onwards there were upwards of 400 day students, a majority of whom were not permanently based on Birmingham ; of those who could have lived at home, many chose not to do so, although they lost financially by becoming independent. When the three-year course had started, most of the third-year students, who could no longer be housed on the campus, went into approved lodgings found by the college lodgings officer ; there they usually established a happy relationship with their landlady, who welcomed both the rent and the companionship that the arrangement seemed to offer. But this was not really what most students were seeking, since it involved restraints upon their freedom, and, in the event of conflict, the likelihood that complaints would be brought directly to the college authorities. They chose, therefore, as they were entitled to do, to find their own accommodation, sometimes in pairs or larger groups of four, five or six. They were often in ghastly conditions, poorly fed and sometimes ill. Some became involved in dispute with unscrupulous landlords and must have been grateful for the assistance that Brian Strand, Sam Palmer and others were able to give. In 1968 Principal Buckmaster tried to supplement the off-the-campus accommodation, by buying some houses in Pretoria Road, but unfortunately the City Housing Authorities imposed a ban. For some years the old convent hostel near the Pelham provided rooms for between 20 and 30 students and for two years between 1969 and 1971 the college leased a curate's house standing empty in Anthony Road from the Parish of St. Mary and St. John, and this was sub-let to a group of 7 or 8 third-year girls. For some years, too, women students, particularly graduates, were glad to accept rooms in a Roman Catholic hostel in Highfield Road. It must be remembered, however, that despite the problems and despite any amount of parental anxiety, students chose voluntarily to live in independence, knowing full well that they would encounter difficulties ; at least no one could continue to assert that teachers in training had been sheltered from contact with the outside world.

It was to be expected that 400 day students would exercise an important influence upon the residential life ; the college campus remained their real base and the centre of their "culture" ; many had boy or girl friends still resident on the campus and they expected to be able to use the residential facilities almost as readily as the residents themselves. This led to the overcrowding of common rooms, particularly the Bar, although it helped to preserve the legend that the college was still a community. The College was fortunate in 1969 to obtain the services of Mrs. Becky Druce as Housekeeper from Bishop Lonsdale College at Derby.

The Michael Parker Building, New Library and Lyttleton.

Prior to her appointment, there had been some friction between her predecessor and the students, but Mrs. Druce was able to tread successfully the difficult and delicate path between her responsibilities to the college and the "freedom" of the students. When she grumbled, as she had occasion to do pretty frequently, about the state of the Common Rooms, the Student Union Officers, aware that she would be difficult to replace, would take rapid action to put things right.

The advent of the direct cash grant system contributed still further towards the tendencies that we have already noticed in the years after 1968. The Governors were invited during the spring of 1971 to participate with a small group of other colleges, voluntary and state-controlled, in a scheme whereby resident students should receive their whole grant in cash and pay both for their meals and for their rooms, in the same way as Oxbridge students had done from time immemorial; readers will recall that, previous to this, fees in voluntary colleges were paid directly to the College from public funds and the resident students received full board and lodgings free, their grant consisting of an allowance for personal expenditure. Why St. Peter's was selected to share in this enterprise was not made fully clear, but one might justly infer from it a compliment from the D.E.S. to Commander Heathcote for his outstanding administration. The Governors were, as ever in things financial, cautious and needed to be persuaded that they would not have to meet any losses incurred. But they agreed and the scheme which the Principal had produced in collaboration with the D.E.S. was unfolded. Most attention was directed towards the catering element, but it would be well to state that the College was expected to maintain the structure of the buildings and pay for light and heat from their receipts from room rentals and from a small element of the tuition fee which was appropriated to teaching accommodation. To make it more difficult, the College was required to estimate its expenses (during a period of increasing inflation) and if it did make any profits in one area they could not balance the losses on another; it seemed improbable, however, that there would be any "profits".

In catering, the College undertook to operate a fully cash-based system, unlike some colleges which preferred to introduce a system in which students paid a global sum and received set meals in return. The difficulty with the Saltley system was that if students elected to spend their money outside college, then there could be heavy losses, because the overhead charges, especially salaries and wages, had of necessity to be met. To do this, the Student Union and Academic Board agreed that all who took part in the scheme should pay a Dining Hall subscription and that to off-set this the prices of the food which they purchased in the cafeteria would be significantly cheaper than in outside restaurants. The most difficult step was to persuade the students that the arrangements were still not viable unless they all joined the Dining Hall club; there could be no exceptions for day students. Indeed, this was fair, because otherwise the residents would be subsidising day students' meals and frequent use of the catering facilities. But what about day students who claimed that they never used the residential buildings, not even for

Saturday night dances? Here the alliance between the College administration and the student union officers held firm and only a handful of exceptions were permitted; some students, usually graduates, asserted that they would not pay their bills, but in the end they did so almost to a man. During the first year of operation students grumbled loudly about the level of the prices and proposed to do the catering themselves; but the union officers were encouraged to share in the price fixing and once the catering establishment had become fully familiar with student needs and how best to cope with them, the complaints died away.

The following year the College was asked to repeat the experiment and thereafter it was continued at the students' request and in anticipation that the D.E.S. would introduce it compulsorily elsewhere. If one were to attempt to strike a balance, one must accept that it was popular among the resident students,d espite the occasional friction incurred as a result of the Principal's insistence that accounts should be settled at the time that grants were distributed. The resident students relished the economic freedom, although it was neither possible nor desirable for them to be equipped with elaborate cook-it-yourself facilities in their rooms or corridors. It meant, however, the end of communal feeding and, although as much as possible was done to improve the dining hall decor by dividing the long oak tables into small ones and the provision of curtains, it was hard to prevent the cafeteria system becoming slummy. Discipline was not easy to enforce and the catering officers, who were expected to make a profit, were concerned not to turn customers away by imposing a strict regime. This applied especially to the graduates who enjoyed a smoke and cup of coffee and perhaps a game of bridge after their midday lunch.

The catering accounts were £3,000 in arrears at the end of the first year despite severe economies before the scheme began, including the redundancy of many of the kitchen staff, some of whom had worked in the college for many years. Commander Heathcote wrote:

"Because of the anticipated reduction in the demand for meals, about one-third of the catering staff became redundant. Every effort was made to act as sympathetically as possible to those concerned, and the Governors allowed extra money to be paid to those leaving who had served the College for over two years. Many of the staff had lengthy service to their credit, in particular Mrs. Morris and Mrs. Moss. . . . "

The other sufferers under the cash grant system were the academic staff although, perhaps, they deserve less sympathy. They were free to join the Dining Hall club, but if they did not they would have to make their own arrangements for all meals, except the morning coffee. They were asked whether they wished for waitress service but rejected this on the grounds of cost. This meant that they would purchase their dinner through the same process as everyone else and they chose to sit at the same tables as the students in the body of the hall. This was indeed democratic and impressed old students with memories of different arrangements. But in fact fewer of the staff took meals at college as the years went on and those who were missing included some of the most senior members. There was some loss of fellowship in consequence as well as of efficiency of communication.

Hospitality became something of a problem. Under the scheme the D.E.S. agreed to a Governors' allowance, so that an official guest of the college could be entertained with a "Governors' Ticket", but the guest would normally queue and select his meal with the rest and sit in the body of the hall, unless a table had been put on one side. In the evening it was far too costly to keep the kitchen staff at college after seven p.m. and guests invited by staff and students to societies or dramatic performances would normally be entertained privately in rooms or treated in the Bar. One would hasten to say again that this was no different from Oxbridge in the Thirties, unless one were fortunate enough to be entertained in lavish style in the Senior Common Room.

Communication had been a problem at Saltley throughout the post-war years and much idle rumour prevailed. Things improved a bit with the extension of the offices and an internal telephone system, and, after 1974, the opening of a Union Office just off the administration corridor. Student Union officials were keen to instal a Tannoy speaking system, which might have been an improvement upon the practice which developed of ringing a handbell in the dining hall when matters of importance had to be announced. The normal method of communication was by notice board ; by the Seventies virtually the whole of Saltley's long corridor had its walls decorated with such boards ; if there were any spare wall space, then before long notices would occupy it. As the need to attract attention increased so the notices became ever larger, until the day came when the Student Union took over the whole corridor to advertise an Open Meeting. One notable improvement in communication occurred as a result of the increased size of the college and that was the appointment in 1970 by the Student Union of a permanent paid secretary, working about half time. It would have been hard for them to have found anyone more suitable than Mrs. Hilary Rees who filled the post for a number of years. She provided the Student Union with much needed continuity in its administration and she was absolutely loyal to her employers and everywhere popular. The whole college was much saddened when she died after a short illness in 1975.

An innovation introduced by Principal Buckmaster was the publication each term of a series of Principal's Broadsheets which were informative and on occasion provocative ; but they were useful and distributed widely. The Student Union, less frequently, produced its own Broadsheets along similar lines and other groups, like the new Socialist Society, skilfully copied the Principal's journalist style. Even individuals now and then turned their talents seriously or in fun in this direction and it was fortunate that the Principal himself first encountered one 'rogue' edition before it had been generally distributed and so saved the third-year students from leaving a specimen outside the surgery door the following morning. The College Magazine, "The Salt", continued publication until 1972, except for the year 1969/70 when the Students' Union produced their own "Assault". The magazine had been strongly subsidised over the years and, as inflation developed, there no longer seemed any way that it could be produced from public funds. With the retirement of Philip Dunn, the "Salt" lost its chief driving force; instead the Principal wrote a much more detailed annual report for submission to the Governors so that the College records might be maintained.

In 1968 the Student Union Council remained the central authority for the conduct of student affairs. During 1969 the students published the first edition of their new constitution. This was a quite remarkable document and a tribute to the small sub-committee of constitution makers which produced it ; it contained a detailed set of standing orders and bye-laws with instructions for the operation and responsibilities of all union officials, although it was never completed. Copies were available for perusal in the Student Union Office and in the College Library, but it was so lengthy a document that only those who compiled it, either knew what it contained or understood it. While Keith Sach and John Thompson were Presidents a real effort was made to implement this constitution and the meetings of the Union Council were invariably lively and usually lengthy. On the whole the Councillors gave a friendly but cautious welcome to the Governors' representative in their midst, who soon became the oldest member ; he usually refrained from using his vote, except on procedural matters, and the student members rapidly lost any inhibitions his presence might have induced. Gradually, however, the S.U. Council declined in importance and its meetings became shorter and poorly attended. This was partly due to the fact that students in general were not prepared to give so much time to the conduct of student affairs, unless there were some specific cause that needed espousal, and they were on the contrary ready to leave complicated financial matters and the conduct of relations with the college authorities in the hands of their officers. The decline in the Union Council also reflected a national disenchantment at that time with representative democracy and a preference for more direct appeals to the electorate by means of open meetings and referenda. The St. Peter's Union Council became quick to put an issue before a student open meeting rather than be forced themselves to make a difficult decision.

At St. Peter's during these years the students showed little sustained interest in political issues outside the College, although the Sach reforms had introduced a Vice President (External) whose function it was to co-ordinate activities of the Union outside the campus. For a time the Union was represented on the Birmingham City Trades Council and the Union Council was asked to consider motions about South Africa or the use of troops to keep order in Northern Ireland. Councillors, however, soon became restive and said that they had not been elected to deal with this sort of business, which partly explains why politically motivated students preferred to make their appeal to open student meetings where they could anticipate some popular support. On the other hand St. Peter's students were ready enough to take up genuine student or teacher causes ; under Keith Sach they sent their own "evidence" to the Parliamentary

168

committee on teacher education and a further document to the James Committee and deserve much credit for both pieces of action. They loyally played their part in protest activities arranged by regional or national N.U.S. leaders; they contributed from their meagre funds to send representatives to student conferences and ceased to do so only when they felt they had been let down by others' inefficiency or by failure to give their point of view a fair hearing.

If the Union Council were reluctant to become too involved in external politics, they saw themselves as the guardians of the Saltley traditions. During this period the traditions which seemed to them most threatened were those concerned with Christmas — the Ball, the Dinners and the Link. Various factors conspired against these traditions — the large increases in the size of the student body, the direct cash grant system and cafeteria service, the prolongation of the third-year final teaching practice towards the end of term; one year, the black-outs imposed by the power strike caused the cancellation of the Ball until the following term. The Principal decided that the most reasonable solution was to have a series of dinners, culminating in a Third-Year Dinner which would preserve as far as possible previous practices. The student union clung tenaciously to the Link, although there were difficulties here, since the increased numbers of one-year students (chiefly graduates) did not appreciate fully the serious character of the proceedings; and, when, the official ceremony completed, unofficial imitations more closely tied to the Zulu Warrior song resulted in unreasonable damage in parts of the College, the administration was not amused. In subsequent years the Union Council threatened severe action against those who marred the event by unruly behaviour. In June, the end-of-course celebrations tended to become more and more a departmental affair and the Principal visited each department in turn to bid farewell to leaving students; the "going-down" service of old, rather formal, but often moving, was replaced by a midnight communion service, which caught the mood of the occasion well. The last Sunday of the academic year remained during this period, an occasion for visitors to the College; it was called an "open day" but apart from the annual Art and Craft Exhibition, which year by year grew in variety and interest, it was in no sense an occasion in which the College put its work on display. After 1968 the proceedings were in the hands of the Student Union Officers; in some years they fought out seriously the events of the inter-year athletics and tennis competitions and in other years they produced a light-hearted programme with quantities of water splashing about; there was nothing light-hearted, however, about the final of the annual 5-a-side football competition which was conducted with all the gravity of a Wembley Cup Final. It was always good weather on this last Sunday of the year and St. Peter's looked its attractive best with plenty of friends and parents and a great many of the staff and their families parading with, seemingly, a new generation of little children every two or three years.

Not all traditions were old ones. There was, for example, what was known as the "Saltley Venture" which lasted for a few years; a Liberal

Councillor conceived the idea of bringing some joy into the lives of a few Saltley old folk and with the help of a group of girls living in Adderley Block arranged Christmas dinners and afternoon tea-parties for elderly people living on their own in the district. If this was good publicity for the Liberal Party, no one lost by it very much and one of the locals who was behind the movement was to be one of the sponsors who presented the local petition to try to save the closure of the College in 1975. It became the custom for local communities to hold a small annual fete one Saturday afternoon in June ; this was another day when it was always sunny, as hundreds of Saltley folk put up their stalls on the College field. "Saltbuild" also clung tenaciously to its traditions with student officers and staff co-operation, although as the need to raise funds declined there was more concentration upon the summer show and less upon jumble sales ; in 1970/71 the sale raised £135 and the following year it was almost equally successful. The summer show would last three or four nights and would be aided by a bar with intervals for cheese, winkles or other suitable eats. In 1970 the show was a Mississippi Show Boat, in 1971 a 1940's Show and in 1972 an Edwardian Show ; the Edwardian musicals were probably the best.

The College clubs remained as strong as ever and, with the introduction of Midland and National League and Cup competitions in Colleges of Education in many sports, there were full fixture lists and problems for club officials to pay for all the travelling. The clubs generated a high spirit and maintained a general excellence of standards, with an outlook almost bordering upon the professional ; in these circumstances individual stars were unnecessary ; but the tall and powerful Geordie, John Inchmore, attracted attention as a footballer and cricketer and many will have seen him playing cricket as fast opening bowler for Worcestershire ; a few years later, Howard Cooper, became opening bowler for Yorkshire and for a short period Cooper and John Woodford from the Sixties were playing in the Yorkshire team together.

There continued to be, too, much dramatic entertainment, varied in character, stimulating and often challenging, although there was a move away from the College Play of earlier years. Much of the drama work was undertaken in the round and one recalls among many fine productions that of "The Crucible", which was the last performance to be produced by Ida and Philip Dunn. The Drama course established the tradition of a performance for school children during the Lent Term, usually a Pantomime ; one was written and produced by the Union President, Russ Howarth, and attracted much praise.

But the outstanding achievements during the late Sixties and the Seventies went to the credit of the Music and Choral Society under the auspices of Harry Jones, who had come to the College in 1967 as second music tutor. Harry Jones had established close personal contacts with the C.B.S.O. and the Arts Council and he was able to attract many distinguished musicians to perform in the Chapel in Lunch Hour or Evening Concerts ; these included John Williams, the Zimryah Choir and the Lindsay Quartet. A group of modern composers came to give talks about their art and these included Malcolm Williamson (now Master of the Queen's Music), Thea Musgrove and Cornelius Cardew ; among other speakers Friedelinda Wagner attracted a large audience to hear her forthright views on the production of her grandfather's masterpieces. During the Seventies the B.B.C. gave an Invitation Concert, which they recorded for later broadcasting ; a disturbance in Bridge Road necessitated a second playing.

But the real joy was that for nine successive years from 1968 the Choral Society performed at least one major choral work ; the orchestra was specially invited by Harry Jones who conducted each work himself, both for rehearsal and performance, and also found the celebrity singers for the soloists ; the choirs came mostly from the College students, although they welcomed friendly assistance from one or two grammar schools. The works which were performed included Haydn's Creation, Requiem Masses by Mozart, Verdi and Faure and the delightful but more secular Carmina Burana ; the programme included two full length and never-to-be-forgotten performances in 1969 and 1976 of Handel's Messiah. The choral singing invariably reached a high standard of musicianship, but succeeded in retaining a youthful zest and enjoyment that made it typical of collegiate life at its best.

6 THE YEARS OF CRISIS (1969-78)
Chapter 29

Since 1945 training colleges had been subject to much public criticism, quite proper, but prejudiced and ill-informed, and towards the end of the Sixties this increased in volume and attracted attention from the national and daily press as well as educational publications. Indeed, criticism of those who train teachers to teach has rumbled on, since they present a handy target for those who decry the shortcomings of the whole educational system ;   this extract from a 1976 "Daily Telegraph" illustrates the point :

> "College lectures who preach trendy theories to impressionable young student teachers were blamed yesterday for the falling standards in schools. A report by the National Association of Schoolmasters and Union of Women Teachers . . . called for urgent improvements in the way teachers were trained . . . The present system of training is unacceptable because initial entry qualifications are too low and the academic quality of the courses is often lacking in intellectual rigour. The system does not have much concern for the practical problems of the teachers work . . . Mr. Fred Smithies, assistant general secretary of the association, said . . . 'We should never have given so much responsibility for training teachers to so many people who know so little about the schools where students would teach'. Mrs. Kay Wareham, president of the Association of Careers Teachers . . . said, 'Over the years I have noticed a steady deterioration in the standard of both students and their tutors. I see inadequate lesson notes and preparation, spelling mistakes on the blackboards, bad grammar and poor diction'."

These were sweeping generalisations which it would be difficult to substantiate ;   the students that were trained had been taught by the schools and recommended by them as suitable recruits for training ;   the training was in the charge of tutors who had been recommended by Headmasters as equipped by experience to train them. It may be that the steady flow of criticism was in reality as much anti-University as it was anti-college, although some University lecturers themselves joined the stream of critics. Many complaints were mutually contradictory and reflected the weaknesses in those who made them :

> "As we back reeling from 'Times' correspondents who tell us that our academic standards are appalling we are bitten in the rear by the young teachers who think we are far too academic and it is our professional standards which are appalling. The N.U.S. vultures swoop on our grandmotherly umbrellas."
>   (The Principal of Nottingham College in the "Teacher", 1969).

Although it was the intensity and the ferocity of the attacks which was important rather than the specific complaints, the most informed and serious of the comments about teacher education dwelt on some three issues. First was a call for the government to establish a Royal Commission to conduct an exacting and searching enquiry into teacher education and to recommend how to put it right. The Government was less enthusiastic despite its sensitivity about the public concern ; Royal Commissions took too long and were perhaps a bit too independent in their proposals ; instead, the resurrected Parliamentary Select Committee on Education, a formidable enough body, was asked to turn its attention to teacher training and A.T.O.'s were required to institute internal investigations.

Secondly, there was the issue of control. The most recent advice from the Robbins Report (1963) had favoured University control, both academic and administrative, by Schools of Education. Was this sound advice ? If teacher education was as bad as so many were suggesting, the blame surely must lie with those who controlled it ? In any case, Local Education Authorities provided students with their grants, permitted them and college tutors to conduct teaching practices in their schools and they employed the students when their training was over. Ought they not to occupy a major place in the policy-making ? Ought not teacher education to lie firmly within the sector of Further Education, which was under the authority of the L.E.A.'s rather than within the University sector, which was not ?

Thirdly, was the question whether teachers ought to be trained in monotechnic institutions, which characterised all existing colleges of education, or in diversified institutions. Indeed there was already in 1969 a small number of Polytechnics which had been allowed to have their own Teacher Education Departments, although their students received their certificates from the appropriate University School of Education. This became one of the decisive issues in the long debate which was to follow. As a problem it had been aggravated by the institution of the 3-year course and 4-year B.Ed. course. 2-year trained students had usually been prepared to complete their courses and gain their teaching qualification, even if their commitment to teaching was still uncertain. But after 1960, if during your first year as a student you concluded that you couldn't face a life-time in the classroom, you were strongly disposed to withdraw from the course, and during the Sixties the number of voluntary retirements of students from colleges of education had increased by almost alarming proportions and this constituted a waste of effort and money on all sides. The influential N.U.T. and the N.U.S. came out firmly in favour of diversified institutions, Jack Straw, President-elect of the N.U.S. arguing in October 1969 :

"Perhaps complaints from students in Colleges of Education that they are processed in 'teacher factories' may sound a little emotive and exaggerated, but the essential analogy is a valid one. From the moment when he is accepted into a college the student is on a single line conveyor belt. There are no series of job options facing him upon the completion of his course, as there are for his more fortunate graduate contemporary, (even the vocationally trained one). You either teach, or drop out of the race. Of course there are some compensations. The security, that from the moment one steps into a college, unless something drastic and unusual such as an examination failure occurs, one's way is clear through a comfortable job, from which dismissal is almost impossible (except for immorality but never incompetence), must be pleasant. But I am not sure whether it is of benefit, in the long run, to either the individual teacher or the child in the classroom. But even by the government's own standards this policy is not working. As the 1965 Report of the National Advisory Council on the Training and Supply of Teachers showed, of every 1000 male non-graduates entering teacher training only 700 are left after five years teaching, and only 600 after ten . . . "

Jack Straw's explanation for students' and teachers' withdrawal from their chosen profession was by no means exhaustive, but his advocacy of opportunities for students to be able to move more easily from one line of study to another received strong support from other places, including the senior common room at St. Peter's. As we shall see hereafter, this was an issue which was to have the most serious consequences for St. Peter's, and it is important for the reader to understand that the Principal and staff firmly advocated the provision of diversified courses as soon as it became a significant question, since there were serious doubts whether the College could have sustained a monotechnic role for a prolonged period.

The Parliamentary Select Committee was barely able to complete its enquiries or digest the information it had acquired before the dissolution of Parliament in June 1970 brought its work to an end. In any case its careful and detailed study of teacher education was rapidly overtaken by other events, so that it may have received less publicity than it deserved. Scholars who have occasion to scrutinise the Committee's Report will doubtless note that Appendix 19 of the printed evidence was submitted by the Students' Union of St. Peter's College. This was an achievement of the Student Union executive under Keith Sach's chairmanship, which pausing from its self-imposed mammoth task of constitution making, dashed off its conclusions on the structure of teacher education. These were ambitious. They proposed that all students should have a four-year course ; the first year of which should be a "foundation year in all establishments of higher education . . . to permit flexible entry into H.E. without the commitment to teaching as a career at the age of 18". One year of the course should be spent in school on teacher's full pay ; at the end of the course, the C.N.A.A. should award a Pass Degree, a suggestion somewhat inconsistent with an earlier call for close University links. Finally they pressed "the Government to set up an independent national enquiry into Teacher Education".

The Principals of the Church Colleges had also been in Conference and with Saltley's Principal as their secretary submitted their booklet of evidence in which they stressed their willingness :

"to continue to meet challenge, remain loyal to their Christian foundation and tradition and play their part in the nation's higher education into the 21st century."

They added to their report D.E.S. projected figures for students in full-time higher education, recently published in the "Times Educational Supplement" indicating a doubling of the students by 1981 and they deduced :

"There would, therefore, appear to be a strong case for extending the range of courses in some colleges of education to provide general degrees in arts and . . . science. This development would have the great advantage of enabling young men and women to transfer between vocational and non-vocational courses in the same institution, and provide a flexibility analogous to that of the American 'college of liberal arts and sciences'."

In the meantime, Edward Short, Secretary of State for Education, himself a teacher trained in a Church College, had unleashed his own enquiry by inviting the Directors of the A.T.O.'s to institute a review of their own structures and courses during which time they should consult teachers, students and H.M. Inspectors. The scope of the enquiry should, significantly, include in-service work for teachers. In the West Midlands St. Peter's played little direct part in the subsequent activity ; indeed the Students Union wrote a letter to the Secretary of State rejecting the idea of internal spring cleaning :

"I was dismayed to read yesterday Press reports that you were considering asking the Chairmen of Area Training Organisations to carry out an enquiry into the education of teachers in their areas . . . A national and independent enquiry into teacher education is the only possible way in which these problems will be adequately investigated . . . "

The enquiry nevertheless proceeded. A committee was established, which divided itself into four sub-committees, most of the members of which were co-opted from the various interested parties, but were under the chairmanship of a member of the School of Education, except that which investigated Teaching Practice arrangements, which was chaired by Dr. Cornwell. Bill Powrie was co-opted to Sub-Committee D investigating postgraduate courses, but no other member of the Saltley staff was called upon to participate. This sub-committee D was the only body which visited Saltley, but full written statements were made about St. Peter's courses and organisation for the other sub-committees. In December 1970, the St. Peter's Academic Board replied to a request from the School of Education for comments upon the A.T.O.'s structure in critical terms :

"One of the less successful aspects of the School of Education has been that it has failed to bring the staffs of Colleges together save for the formal Boards of Studies which in any case affect but a proportion of the College staffs . . . The A.T.O. has tended to become an administrative organisation, rather rigid in its conservatism and adherence to 'regulations', often out of touch with the real needs of

Colleges, their students and their courses. The size of the A.T.O. with its 17 colleges does not help, making both numbers and geographic distance excessive for fruitful discussion of mutual problems and involvement in future decisions."

Nevertheless the sub-committees completed their investigations with commendable speed and their reports were circulated. The exercise exposed the superficiality of many of the complaints and indicated that both the School of Education and its affiliated colleges were self-critical and anxious to give general satisfaction. Indeed criticisms had been muted and few could have supposed that the Robbins decision to leave teacher education in the hands of the Universities was about to be called into question. While the quotation above may reveal criticisms of the University procedures from the St. Peter's staff, there was at that time no doubt where the academic future of St. Peter's lay :

"I, on behalf of St. Peter's College, know that the College Governing Body would wish the College to remain within the School of Education of the University of Birmingham and to continue and further develop the long and profitable association that it has been the privilege of the College to enjoy since the foundation of the University."
(C. Buckmaster to the Chairman of the Delegacy, March 1971).

Before the completion of the Short Enquiries, however, Edward Short was himself out of office and his place was occupied by Margaret Thatcher in the Heath Government. On December 8th the new Education Secretary announced in Parliament that she had set up a small "expert committee under the chairmanship of Lord James of Rusholme (at that time Vice Chancellor of York University) to make an intensive study of the education and training of teachers"; its terms of reference were terse but comprehensive, and they included the role of all the bodies at that time involved, including the universities. Since it was a Departmental Committee it would have its temporary offices in and would work from the Department in Curzon Street. It was given twelve months to conclude its operations and it rapidly became apparent that this Committee with its close contacts with the chief civil servants in their offices down the corridor was to be unusually significant for those who worked in teacher education.

It seems to be accepted that Hugh Harding was the civil servant who exercised most influence over the reorganisation of teacher education, although we must recognise that the final responsibility lies with his political chiefs. Harding had already given some indication of his own personal "reflections" upon "the problems of teacher education over the next ten years" when he had addressed a special D.E.S. conference of Principals of Colleges of Education at York in June 1970. He warned his audience against drawing conclusions from his "reflections" about "the tenor of advice which may be given to Ministers", but it is certainly tempting to suppose that Lord James and his assistants had listened carefully to Harding's opinions. At York Harding had been careful not to commit himself to any confirmed line of thought, but by the questions he posed and the arguments he presented one may perhaps be forgiven for seeing future developments mapped out : "academic, financial and administrative control of higher education should go together"; "mono-technics are educationally undesirable" ; "we should need to contemplate a two (year) plus one pattern of training in which the first two years led to a qualification comparable with the Higher National Diploma", and "the inadequacy of the provision for in-service training of teachers is generally recognised".

As the James Committee got down to its task, it became increasingly necessary for the Church Colleges to think and act together, since a reasonable inference from the Harding speech was that the voluntary sector could become redundant. There has been little occasion in this narrative to refer to the Church Colleges Council since the retirement of R. J. Harvey and Canon Platten. Canon James Robertson as Harvey's successor had established a friendly and close relationship with Principal Buckmaster, and his inspiring leadership and shrewd judgment had made him a much respected figure in the Colleges. There had been a series of changes in the structure of committees and responsibilities, especially after the Church Assembly had given way to Synodical government. The Church Board of Education became directly responsible to Synod in 1970 with the Bishop of Blackburn as its Chairman and the Rev. George Whitfield as its full-time Secretary ; this body operated three Committees, one of which, the Higher Education Committee, was under the chairmanship of the Vice Chancellor of Durham University and had Canon Robertson as its secretary and a "College Support Group" of which the Rev. C. Buckmaster was a member. In addition, the Council of Church Principals, an unofficial gathering of the 27 Church Principals with no corporate responsibility of its own, maintained an important link between the Colleges and the Church and became an increasingly important forum for the Principals as the crisis of the Seventies gathered pace. In 1970, however, it did seem that there had been some decline in the part played by the Church central authority in planning since the days when the Central Board of Finance had paid the Governors' share in capital expenditure, as this letter from Principal Buckmaster to Canon Robertson indicates :

"Dear James,   22nd May, 1970.
    . . . . Two matters . . . make me anxious. You have spent enormous time and trouble in allaying fears on the expansion of colleges and the allocation of central funds . . . This was a major task . . . but it seems we are not to be consulted as a group of colleges on size increases and I quote Lincoln's apparent move to 850 students without consultation, in spite of the serious shortage of student numbers in other colleges and unallayed fears on the part of Hockerill and Culham. You have hinted that money from central funds will be available again perhaps in very limited amounts. Who will allocate this money and on what basis will it be allocated ? One Principal assured me that money had been allocated and two other Principals knew nothing about it . . ."

The Council of Principals found itself to be divided in its opinions and in effect submitted two different proposals to the James Committee—either that "the natural evolutionary point for most colleges would be the university to which they were affiliated" or that "it would be possible to see a large number of colleges federated into a national, autonomous institution with degree awarding status . . . " They were strongly agreed on some points ; "we are not attracted to affiliation with Polytechnics" : "we want to resist the current pejorative of the phrase 'monotechnic'" ; "we are still of the view that our tradition and style enrich the total pattern and that our principled commitment is still necessary and honourable (sic) within a changed and changing society . . . " Saltley's Principal was one of the four persons who presented the Church submission to Lord James and the occasion seems to have been the opportunity for mutual understanding and even some hilarity. The James Report was published in December 1971. As it was a Departmental consultative document the Secretary of State did not need to disclose her own views immediately or, indeed, at all. She announced that she would allow twelve months for a further discussion of opinions during which time she would discover from all the institutions, who were directly involved, their reactions to the James proposals and would then determine her policy. The James Report was, however, a significant land-mark in the changes that have revolutionised teacher education in England, although its proposals were not put into force to the letter. The Report proposed to replace the University-controlled A.T.O.'s by Regional Councils and to separate the personal from the professional training of the student by means of a two-year Diploma of Higher Education (first cycle) devoted to special and general studies, followed by a further two-year professional training (second cycle) which would culminate in the award of a B.A.(Ed.). It is not necessary here to go beyond these recommendations, although those for a third cycle devoted to in-service training received universal approval. The Report was criticised on the grounds that it ignored the financial implications of its proposals and it did not attempt to study deeply the problems of government of the colleges which might emerge ; but two recommendations in particular received close attention in the colleges :

"The new system would allow great possibilities of specialisation within a framework of diversity . . . It is to be hoped that the voluntary bodies would agree to a widening of functions for their colleges so that all could share in the same advance . . . Financial arrangements for these colleges would continue as at present." (5.36).

"Groups of two or three colleges might choose to amalgamate . . . Different forms and styles of amalgamation should be encouraged and could lead to a rationalisation of effort . . . Nor should planners overlook the possibility that some colleges might close or be made over to other educational uses." (5.37).

The Secretary of State, Mrs. Margaret Thatcher, published her own statement of education policy in December 1972 in a White Paper entitled : "A Framework for Expansion". Most of this document was devoted to

178

Higher Education and in particular to her plans for the reform of teacher training. She accepted many of the recommendations of the James Report and proposed to replace the A.T.O.'s by Regional Planning Committees, although she hoped that Universities would continue to validate the academic elements of courses, since she did not propose to create any new body specifically for that purpose ; she put the Universities on the spot, however, by coming out in favour of a three-year B.Ed. Degree Course and welcomed the "declaration by the Council for National Academic Awards of its willingness to participate in such validation". She favoured the proposed Diploma of Higher Education, designed both for the first two years of a teacher education course and more diversely for those with other vocations in mind. The ten paragraphs under the heading of "Colleges of Education" were studied closely ; they repeated the warning of the James Report that "some (colleges) must face the possibility that in due course they will have to be converted to new purposes ; some may need to close" ; and added the warning that, "if the colleges of education are to find a fuller and firmer place in the higher education family, their staffs must face major changes". The White Paper suggested possibilities of mergers between colleges and integrations with Polytechnics or Universities, but gave no hint of the process whereby this might be achieved, although it stated that "a college which expands and diversifies . . . will not be easily distinguishable from a polytechnic or other further education college". Many vital questions especially of of procedure remained unanswered but a D.E.S. Instruction to Local Education Authorities in March 1973 significantly entitled Circular No. 7/73, "Development of Higher Education in the Non-University Sector", supplied a few of the answers.

As the contents of circular 7/73 were being fully digested, it became apparent that the crisis surrounding teacher education had deepened and that the whole teaching profession was about to be engulfed in a major calamity brought about partly by overproduction of teachers, the consequence of some error in predicting or computing the future school population. One cannot write with any authority about when the false prophecies were discovered ; there have been hints in the Press that the D.E.S. lost confidence in the figures before 1970, although it is difficult to square such rumours with the fact, reported on an earlier page, that in March 1973 — the very month in which Circular 7/73 was issued — the D.E.S. agreed to the new Library building at Saltley at an estimated cost of £214,000.

School population projections were based largely although not entirely upon forecasts of the birth rate. This had risen steadily from the War until 1964 but had fallen in the second half of the Sixties ; it had been supposed earlier that after 1970 it would rise again sharply and by the end of the century it would reach perhaps one million a year. In fact the birth rate continued to decline sharply after 1970, although official predictions in 1974 still expected a recovery in the rate in the late Seventies and Eighties, but a further decline after 1990. Predictions for total school population followed similar lines, that is if one allows for the five-year gap between birth and school attendance. The forecast of school population made in 1972 showed no decline at all and predicted an expanding school population to over ten million in the late Eighties. The total school population in fact increased from under 7 million in 1960 to about 9 million in 1975, which thus justified the runaway expansion of the Sixties and was explained by young people continuing longer full-time schooling, so counteracting the decline in birth rate. The forecast in 1974, however, showed a sharp decline and it was predicted that the total school population in 1990 might be something like 7 million (the 1965 figure), although it would probably rise again after that.

Faulty birth-rate forecasts were not alone the cause of an embarrassing situation in which the Government found itself. One of the factors that gave rise to the large expansion of colleges in the Sixties was the high wastage rate, particularly among young married women teachers leaving school to have their families. Now in the Seventies these women were returning more quickly to the class-room. Many people argued that this was the moment when the Government might easily achieve a notable social advance by reducing the size of classes throughout the land to under thirty and thus absorb the surplus teachers into the system. Unhappily it was not to be. In October 1973 the fourth Arab-Israeli war broke out and with it came the Arab oil embargo and fuel crisis in countries of the west. This was followed in Britain by economic and industrial unrest, two General Elections in 1974 and a change in political leadership from Conservative to Labour. The political change hardly affected higher education policy, since the new Government was faced by rapidly accelerating inflation and an immediate threat of mass unemployment, so that economic solvency and stability could only be achieved in the opinion of the Treasury by severe cuts in the spending departments, both national and local. During the next five years the D.E.S. officials proceeded to apply cuts in teacher training ever more firmly and one must not be surprised that these officials may have preferred the idea of polytechnic-type institutions where they could more easily regulate the numbers of student teachers in training than in small colleges devoted to a single monotechnic function.

Circular 7/73 gave the first clear intimation that this was to be the new policy :

"the number of full-time students in initial teacher training will be reduced from 114,000 to 60/70,000."

A small crumb of comfort was offered :

"The Government's plans require provision for some 335,000 full-time and sandwich higher education students in England and Wales in 1981. This compares with 204,000 students in 1971/72 and implies a net expansion of some 130,000 . . . This would leave provision to be made for 155,000 students in colleges of further education and the colleges of education, which at present accommodate some 138,000 students on advanced courses, and would require provision for a further 17,000 students."

The competition for these 17,000 students was likely to be a fierce one, and the news of the declining birth rate must have raised doubts about how many candidates would be available to profit from the expanding resources of higher education, released by pruning the teacher training element.

There was, moreover, one further significant clause in Circular 7/73. Local education authorities were required to submit by November 1973 a plan for the future development of the higher institutions in their areas and under their responsibility and "to consult also with the voluntary colleges of education . . . and to take into account their potential contribution both to teacher education and higher education more generally".

Voluntary colleges had seen themselves as national institutions and that they should come within the formal planning arrangements of the local education committees was a novel development in Church-State relationships, although, of course, the existence of aided schools, owned by the Church but maintained by the local authorities, might have been held to constitute a precedent. Where a local authority, like Warwickshire, had only a single college, a voluntary one within its area, one may suppose that there would be no conflict of interests ; where, however, the local further education committee had a direct responsibility for a Polytechnic and two or three colleges of education of its own and was now required to fit the future of three voluntary colleges into its plans at a time when there was a call for retrenchment all round, the problems to be resolved were delicate indeed. This was the situation in Birmingham.

It was complicated by Local Government reform due to be put into effect within twelve months and by the further requirements that Local Authority Officers were to consult with their neighbours, so that a regional plan could be established. To bolster this concept of regionalism, the D.E.S. published in Circular 7/73 its proposed revised figures for teacher training places in 1981 on a regional basis. How far the real responsibility for the recommendations that the Birmingham Chief Education Officer was to be called on to make lay with the regional panel of Directors, or how far with the local education committee remained obscure.

This was the background in which St. Peter's, the only Anglican college of education serving the population of 5 million people living in the West Midlands, was called on to fight for its existence during the next two and a half years.

Chapter 30

It is time that we turn our attention from the national to the local scene and examine more closely the impact of the James Report in December 1971, "A Framework for Expansion" in December 1972, and "The Development of Higher Education in the Non-University Sector" in March 1973 upon St. Peter's College. It was clear that large changes were impending and there was naturally much anxiety about the future, although this was allayed somewhat in March 1973 when permission

181

came through for the construction of the Library/Education block. Discussion on the staff was lively and well-informed ; at least one whole day was spared from normal routine to allow the staff to go into conference and all listened attentively to colleagues, like John Pick and David Fontana, who had had experience of work in much larger institutions than St. Peter's. All over the country academic boards and councils were forming their think-tanks and busily engaged in conjecture and discussion. In November 1972, for example, the St. Peter's staff received a letter from the academic board at St. Paul's, Cheltenham.

"We deeply regret that the post-Jamesian time has seen no vigorous initiative on the part of Bishops or Principals to explore the possibility of setting up an Anglican University of Education composed of all, or the majority, of the twenty seven colleges bound into a federation which would preserve their existing traditions and award its own B.Ed. degree to the greater majority of the students . . . What is needed . . . is a ground-swell of opinion which will lead each academic board to send an effective representative . . . to a meeting at St. Paul's on Saturday, December 16th."

St. Peter's agreed to send its Vice Principal, but, alas, the meeting was not held and no more was heard of the idea.

The staff were concerned that no avenues should remain unexplored and some were interested to examine the possibilities of alignment with the Birmingham Polytechnic and validation of work by the C.N.A.A. What remained unclear in 1972/73 was how far the autonomy of the College would be jeopardised by such a move. The need to take some sort of initiative was high-lighted by a Principal's Conference at Oxford in April 1972, which was addressed by the Secretary of State herself ; the A.T.C.D.E. report stated,

"The problems of colleges which co-existed in urban areas with universitities and polytechnics were raised. The Department emphasised the difficulties of expanding colleges which found themselves in this situation. There was, however, no clear resolution of this problem. One got the impression that every case would be looked at on its merits, and that solutions would be pragmatic and hence considerably varied. The Department emphasised that more initiative remained with colleges than perhaps they realised. Both local authorities, and subsequently D.E.S., would look carefully at workable proposals. There would be no attempt to impose a straitjacket. The real test of a scheme would be whether it was likely to work . . . "

The staff were realistic in understanding that the initiative which the circumstances called for could come only from the Principal, supported by the Governors, and frustrating though it might seem, they were called upon largely to be spectators. The Principal, Charles Buckmaster, was resourceful and argued skilfully and with good humour, seeking throughout the coming years to maintain the morale of his colleagues and students. He was assisted most notably by the Chairman of the Governors, Laurence Brown, diocesan Bishop of Birmingham, who participated personally and with persistence and charm in detailed negotiations to preserve an assured future in Higher Education in Birmingham for St. Peter's.

The College Governors had their first serious consideration of the implications of the James Report at their meeting in June 1972. Principal Buckmaster sketched the situation and suggested :

"that the Governors should examine the alternative possibilities which would be open to this college in readiness for taking positive steps for the future when the Minister reported. It appeared that the two main alternatives were either (a) to form some association with other voluntary colleges in the Birmingham area to form a unit offering some 2,000 places, the minimum considered viable in the future, or (b) to attempt a closer link with the University of Aston."

During the subsequent discussion the Vice Principal gloomily but accurately forecast that

"the voluntary nature and collegiate status of colleges such as this would almost certainly be lost as there was little hope of a college being able to exist as an independent unit."

Professor Joselin stated the opinion that "an association between the College and the University of Aston could be mutually beneficial." As a result the Governors appointed a Working Party to consider the future of the College with the Chairman (the Bishop of Birmingham), Bruce McGowan (Headmaster of Solihull School) and George Ison (Chairman, Old Students Association) to join forces with a number of the staff and the President of the Students' Union.

Readers will recall that after earlier private talks between Canon Platten and Sir Peter Venables, then Aston's Vice Chancellor, K. L. S. Stretch, Pro-Vice Chancellor, became a co-opted member of the Governors and he was succeeded in 1969 by Professor Joselin, Professor in Education and Dean of the Faculty of Social Sciences. He now proved excellent in maintaining the pace of negotiations between Dr. Pope, the Vice Chancellor in 1972, and Principal Buckmaster. Dr. Pope, hoping to extend the sphere of activities of his Social Sciences Faculty and to deepen his contacts with the community, seemed eager to do a deal and the College Working Party "unanimously decided to explore the possibility" and suggested that a "Joint Working Party, representing the two institutions should be established as a matter of urgency". There were doubtless some reservations on both sides and one of these was the warning issued by the A.T.C.D.E. to colleges not to undertake specific commitments until the Secretary of State had published her promised White Paper. It was a wise caveat, diminished unfortunately by a personal letter from Stanley Hewett, the General Secretary, to Principal Buckmaster, in which he said that the A.T.C.D.E. communiqué "was not intended to put the brake on any college negotiating a relationship with a University".

In fact negotiations proceeded swiftly during the later summer and autumn of 1972. Each side produced a Memorandum and the two Papers were put together to show the areas which would require amplification and discussion; there were few points of disagreement, since it was anticipated that Dr. Pope as the senior member in the discussions would need to develop his proposals fully before the College Governors and Academic Board could determine whether they could be accepted. The discussions were of necessity confidential since it would have been impolitic to broadcast their details before they had been submitted to the Aston University Senate. The negotiations included two informal meetings between the Vice Chancellor and the College Chairman in which, presumably, questions affecting the status of the College and the character and future of its foundation were asked and answered.

The proposals that the two sides finally agreed postulated a two-stage development dictated by the quinquennial system of operating university grants. The first stage, which Dr. Pope anticipated would begin in September 1973, would have lasted up to ten years and was concerned with academic matters, St. Peter's taking degree courses of the University, but its finance coming from sources other than the University; during this period the Governors would retain their autonomy, reinforced, one supposes, by representatives of the University, but the University would be involved in all staff appointments. The second stage, after ten years, would cover the absorption of the College into the University, a group of Foundation Trustees remaining to "be ultimately responsible for the College premises".

By the Stage 1 proposals, St. Peter's, with a two 'A' Level admission requirement, would take only degree course students. The ordinary degree of three years would be a Combined B.Sc. degree, involving three subjects, one of which would be Education. Most, although not all, of the teaching for the degree would be at the College and "students who proved their academic ability would be allowed to proceed to Aston for a fourth year to complete an honours degree. Staff who had been allowed to teach for the Birmingham University B.Ed. degree would be eligible to teach for this degree; additions would need to satisfy Aston University requirements. It was proposed that each year should consist of three academic terms making 30 weeks and supplemented by "ten weeks of professional aspects of teaching in schools." Since Aston University would not be involved in teaching or assessing the professional work, which would remain under the control of an A.T.O. or regional committee, it would be possible to build up a cadre for professional work of those staff who would not be needed for the degree teaching. Thus the interests of the existing staff would be safeguarded.

The scheme was not set forward for full public criticism either by Governors or Academic Council and one may suppose that there were many points of detail that needed clarification, especially in financial matters. It is well to recall that these agreements were reached in the autumn of 1972 when most other universities would have looked with extreme caution at the idea of a 3-year B.Ed. degree. Here Aston University was proposing to apply the same standards and give the same

184

award to St. Peter's students as it gave to its own students. With hind sight one knows that in 1975 other universities (including Birmingham) agreed to accept a three-year professional B.Ed. degree and one may guess that had this scheme or something like it gone ahead, there might have been pressure on Aston University to agree to something rather different. In December 1972 it still looked pretty good.

On January 16th Dr. Pope had a final meeting with the Bishop of Birmingham and Principal Buckmaster and the last amendments to the agreed memorandum were made. On 25th January Dr. Pope laid the document before Sir Kenneth Berrill, the chief D.E.S. officer who dealt with the University Grants Commission, and thus was able to exercise a veto. Early in February 1973 Dr. Pope distributed a report from which the following extracts were taken :

"The Officers of the U.G.C. offered no criticism of the concept of combining the educational training with our combined honours scheme. I therefore assumed that there was no basic objection to the educational aspect of the paper . . . "

". . . . it was agreed that affiliation with St. Peter's College was not adequate and I was asked to draft a final paragraph, 'Complete Integration with the University of Aston'."

" . . . I assumed that the teaching up to ordinary degree level would be at St. Peter's College . . . At our informal meeting, the officers of the U.G.C. were entirely opposed to this suggestion and were quite adamant that all teaching should be at the University of Aston. . . In principle they opposed the idea of two centres of instruction within the University . . . "

This final condition would have meant that much of the post-war reconstruction at Saltley, including the £250,000 Library and Educational Resources Centre, would have been wasted and one wonders in these circumstances why it was necessary for the D.E.S. to take so dramatic a stand when it conflicted with normal British practice of making use of all resources that are available. Perhaps it was that the D.E.S. officials were mindful of other negotiations that they might have to conduct at Durham, Southampton, Exeter or Lancaster. It is worth making the point that at Exeter they agreed not merely to the retention of the site of St. Luke's College (located on the other side of the city from the University) but, indeed, to move the University School of Education there.

Dr. Pope lost no time in drawing up a new proposal in these changed circumstances. St. Peter's College would become a University Village leased by the College trustees to the University for a peppercorn rent and with the Church of England having an interest in the appointment of a Warden who would live in the Principal's house. The concept of a combined degree would be proceeded with but it would be entirely University controlled.

185

"... One would have to assume that we would not automatically take over any member of staff and that the staff should be informed of this. They will then have at least five years during which they can adjust their careers . . . All vacancies occurring at the University of Aston in subjects which might be of interest to St. Peter's College staff should be advertised in the College and, if suitable applicants were available from the College for these posts, then they should be very seriously considered."

The Principal discussed the changed situation with the Chairman and wrote to Dr. Pope :

"It seems to me improbable that the Governing Body will accept your proposal to take over the College building for a long lease paying a peppercorn rent. I think they will take the view that the property has been built up and consolidated over a very long period and they would probably wish it to remain much more firmly in the hands of the Church of England as the providing body than your proposal allows.

"The second serious difficulty would be accepting your proposals for the college staff. I am certain that the Governors would wish to see that the Principal and staff are safeguarded in a much more direct manner than you have indicated in your document. . . "

The Principal's opinions were endorsed by the Working Party in February and the full Governors' meeting in March, but with regret.

It was unfortunate that these promising proposals had met such intransigence at the D.E.S. and, with hind-sight, one may wish that the Governors had persevered with them instead of allowing them to fizzle out so tamely. One may state, again with hind-sight, that they represented the best prospect for St. Peter's in Saltley and it is sad to realise that they had in fact been abandoned before the publication of Circular 7/73 called for such probings to be commenced.

Another of the possibilities which emerged from a consideration of a "Framework for Expansion" and Circular 7/73 was that of some form of federation of colleges in the West Midlands such as was under discussion in Derby and Cheltenham. There was a variety of possibilities here which needed to be explored and St. Peter's welcomed the invitation in May 1973, from Miss Rigg the retiring Principal of the City of Birmingham College, for the Principals and Vice Principals of the Birmingham colleges to meet informally over a working lunch at Westbourne Road. Principal Buckmaster, armed with a Memorandum which sketched out the possible skeleton for such a federal structure and strongly supported by St. Peter's Vice Principal, failed to take the meeting by storm. Other Principals could not or would not commit themselves to so forward a statement of aims ; the Principal of Newman said that such proposals were premature and the rest agreed with him. They were, however, prepared to think about it and to meet again.

Before this second meeting occurred, the St. Peter's Academic Board (Secretary, W. Powrie) had posted invitations to the Secretaries of other Academic Boards in the A.T.O. to a meeting at Saltley to discuss federation. This ran into severe trouble since other Boards were constituted differently from that at St. Peter's and some Local Authorities may have been affronted by this display of initiative ; no offence had been intended and it seemed a logical and proper step in accord with Mrs. Thatcher's statement at Oxford in April. The meeting was held ; a few observers attended and a full contingent from Hereford including its Principal. In view, however, of the disapproval of the Birmingham Principals, Principal Buckmaster decided to proceed no further, to the chagrin of his own colleagues. These were hard days.

The second meeting of Principals and V.P.s at Westbourne Road, held under the cloud of disapproval arising from St. Peter's Academic Board's impetuous action, resulted in no more than a restatement of the previous points of view and the concept of a Federated College of Higher Education for Birmingham was virtually dead.

In November 1973 the St. Peter's Governors decided that it was time for a more searching attempt to discover the reaction of the other two voluntary Colleges, Newman and Westhill, to some form of merger. The Chairman was much attracted by the prospect of a Christian College in Birmingham and agreed to undertake informal enquiries with the Chairmen of the other two Colleges. He had little success but persevered over many months. Newman College had been selected by the Roman Catholic Education Council as their Midlands Centre for training teachers and in order to preserve this college they were to sacrifice their colleges at Nottingham and Rugby ; the R.C. hierarchy were unlikely therefore to view a merger favourably. Similarly Westhill was a unique college and alone represented the interests of the Free Churches in teacher education in England ; one must understand therefore its desire to retain its identity ; the possibility of a link with Westhill remained, however, and it will be necessary later to make fuller reference to this.

Certain of the College Governors were interested at one time in promoting a merger with Hereford college with which St. Peter's staff and students had often maintained close professional and social associations, and which, like St. Peter's, was anxious about its future role. The subject was discussed in the Governors' meeting in June 1975, but, since cuts in numbers had by then become so serious, it was unlikely that the Church Board of Education would have agreed to support the survival of Hereford college at the expense of its own quota, and the idea was abandoned.

Under Circular 7/73 the man upon whose shoulders fell the responsibility for formulating the Birmingham plan was K. Brooksbank, the Chief Education Officer and successor to Sir Lionel Russell, whose deputy he had been. The Chief was no stranger to Saltley since he had been a popular visitor to several of the student revues during the Fifties. The Governors of St. Peter's were disappointed when he was unable to join the Board after Sir Lionel retired and, although the Deputy Chief became a member, the association between the City and the College was never quite so close after 1968.

It was not until 1st May 1973 that Chief Brooksbank made his first move and this was to visit Principal Buckmaster informally at Saltley accompanied by the Officer in charge of Further Education for the City; the Vice Principal was also present. The Chief explained that this was the beginning of an itinerary that he proposed to make to each of the institutions involved in his city plan and that, with a totally open mind, he was genuinely seeking information. He listened as the Principal expounded the views of the college academic board about the future. The Chief was pleasant, urbane but, for the most part, uncommunicative. He did say, however, that he was not prepared to accept the proposed cuts for teacher training in Birmingham and would be discussing them directly with the officers of the D.E.S. He said also that he was surprised that the academic boards of the colleges had taken no steps towards the discussion of a federal structure for teacher education in the city; he enquired closely what the Principal supposed would be the reaction of the College Governors to some form of federal association and what was the plan of the Church Board of Education for Saltley; he was surprised to learn that there was no such plan and seemed unprepared to accept that the College Governors were fully autonomous. Throughout the meeting which lasted about an hour he was friendly but reserved.

The next event was momentous. Shortly before the commencement of the new academic year in September 1973 Principal Buckmaster was invited to the education committee's headquarters in Margaret Street for a further meeting with the Chief; again he was accompanied by the Vice Principal. The Chief stated that in view of the city's long association with the College it was only fair that he should give the Principal some inkling of his proposed plan, although the information was still necessarily confidential. He had determined, he stated, that the city colleges should be merged into the Birmingham Polytechnic; he spoke briefly about the other two voluntary colleges; Westhill as a centre of excellence in religious education and already offering some diversified courses, and Newman, opened in 1968 at the city's request, continuing to fulfil its present functions; he was sorry that he could see no points for further growth at St. Peter's, although he hoped that the Church Board of Education would still maintain the premises for teacher training purposes; he agreed with the Director of the Polytechnic that there was no question that St. Peter's could be merged into the Polytechnic; when it came to diversified courses, he was prepared to consider any proposals, but he could not think of any courses which St. Peter's might undertake which the Polytechnic could not do better. The hearts of the listeners turned cold.

There was a series of subsequent meetings between the College Governors, led by their Chairman, and Chief Brooksbank; the Chief never budged from the stand which he took in September 1973; he acknowledged the past value of the role that the College had played in the history of education in the city, but it was up to the Church, whose College it was, and not to him, to determine its future. He remained adamant that there could be no place for St. Peter's in a diversified role in the city's higher education scheme of things.

The Principal and Vice Principal asked a number of questions. Would Saltley be given any priority, for example, for training of craft teachers and men P.E. teachers? The Chief agreed that once the D.E.S. had accepted the general plan there could be a second stage of discussion during which it would be possible to bargain about the detail of courses. Where the Principal and Vice Principal failed was to challenge the ruling that St. Peter's should be denied any opportunity to join the Polytechnic ; the subject had been briefly discussed in an academic board meeting and some of the staff felt that the possibility ought to be followed up ; there is no knowing how the Governors would have reacted, but it is worth noting that at St. Matthias College, in Bristol, where the situation most nearly compared with that in Birmingham, staff and Governors eventually agreed to integration with the Polytechnic. That the opportunity even to consider this was denied ought to have been contested vigorously.

St. Peter's was unfortunate in the order in which these events occurred. The decisions taken by the local authority rendered the situation of the College serious, if not yet critical ; had they been made six months earlier, it is possible that the Governors would have been attracted by the final offer made by Aston University's Vice Chancellor, resulting from his negotiations with the D.E.S. In that case the story would have developed along different lines.

An emergency meeting of the College Governors was summoned for 11th October, by which time a preliminary draft had been received of the Education Committee's reply to Circular 7/73. It contained this paragraph :

"St. Peter's College
Founded in 1850, the future of St. Peter's is for decision by the Church of England in the context of the Church's commitment in the country as a whole. If it is decided to retain St. Peter's College at its present size then it could be envisaged that the college could make a valuable contribution in spheres not adequately covered by others, for example in craft education and physical education. This would be of great value to authorities in the West Midlands and Birmingham in particular."

The Principal made an oral report of the events recounted above and emphasised that if the D.E.S. refused to accept Birmingham's proposed teacher training statistics "there would be no long term future for the College". Robert Prosser speaking for the staff, warned that "if the teacher training figures used by Chief Brooksbank were wrong, then the

189

College would need its share of a diversified role". The Governors were highly indignant at the qualified terms which had been used to describe the College in this official document to central government and noted a sharp contrast in the attitude towards the other two voluntary colleges. They resolved to make a formal protest and to request a hearing before the Chairman of the Education Committee.

This meeting duly took place on November 26th with Councillor Ms. Sheila Wright in the chair. The Governors amplified their objections to the statement about the College and Ms. Wright insisted that it should be rewritten in terms that they approved of. But there was no agreement to change the proposed role for the College or investigate diversified courses. The Bishop of Birmingham tried unsuccessfully to convince Ms. Wright and Chief Brooksbank that there could be no national Church of England plan for its colleges.

There were two consequences which followed from these interchanges with the local education authority which no subsequent pressures were able to rectify ; first, that if the D.E.S. approved of the authority's plan (as it did) then St. Peter's was doomed to remain a small monotechnic institution as long as it could continue to recruit teacher training students ; and secondly, that the local authority was not able or prepared to offer to the Church of England college in Birmingham that encouragement and support that was evident in many other parts of the country ; both these factors influenced the Church Board's final decision about its colleges, when at last it was made.

Chapter 31

During the winter and early spring of 1974 one sensed a deepening of the gloom in the Senior Common Room occasioned by the long uncertainty and by informed predictions in the educational press under such headings as, "The Knives are out". During the previous year a number of the experienced members of staff, Colin and Rita Jones, Michael Berry (to be Vice Principal of Christ Church, Canterbury, and subsequently its Principal), John Pick and David Fontana had taken new appointments, shortly followed by Geoffrey Brown and David Hill. There was still no real difficulty in filling the gaps and Brian Spence was welcomed from Sunderland Poly to be head of the Education Department in Fontana's place.

A notable departure in another field was that of Canon James Robertson, who in November 1973 had composed for the Church Board of Education a printed memorandum entitled, "The Future of the Church Training Colleges", which was to have unforeseen consequences for St. Peter's. At the Governors' meeting in March 1974 the Chairman referred to the "sombre tones in which the future of St. Peter's was expressed" and one wonders why the Governors did not voice a stronger protest at the information which was on sale (price 19p) at the Church House Bookshop for all to read. It certainly depressed Saltley staff who may have come by a copy:

"Birmingham presents a problem comparable to that of Bristol in terms of a large urban complex over-stocked with institutions of higher education . . . .

". . . a huge problem is created for St. Peter's, Newman College (R.C.) and Westhill College (Free Churches), with little specified future within a Birmingham submission to the D.E.S. . . . . It has not yet been possible to make any decisions but there are several possibilities.

(i)   To form a 'voluntary' complex of the three colleges, named above, on an ecumenical basis, to enable diversification ;

(ii)   To keep a monotechnic role with a combination of specialist work and in-service work ;

(iii) To realise the assets . . .

(iv)   To plan with Church and Government to be reborn like St. Mark and St. John College in another area of need . . . "

The Principal reviewed the situation for the Academic Board in February 1974, and the meeting was minuted thus :

"Following a full discussion it was noted that despite the numerous formal and informal negotiations that had taken place, St. Peter's College still had no clear indication about its future position and role. Academic representatives on the Governing Body were requested to press the Governors for some action on this important matter."

The Governors' meeting a few days later was unhappily not able to offer any further advice or firm opinion after it had listened to reports from its Chairman and the Principal ; responsibility for any fresh initiative rested squarely with the Principal.

It was against this background that the Principal received a letter from Canon Whitfield, secretary of the Church Board of Education :

"Yesterday evening I had a visit from Gordon Bessey, C.E.O. for the new Cumbria Education Committee, of which the possibility had been mentioned by Hugh Harding some weeks ago . . . .

"Bessey is of the opinion, to which the D.E.S. has been sympathetic, that Cumbria has a strong case for a developing centre for higher education with opportunities for teacher training and diversification in other academic disciplines . . . What they would like would be a dual college shared with the Church . . .

"He asked me whether there was any Church College thinking of a move and I said that, although at the moment you were pursuing other possibilities, it was not impossible that in the end St. Peter's might decide to recreate itself elsewhere. How likely this possibility is I am, of course, in no position to estimate, and all I said to Bessey

Was that I would mention to you the proposals he had outlined. So there you are."

In view of the controversy engendered by this Carlisle project it is well for readers to note carefully its origins and to understand that the Principal would have failed to fulfil his obligations to his colleagues unless he had examined the new possibilities thoroughly.

In fact negotiations proceeded smoothly and affably between Principal Buckmaster and the Cumbrian C.E.O. during the early summer months and before the end of June 1974 a scheme was in being, although it had not yet been divulged beyond a small group of persons who maintained the strictest confidence. It was proposed to create a new College at Hadrian's Camp, an abandoned army camp site, north east of the city of Carlisle, by linking Saltley and a local authority College of Art ; the document of merger was to be similar to that by which Bishop Lonsdale College in Derby was to be joined to a local authority college and both the Governors of Bishop Lonsdale and the Church Central Board had approved its articles. The courses at the new college were to be higher level courses validated by C.N.A.A. The St. Peter's staff, or those who elected to do so, would form the original teaching cadre with the staff of the Art College for the new college ; the Saltley assets would be realised and put into the new venture.

The academic staff were informed during the last week of June and the immediate reception of the plan seemed strongly favourable and the relief was evident in many faces. The Chairman of the Governors was less enthusiastic and the Governors' meeting on 24th June showed a divided opinion, despite the support for the project of the Bishop of Coventry, Cuthbert Bardsley, making his last appearance at Saltley. The Governors resolved to call a special meeting for October 7th when they would make a decision ; in the meantime the Principal was given permission to issue a statement to the Press, and to proceed with negotiations.

At the beginning of the new academic year, in September 1974, it was evident that the opinions of some of the staff had hardened against the project and there was a call for joint consultations between Governors and staff before decisions were made. The special meeting billed for 7th October failed to live up to its promise, despite the fact that it was held, ironically enough, in the newly-opened Library and that Hugh Harding from the D.E.S. and David Bungey, the new secretary of the Church Colleges committee, were present ; Councillor Ms. Sheila Wright and Education Chief K. Brooksbank had also been invited but were unable to attend. The twenty-two Governors present included, besides the Chairman, the Bishop of Worcester and representatives of all of the five dioceses involved. It was evident that if the issue of a move to Carlisle had to be put to the vote, the result would be hard to forecast, since there was a strong historical and emotional attraction to Saltley. Indeed the longer the arguments were pushed to and fro, the harder such a decision would have been. What was apparent, however, was that no decision could yet be made. There was disagreement, which could only have been resolved by the presence of Birmingham's C.E.O., about whether St. Peter's could be allowed to diversify or not, if it stayed at Saltley; Councillor Hargreaves insisted that the C.E.O. had been misunderstood and Hugh Harding stated that a C.E.O. could not veto diversified courses submitted by voluntary colleges despite D.E.S. Circular 6/74 which required voluntary colleges to submit applications for F.E. courses through the L.E.A. The Governors, too, wanted to know much more about the possible sale of the college and the financial problems the move to Carlisle would involve ; these would need to be discussed with the L.E.A., whom Harding thought to be the likely purchaser of the College. In the end the Principal proposed that Cumbria be asked to wait a further four months for a decision while investigations were made, and the meeting broke up.

As a result of this meeting the Governors sought a further review of the situation with Ms. Wright and Chief Brooksbank and a report was made to the ordinary meeting of the Governors in November. The Chairman of the Governors :

"expressed his difficulty in reconciling the willingness of the Local Education Authority representatives to meet Governors with their unwillingness to consider the College as an integral part of the area's educational system."

Chief Brooksbank firmly rejected for St. Peter's any prospect of 'A' level courses, general Dip.H.E. courses, or urban study degree courses, all of which had seemed areas of usefulness that the College might fill. He suggested that the Bishop and the Principal should arrange an appointment at the D.E.S. with Ms. Wright and himself to discuss how the purchase of the College site might be effected.

The appointment was duly made and the foursome proceeded to London one day late in mid-December 1974 to a meeting which was completely abortive. Met by Harding, they were told sternly and forcibly that a new crisis had blown up and teacher training numbers for both the Voluntary and the L.E.A. Colleges were about to be severely curtailed once more ; the Carlisle dream was over and the Bishop and Principal were warned that it was inevitable that the Church of England would need to close "four or five" of its Colleges. Dejectedly they returned to Birmingham, Principal Buckmaster to report to his colleagues the next day that he was sorry but that he could not yet see any light at the end of the tunnel.

It was not true that the College sought to move to Carlisle. The idea was the product of James Robertson's pamphlet "The Future of the Church Colleges of Education" and of contacts existing between the D.E.S. and the officers of the Central Board of Education. Principal Buckmaster did no more than his proper duty in conducting the negotiations to a point at which others would make the necessary policy decision. The project was greeted with enthusiasm by some members of staff and rejected as firmly by others. The Chairman of the Governors was known to have powerful reservations and certainly did not wish to lose the College from Saltley and his Diocese; his reservations were probably fortified by a letter received from the Headmaster of Cardinal Wiseman Comprehensive School and containing supporting signatures from more than 60 well-known secondary school Head Teachers in Birmingham :

> "I ask that, at your meeting in January, you will decide to remain in Birmingham as a college specifically for the training of students for the teaching profession or, at least postpone yet again a final decision until there has been a meeting between representatives of the College, its Governors, the L.E.A. and the schools."

A copy of the above was sent also to Chief Brooksbank, who returned it all to the sender with a note appended :

> "If the issue were as simple as to secure the retention of St. Peter's by enlisting signatures I would be very happy indeed. May I assure you it is not nearly so simple and that the Authority have been closely associated with the Governors of the College. I am afraid that I cannot undertake any action on your letter at all as I think it would only cause embarrassment . . ."

The Governors had made no decision and, in view of these reservations, no one can say how they would have voted. They were never required to do so; and in view of the complications that would have attended any attempt to sell the College at that time, the probability was that there would have been no move to Carlisle unless it had been willed positively by the D.E.S. and with the acquiescence of the Church Board of Education.

Chapter 32

When the Carlisle project terminated, there was little more that the Principal of St. Peter's or its Governors or staff could do but sit back and watch the progress of events in London, where the fate of the college would be determined in a series of meetings between D.E.S. officials and the officers of the Church Central Board of Education, Canon Holtby, now secretary of the Board, and David Bungey, secretary for the colleges of education.

The new crisis of numbers at the end of 1974 was accompanied by a letter from Harding at the D.E.S. to Canon Holtby in which he confirmed that "the effect of this downward revision will be a reduction of training places at Church of England Colleges of Education of the order of 50%" and that, "allowing for the proposals which have already emerged about the future of individual colleges, it may well be necessary to close as many as five Church of England Colleges". The Church officers hastened to make an appointment to see Harding and to summon a meeting of the Council of Church Principals in January 1975.

The meeting at the D.E.S. revealed that teacher training places were to be reduced in Church colleges by 1981 from 19,000, the figure quoted in the White Paper, to 9,800, which would include in-service and post-graduate places ; further, that figures had already been agreed for sixteen of the colleges and these would absorb 7,000 places ; this left 2,800 places for the remaining ten institutions ; two colleges, St. Luke's, Exeter and St. Mary's, Bangor were merging with universities and "no teacher training places would be debited against the Church Colleges allocation". Unfortunately the D.E.S. departed from this policy later with St. Luke's who were subsequently given 500 of the places. Harding made "suggestions as to how the division could be arranged" and it is quite clear that from this time the D.E.S. policy was that some colleges must close and St. Peter's held a high place on that list. When the Church officers suggested that colleges could be saved by cutting down slightly numbers already agreed, Harding rejected this argument with the unconvincing reply, "that the D.E.S. had already made optimistic allowances for diversification and could not afford to run any further risk of colleges with empty places".

It is reasonable to suppose that the D.E.S. may have had good political reasons for sticking so firmly to its policy ; a number of Local Education Authority colleges were on Harding's short list for closure and with some of these he was in for a fierce local battle ; the Roman Catholics had agreed already to close some of their colleges, including as already mentioned a costly new college at Nottingham ; so that the Church of England must be seen to be making an equal sacrifice with other providing bodies. There is no evidence how far the Church officers were disposed to resist Harding's pleas that "colleges whose future was already agreed would not be reviewed and revised by tne Church", in order to retain colleges in being whose future remained to be determined. Certainly the stated policy of the Church was to keep all colleges open, since "if decisions are made to close any of the Colleges, it is almost certain that they will never be opened again".

The net result of the meeting between Harding and Holtby in January was that the Church Board of Education was to make up its mind how the remaining places were to be distributed and which institutions were to be closed ; and it was given until December 1975 to do so. It was argued that the Church had absolute freedom of decision, but it is clear from the previous paragraph that this freedom was within a most restricted background and that in practice the Central Board had little choice and that an unenviable one. One is bound to say that the D.E.S. had played its hand with Jesuitical cunning so that any responsibility for the dissolution would lie not with Central Government or with Local Government, but with a small body of sincere and dedicated Churchmen seeking to make the best out of a bad situation. Whether the Central Board was wise to accept this responsibility in the circumstances of the time would be open to much debate.

The immediate consequence of the meeting in January was that the Central Board established a small fact-finding sub-committee which visited

Saltley in March 1975 but published its findings just before it did so, which seemed an odd way to proceed! The Board determined to put its problems before a conference to be held at York, inviting College Governors, Principals and uncommitted members of the Board. In addition to Principal Buckmaster, the Vice Chairman of the Governors, the Venerable R. B. Ninis, Archdeacon of Stafford, attended between 17th and 18th April. A special meeting of the College Governors was called to hear the results ; nine points were agreed at the conference, one of which was that there should be a "national confederation of autonomous colleges with an overall developing strategy with each College being considered as part of a national complex" ; another was that "the Board of Education should have the authority to negotiate on behalf of Church colleges as a whole." . . . a new Working Party was to be established to work out the details of its strategy for the Central Board, and Archdeacon Ninis was made a member of this body. The Governors were now asked to approve these findings and to accept the decision of the Central Board, whatever this might be for St. Peter's. They did so in somewhat vague terms :

"this Board of Governors welcomes the decision of the Church Board of Education to draw up an overall strategy for the complex of Church Colleges. They would re-state the confidence they had in the future of St. Peter's, Saltley, by its unique central geographical location available to a very large population, its vital concern for children and young people who live in urban areas, and its ability to serve both Church and State in a wide range of educational situations."

Throughout the summer of 1975 the Church colleges under suspended sentence waited to learn the judgment of the Working Party. The freedom of the Church to determine its policy was jeopardised by two further letters from the Department to the Board during May, one of which restated the numbers agreed but included the St. Luke's figures (500) as counting as part of the Church's element. The other spelt out the arguments and among other statements added :

"The situation in the West Midlands demands a reduction in voluntary college places comparable with that we are requesting from the local authorities. We see no way in which this can be achieved without the closure of St. Peter's . . . "

So concerned were the officers of the Board about these two letters that they sought an interview at the D.E.S. with Lord Crowther-Hunt, who as Under Secretary of State dealing with Higher Education, took political responsibility for the decisions of the Department. The deputation included the Bishop of Blackburn, chairman of the Central Board, and two college Principals. The meeting resolved little and Harding strongly maintained his fortified position ; Lord Crowther-Hunt repeated what he had said in public that "closure was the wrong word to use about colleges which were ceasing to train teachers" and "he hoped to be able to ensure that all Colleges were used".

During late July the national Press published a statement that the D.E.S. had agreed to the closure of a list of colleges, which included St. Peter's, Saltley and Culham ; since the York Working Party was not due to finalise its report until early September nor the Church Board of Education to consider its findings until October, it is clear that this was a bad breach of confidence by the D.E.S. either by accident or with the design of forcing the issue.

The Working Party report was received early in September. It was a long document, carefully and thoughtfully presented and it indicated that its members had taken much trouble in setting out their conclusions ; a copy of it with its appendices giving Church statements of its meetings with the D.E.S. was published in full in the College Minute Book. About St. Peter's it stated simply : "St. Peter's has met disheartening problems from the outset of the reorganisation. It cannot expect any support from the L.E.A. which has severe problems of cut back in its own colleges . . . " and in its recommendations the report repeated : "St. Peter's seems to have no future at all in Birmingham in spite of the most strenuous efforts to reach an agreement with the Local Authority." In a similar category, although far from identical, were St. Matthias, Bristol ; St. Katherine's, Liverpool ; and All Saints, Tottenham. The report concluded :

"The Working Party is far from happy in presenting these proposals. It knows that they will cause great distress but they have been arrived at after long and earnest consideration. The disappearance from teacher training of so many famous city colleges which have served the Church and the nation so well and for so long can only be a matter of the deepest regret but there seems to be no possible alternative . . ."

A special Governors' meeting on 22nd September considered the Report ; as was only to be anticipated, the Report met severe criticism particularly on the grounds that :

"it seemed to have ignored the fact that it was establishing the direction the Church would be taking in further and higher education for the next thirty years. It had failed to see that the urban colleges were in the forefront of the mission of the Church and it had not outlined any new roles for its colleges. In short it had abandoned the city colleges."

These views stated by the Principal were warmly endorsed and the Bishop of Worcester "proposed that the Principal should put his views in writing and, with the Chairman's approval, give them as wide a circulation as possible". It was agreed, also, that in view of the Report, the Governors should make one further approach to the L.E.A. "for some diversified courses to support the 400 teacher training places for which the Board of Education would be asked" ; the Chairman, Vice Chairman, Principal and Miss M. Rolfe, one of Birmingham's Head Teachers, were deputed to take on this forlorn hope.

With the commencement of a new academic year, staff and students returned to learn of the almost certain closure of the college. Staff had found the months waiting for decision not only full of anxiety, but also frustrating because of their sense that there was little or nothing they could do which would affect the issues. They now resolved to mount a campaign to persuade those at Church House, at Elizabeth House where Fred Mulley had taken over from Reg Prentice and at Margaret Street, Birmingham, that they were in danger of sharing in a calamity. A committee was formed with John Bradford chairman and Pat Brookfield secretary; they were joined by the chairman and secretary of the Old Students association, the President and other members of the Students' Union, the Principal of the College and other friendly persons. They set out to arouse interest in their cause and understanding of the problems, and to make as public as possible the arguments that seemed to justify the College's continuance; in particular they wanted to influence opinion locally and nationally in the Church and in politics, by means of Press and Television and personal contact.

The arguments to maintain St. Peter's on its Birmingham site had indeed strengthened during recent years and they were equally strong whether viewed through national or local eyes or of those concerned for the continuation of the Church's mission. St. Peter's was one of the few colleges in a genuine inner ring situation and was surrounded by a multi-racial society, complex and deprived; in Birmingham, perhaps more than other cities, the eastern side of the city had been neglected and starved of civic institutions; there was a most serious economic decline and withdrawal of work and capital from the area. Even a stay of execution for five years to give the College an opportunity to demonstrate whether or not it had any "growing points" might have been environmentally sound policy.

It was not to be expected that a campaign such as had been embarked upon could be executed without acquiring enemies as well as friends and those who advocated the cause of the College did so at some personal risk that they could have given offence. This was well illustrated by an article by the Rev. Brian Rice, Birmingham Diocesan Director of Religious Education, in the "Church Times" on 10th October, which gave publicity to the problems which the Church Board of Education were about to decide upon and asked for public debate of the issues.

It would not be possible to describe all the activities of the Committee, but a number of memorable events occurred. One Friday afternoon, lectures were suspended and a large proportion of the student body determined on a protest march. Led by the S.U. President, Mike Crowston, and carrying their S.U. Banner, they marched to town; when they reached the Cathedral the doors were flung open and, greeted by the Provost seated at the organ, they sang "Onward, Christian soldiers . . . " and were then addressed by Saltley's M.P., the Right Hon. Denis Howell; they next progressed along Colmore Row to Margaret Street, but received no response from the education offices within. The Chief of Police congratulated Mike Crowston on the orderliness of the protest. The students also gathered a local petition of nearly 5,000 signatures; this was later presented to the Archbishop of Canterbury at Lambeth Palace with a copy (for information) to Councillor Ms. Wright. The body which presented the Petition and also did some lobbying at the House of Commons included the Vicar of St. Saviour's and local teachers, besides members of the Action Committee. The committee was most effective in marshalling support from the local M.P.'s of both major parties who tabled questions and sought interviews with the Secretary of State. One supporter was the Rt. Hon. Roy Jenkins, then Home Secretary, who was alerted to the case by visits to his surgery at Stechford from the Chairman of the Old Students, a member of staff and a resident student. He visited the College and met a number of staff, and certainly spoke to his Cabinet colleague, Fred Mulley, pressing St. Peter's claims. Denis Howell most actively supported the campaign. He had recently made a speech at the Trade Union Congress in which he deplored the way government was withdrawing its resources from Inner City areas and his relations with St. Peter's had always been most friendly. He followed the final stages of the closure carefully and his activities included two letters to the Archbishop of Canterbury, a particularly sharp letter to the Chairman of Birmingham's Education committee on the subject of diversification, and personal interviews with the Bishop of Blackburn and with Fred Mulley. The College received many friendly letters of encouragement, especially from teachers in Birmingham, but none more sincere and affecting than one signed by the Saltley Methodist minister and eighty members of his congregation.

But pride of place in the campaign to save the College must be given to the chairman of the Governors, Laurence Brown, the Bishop of Birmingham ; he was deeply concerned at the loss to the Diocese and to the Church that would be incurred by the closure and seemingly spared no effort, as with a gentle and poignant sense of humour he wrote to his colleagues in Church and State :

"To the Rt. Honourable F. W. Mulley, M.P.   1st December, 1975.

. . . It seems difficult to convince our own Church of England Board of Education that the governing body is not fighting a rearguard action simply to preserve a venerable institution, but that we are endeavouring to avert the loss to the local community, to the educational system and to the Church of a College which has become unique in its location and, I believe, in its relationship to the local community. I fully recognise the delicacy of the judgment which must eventually fall to you to make, but I cannot forebear to observe that it would be quite splendid if it could be demonstrated in this instance that the State was more visionary than the Church."

On 13th November, the Bishop inaugurated a debate in the General Synod of the Church of England, in which he proposed an amendment to the motion accepting the report of the Board of Education. It was a momentous occasion and a contingent from Saltley was present to listen as well as Harding from the D.E.S. The Bishop made two speeches, first a prepared speech and later one unprepared in reply to points raised. It was reported to the author, who was not present, that it was a masterly performance. He carefully picked out the salient points from the recent history of relations between the Board and the D.E.S. ; he pilloried the Birmingham L.E.A. :

"My local authority has spoken honeyed words, but it has made no concessions in student places or anything else . . . "

and finally he criticised the absence of effective long-term planning by the Board :

"As a minimum one Church College in London and one in Birmingham must at all costs be retained. Only through such means can the Church keep in effective touch with all the problems of urban education : truancy, violence, illiteracy, multi-racialism, deprivation and all the difficult social conditions of our large cities . . . "

In the debate there was only one speaker from the West Midlands, a lady from Lichfield who opened with the words : "I cannot speak of individual colleges . . . " ; no other voice was raised, either by the clergy or the laity, on behalf of St. Peter's ; Alan Heawood, once chaplain at Saltley but now speaking as a governor of Keswick Hall, had a few words of sympathy but none of support. Most subsequent speakers, including the Bishop of Blackburn, paid tribute to the Bishop of Birmingham and the validity of the general points which he had made. When the Bishop replied to the debate, he first scotched the "Cumbria hare" which had been raised as a point of order :

"Saltley examined the possibility of a move to Cumbria . . . at the firm suggestion of the Department of Education, encouraged by the officers of the Church of England Board of Education, and with the implication that if we did not do it our hopes for the future were slender . . . ;"

he stressed that the point he was making was that St. Peter's was in Saltley, Birmingham, as All Saints was in Tottenham, London, and repeated his main argument

". . . we believe that the decision so arrived at fails to take account of the vital necessity to retain by the Church certain of its colleges which are firmly embedded in that urban situation which is characteristic of the heartland, indeed the wasteland, of so many of our larger cities."

It was no good. The debate was lost on a show of hands with no need to count the votes. The Bishop's contribution none-the-less made a fitting curtain to the national record of the College. It is printed verbatim in the General Synod "Report of Proceedings" Volume 7 No. 1, November 1975.

The battle was lost. In due course the College received official intimation that the Board of Education had recommended Saltley's closure to the D.E.S. and in February 1976 the further news that its final appeal against closure to the Secretary of State had been dismissed :

"The Secretary of State had decided to accept the recommendations of the Board of Education that St. Peter's, Saltley should close and, subject to what is said below, . . . should have no further intake of students . . . .

"The Secretary of State would hope, however, that even in present difficult financial circumstances, the Local Education Authority would be able to find alternative educational uses for the premises . . . He would also welcome arrangements by which the present Handicraft course at the College could be transferred to the Birmingham Polytechnic . . .

"He would also if it were the wish of the two Colleges, be prepared to consider favourably the possibility of perhaps 200 places being re-provided as part of Westhill College of Education, if the cost of the necessary buildings could be financed by the disposal of the Saltley premises . . ."

An interesting footnote to this communication was that no one in authority bothered to send a copy to the Principal of Westhill College ! For the rest the matters put forward by the Secretary of State may best be left to another chapter.

Chapter 33

It is pleasant to relate that during the dismal events recorded in the last two chapters good relations with Birmingham University had been restored. Readers will recall that before 1939 some Birmingham University undergraduates had resided within the college and that there was a one-year course available at Saltley for graduates wishing to gain a certificate. After the war Professor Jeffreys had maintained a close relationship with the College and Dr. Geoffrey Templeman (before he became Vice Chancellor of the University of Kent) and R. L. Knight were most active and useful members of the Governing Body. Although the University of Birmingham and the School of Education each appointed a Governor to St. Peter's after 1968, little seemed to be done by the University to support the College interests vigorously during its struggle for existence.

During the period that St. Peter's was discussing with Aston University in 1972 its proposed new link, Principal Buckmaster had informed Professor Hilliard at the School of Education and it seems to have been presumed that Saltley would not be involved in any new B.Ed. validation at Birmingham. When the Aston proposal was rejected by the D.E.S., the Bishop of Birmingham wrote personally to the Vice Chancellor of Birmingham University to request that St. Peter's be restored to the list of colleges in active association with the University. By this time the University Senate had agreed to proceed with a three-year B.Ed. degree in line with Mrs. Thatcher's "Framework for Expansion" and in December 1973 the senior members of Saltley's staff entertained a Working Party from the University to a working dinner in which the issues involved were closely examined ; the visitors included Professor R. J. North, the chairman of the working party, later University Pro-Vice Chancellor, and W. R. G. Lewis, the University Registrar. As a result, St. Peter's was readmitted to the small group of colleges which were to offer the new degree.

After the long B.Ed. wrangles of the Sixties, it was splendid that Birmingham was now able to offer a three-year Ordinary degree which included within its compass full arrangements for professional teacher training. But at the risk of appearing churlish and ungrateful one must state that it was not enough. The situation in which St. Peter's found itself in 1974 and after, would have been transformed if only Birmingham University had been prepared to validate ordinary Diploma of Education courses or give other scope (perhaps through ordinary B.A.s) for even a limited amount of diversification of courses. In such circumstances the Chairman and Principal would not have had to beseech Councillor Ms. Wright or Chief Brooksbank (as they did fruitlessly on three occasions) to grant St. Peter's a measure of diversification. Such courses would still have needed to be approved by a Regional F.E. Committee, but it seems reasonable to suppose that supported by so influential a body as Birmingham University, they might have surmounted this hurdle. Leeds University have performed this service for St. John's College, York.

The colleges involved in the new B.Ed. degree were the three voluntary colleges, with Dudley and Shenstone. The group constituted its own informal consultative committee under the genial chairmanship of the Principal of Dudley with the Vice Principal of Newman acting as secretary. The meetings were held at the different colleges in turn and contained three members from each college, Principal, Vice Principal and one academic board representative ; there were a few differences of opinion, but the discussions were relaxed and friendly and made good progress in much detail. Following this, the chairman and secretary established a close rapport with Professor North and the University Registrar, so that the colleges and the University were now more easily able to understand each other's point of view, respect each other's judgment, and make substantial progress towards agreement about the new degree.

The consequence was that the three-year professional B.Ed. degree and four-year Honours degree started with students who arrived at Saltley in September 1975, Saltley's last three-year course intake. The new degree course was structured on module-unit principles and it was therefore necessary to reorganise the certificate course similarly, since there were points, particularly in the professional studies areas when the two courses must come together. The changes involved made it imperative to bring out an entirely fresh edition of the College Prospectus, which became a most interesting and attractive booklet, for it now included all the college course programmes. It is not the intention of this work to evaluate these changes or to discuss the merits and demerits of module-type courses. Suffice it to say that the University agreed to what was a clever combination of module-type and traditional courses which allowed both for continuity and flexibility. At the same time it was possible to maintain the process of three-year continuous professional training which had been the chief merit of the old certificate system so soon to be discarded.

The inter-college group was reinforced during 1975 by Hereford College and later by Wolverhampton Day College, but as the days progressed it became apparent that, when the institutional reorganisation had been completed by the end of the decade, the University of Birmingham would be left to provide for only the two voluntary colleges, Newman and Westhill, from the seventeen teacher-training colleges which had constituted the Institute during the Sixties. It was ironic that soon after the Government closed the University A.T.O.'s in 1975, the School of Education in Birmingham was promoted to the status of Faculty.

The success of these discussions might have prompted the hope that they would lead to some more intimate institutional arrangements between the voluntary colleges, especially to a closer association between St. Peter's and Westhill, an object which the Bishop of Birmingham would have been pleased to achieve from the beginning of the reorganisation. In 1974 when the Carlisle discussions were in progress, there was a suggestion that the handicraft wing at Saltley might be transferred to Westhill and the Westhill governors reciprocated by drawing up a scheme allowing for Anglican representation on their Governing Body ; the idea was firmly vetoed by Harding at the D.E.S., who said the wing should go to the Birmingham Polytechnic, which equally firmly rejected the idea in 1976.

The Church Board of Education favoured a link between St. Peter's and Westhill, although there is no evidence that the officers of the Board themselves took any initiative. When in 1976 Professor Niblett undertook an enquiry for the Board into the future of the colleges, he wrote :

"There may be instances where part of a College might merge with another college, as seems to me commendable in the case of St. Peter's College, Saltley, in relation to Westhill College . . . Several Governors of the redundant college would presumably serve on a reconstituted Governing Body of the united college and several members of its staff, after interview, find new posts in it . . . "

It is possible, although improbable, that Westhill might have taken up the offer more keenly had the officers of the Board followed up the Bishop's initiative. It must be admitted that there was little evidence from the staff at Saltley that they had much enthusiasm for the venture ; as other colleges have found, it is a tricky operation to effect such a grafting, especially during a period when the number of jobs is contracting.

However, Fred Mulley's final communication to St. Peter's in February 1976 spoke of :

"the possibility of perhaps 200 places bring reprovided as part of Westhill College."

Once more meetings were held between Chairmen of Governors and Principals, and Westhill responded promptly and seriously with a new scheme allowing for an expansion of Westhill by 200 places on the condition that money would be available from Saltley. Unfortunately no one knew what "reprovided" meant and when the D.E.S. were consulted, their interpretation was that the 200 was a part of the Church of England's "historic share" and the Central Board insisted that the vacancies created by Saltley's closure should be distributed among the Anglican colleges. This ended all idea of a merger, but Westhill drew up a further document which could allow for some memory of St. Peter's to be preserved at their College and their interesting ideas will presumably be considered at some date by the Trustees of St. Peter's.

The D.E.S. was equally unhelpful about its proposal to move the handicraft wing to the Birmingham Polytechnic ; the Polytechnic lacked the financial resources to purchase this expensive collection of equipment and it would have been required to create vacancies from its own numbers in order to absorb Saltley staff and craft student-teachers, which could have involved extreme difficulties. In July 1976 Principal Buckmaster wrote to Denis Howell, still trying to save things from the wreckage :

> "At a meeting yesterday with the Chairman of the Education Committee and Mr. Brooksbank, and with Mr. Smethurst (Director of Polytechnic) present, the decision was made not to take the Craft Course when St. Peter's closes. This means that apart from a prospect of a modest Craft Course in a new complex based on Wolverhampton Polytechnic, and including the present Dudley College of Education, there will be no provision for the training of Craft teachers in the West Midlands area. I will not enlarge upon the folly of this decision."

After further negotiations involving H.M. Inspectors who were presumably much concerned by this state of affairs, it was agreed that Dudley College should commence a one-year F.T.C. course with part-time assistance from Saltley staff and the loan of Saltley technical equipment ; the Saltley wing course would be closed with the rest of the College.

The D.E.S. proved unaccommodating in other negotiations about college courses ; since the decision to close the college had not been confirmed until February 1976, courses for September were already half full. It was reasonable that the 60 or so who had been accepted for the 105 places allowed on the three-year course should be moved elsewhere, since either the college would have had to be kept open till 1979 or they would have had to be transferred at the end of their second year ; but it was less reasonable that the one-year postgraduate course should have had to be moved since it would have hardly affected staffing arrangements or the longer-term plans for the closure ; as many of these graduates had local connections and would have been trained for subjects in short supply, like Mathematics, Science and Modern Languages, there could have been appreciable loss for the West Midlands. Fortunately Dr. Cornwell at Walsall agreed to take, without further interview, all candidates for the one-year course who had already been accepted by Saltley. In February 1976 some twenty-four candidates had already been accepted for an F.T.C. course commencing in January 1977 and after special pleading these were allowed admission ; and by all accounts a splendid group they proved to be.

In staff matters the D.E.S. with the eyes of the teachers' unions upon them proved to be generous in their interpretation of the regulations, allowing the normal staff/student ratios for the college to be withdrawn during the run-down period and giving liberal opportunities for retraining, especially of younger staff. The redundancy regulations, were complicated and subject to a variety of meanings, which the experts did not always interpret the same way. The staff of L.E.A. colleges who were threatened with redundancy during this reorganisation period were usually guaranteed re-employment by their authority, but there was no way such a guarantee could be made to the staff of voluntary colleges ; the Church colleges that were continuing were themselves shrinking and with the best will possible could rarely help. The 1976 and 1977 search for new posts coincided with the crisis of public expenditure and entrants from colleges of education into school, where numbers were also being contracted, were not always popular. There were occasions when Saltley students and the staff who had taught them at college were applicants for the same job. One member of staff made 100 applications, and, after nine fruitless interviews, obtained an appointment at the tenth. It was not all gloomy ; two Heads of Department gained promotion — Douglas Courts in Western Australia and Clive Bond in Leeds/Carnegie ; and a number of others to posts of major responsibility in comprehensive schools or the local Inspectorate.

During the summer of 1976 at the end of the College's year of trauma, came the sad news of the death of Frank Brinkworth, the Head of the Craft Wing ; Frank had had a short illness but, when he made his last appearance at Saltley on the occasion of the lunch given to mark the departure of the retiring Vice Principal, it was apparent to all that he was gravely ill. There was no better servant of the College during the period of this book, nor one held in any higher esteem by staff or students. He was a fine active christian worker and a friend to all ; St. Peter's profited equally from his professional excellence and his personal dedication.

Lord Crowther-Hunt had told the Bishop of Blackburn that "he hoped to be able to ensure that all colleges were used" and the Secretary of State himself had also "hoped that the Local Education Authority would be able to find alternative educational uses for the premises". In the circumstances these were idle promises despite the large sums of taxpayers' and church-goers' money that had been devoted to the buildings. The College did not belong to the Local Education Authority and they had no money with which to purchase it. Nor would the Governors, even if they had wished, have been able to present the buildings to the L.E.A. (or to any other worthy cause) since the law forbids that charitable endowments and benefactions should go for a song. In any case, if St. Peter's ceased to be a residential institution of higher education, it was far from clear to what uses it might be put without extensive and costly alterations. For these reasons the Governors decided that they must make some attempt at realising their assets and invited their agents, Messrs. Chesshire, Gibson and Co., to advertise the sale of the buildings. The brochure which was produced announced the sale by private treaty of :

"A fully equipped Training College for Teachers with fine buildings and facilities capable of adaption for many purposes."

The outside cover showed a fine photograph of the old college, the hall and south block, taken from the roof of the new library and showing a panorama of the city as a background ; in the foreground appeared the running track and the cricket nets and the college trees in full summer leaf. In October 1977 the representative of Chesshire, Gibson and Co., reported to the Governors that :

" . . . there had been between 50 and 100 enquiries for the College property including one or two from overseas. He referred to a number of specific enquiries . . . but there had been no further developments. One of the problems which the Governors had to face was that the general economic situation and lack of finance prevented other organisations which would otherwise be interested from making serious enquiries about the property. In addition there were at least thirty other similar buildings on the market at present with prospects of another thirty within the next few years . . . "

The last two years were in a sense an anti-climax and it would have been strange if it had been otherwise since the issues had been decided. It was remarkable, too, how the chief personalities disappeared into retirement during these years, leaving Principal Buckmaster and his shrinking staff to clear up the final details. Laurence Brown's period of office as Diocesan Bishop ended in 1977 and he was succeeded as Chairman of the Governors by the new Bishop of Coventry, the Rt. Rev. John Gibbs, who had been Principal of Keswick Hall College, Norwich, during the Sixties. Since 1947 the active chairmanship of the College had been with the Birmingham Diocese and the Bishop's efforts to retain a Church college at Saltley deserved stronger support from within as well as from without the Diocese. His sincerity and friendliness in the Saltley Common Rooms were appreciated by both staff and students ; in a farewell party, John Taylor, a staff Governor, expressed in a speech, both warm and witty, the thanks and good wishes of all on his retirement to Salisbury.

From the University Professor Hilliard retired, as the A.T.O. over which he presided broke up, and teacher education in the West Midlands came under the authority of the Chief Education Officers linked together in a Regional Board from which the Church of England Board of Education was totally excluded. K. Brooksbank had also retired as Birmingham's Chief Education Officer and Councillor Ms. Wright stepped down from the Chairmanship of the Education Committee as the victorious Conservatives took over ; from their record in opposition there was nothing to suggest that St. Peter's would have fared any better had the elections swung them into office earlier.

Nationally, Fred Mulley gained promotion and moved to Defence from Education while Hugh Harding retired from the D.E.S. By 1977 Canon Holtby, Secretary of the Church Board of Education, had become Dean of Chichester Cathedral and David Bungey, Secretary of the Church colleges, had retired, so that opportunity was there for a new higher education concordat between church and state to be determined by their successors.

Life and work in College continued with undiminished zest. June 1976 was the last occasion when the College was full of St. Peter's students ; when the College reassembled in September, Anne Brereton had become Vice Principal and there were ten members of staff fewer, many of them senior and long experienced tutors like Courts, Bond and Prosser. Fortunately there was in Birmingham a rich fund of able "temporaries" from whom the Principal could draw to supplement the dwindling numbers of the college staff. In September 1976 there was no entry of first year students, graduates or three-year course, so that numbers were down by more than a third ; fortunately it was possible to rent the spare rooms to Aston University students, who between 1976 and 1978 made a fine contribution to the social life on the campus ; indeed, it would not have been possible to preserve the high standards of the essential services like the dining hall and the bar without their assistance.

At the end of the 1976/77 year, 21 students obtained their B.Ed. degree, 4 of whom, each with a different Principal subject course, achieved award of honours ; this compared well with 1969, the first year of the degree, when only 6 students qualified for their degree. By the final academic year, 1977/78, with the staff further decimated and with only the final third and fourth years left, there were 8 candidates for the four-year degree (spread over six Principal subjects) and fifteen for the first and final batch of three-year degree candidates ; there would have been more, but for the fact that honours degree students, taking a four-year course, had been passed to other colleges at the end of their second year and four P.E. students were also transferred, since the remaining staff could not reasonably cope with these as well as a full certificate course. It must be said that many of the students were aware that in view of the severe national cut-backs there was little prospect of them obtaining employment in teaching at the end of their course. Their anxiety, however, seemed to hang lightly on their shoulders and their resilience in the face of these buffets of fortune was splendid.

During these final years the students were concerned that they should continue to be identified as part of the national student body and, although they did not always approve of the activities of the N.U.S., nevertheless they supported student action locally and nationally with much loyalty. In the spring of 1976 they participated in their most prolonged spell of protest against proposed cuts in public expenditure, the protest taking the form of what was optimistically described as a "work-in". This meant that students would hand in work which they were required to complete, but would not attend lectures ; their specially appointed committee took permanent occupation of the conference room and arranged open meetings of the student body in the dining hall. On the whole the student body supported their demonstrations and withdrew from their lectures, although they continued their studies diligently and took long week-end breaks. Eventually all but the most politically activated became rather bored and perhaps realised that their protest was damaging no one except themselves ; and the work-in was called off.

Perhaps during these last years the students succeeded in recapturing some of the enthusiasm for college life that was evident in the first years after the war, although it is improbable that the post-war students with all their war-time and service experience would have equalled the sales at the College bar of £29,722 recorded in the accounts of 1976. Certainly the life focussed upon the Junior Common rooms lost little of its intensity and regularity in its discos or the convivial routine of songs and dramatic movement which seemed to have become so much a part of a Saltley evening's enjoyment.

In games the College continued to excel, and the well-organised national and regional championships gave them every scope. In 1976 the Rugger club fought its way successfully through the tough competition of the midland region to be narrowly defeated at Stechford by Jordanhill College from Glasgow in the national championship semi-finals ; the college side was full of good players, but had no outstanding ones. The same year the Soccer club were the midland colleges champions and also reached the semi-final of the national championship for the Mitre Shield. During these last years Robert O'Hara, a fourth-year B.Ed. student in 1978, acquired a fistful of medals for his cross-country running and athletics.

It was in cricket that they achieved their best results. In 1976 they were Midland Colleges finalists and Warwickshire Club Cricket semi-finalists, two of their number playing for a British College representative XI ; but in 1977 with only two years to pick from they reached the final of the National Competition in which they were defeated by Borough Road. Their audacity was explained partly by the presence in their ranks of a young man named Ashley White, from Nottingham, that legendary home of noble strikers of the cricket ball ; White showed himself to be a prodigious hitter ; on one occasion during the summer of 1976, playing at college in a light-hearted match between the staff and the Students Union he struck the ball full pitch into the College Quad, a feat that many aspired to but which was only accomplished this once in the post-war years to the author's knowledge.

Similarly the drama traditions were well maintained and demonstrated the informal and experimental nature of contemporary fashion. The drama studio became a popular venue for lunch-time and late night theatre and the regular "Wednesday at One" programme was a lunch-time studio hour when staff and students came together to discuss, perform and enjoy drama. During the closing years there was a strong link between the postgraduate course and the drama work and it was fitting that one of the most recent of graduate students, Tony Hall, should come back on the staff for a year. Other society life flourished and even developed new shoots, when Bridget Agnew formed a Ski-ing club which showed its enthusiasm and expertise by spending a week-end on the slopes of the Cairngorms in the face of the February blizzard of 1978. During the final years Pat Dixon, operating still under the banner of Saltbuild, was tireless in organising barn dances and other entertainments. The

Governors and Old Students, too, had good reason to be grateful to Pat for undertaking the detailed organisation for the valedictory festivities for July 1978.

And so this history reaches its conclusion on a somewhat low key with St. Peter's students similar in numbers to those recruited in 1945 for the first post-war assembly of the College. The 33 years between had been, for an institution concerned with education, unusually full of incident and challenge ; there was no opportunity to become complacent, since there was never any time when the staff were free from problems of expansion of courses and of numbers, until they suddenly found themselves afflicted by anxieties about contraction and closure.

It would be quite wrong to deduce that because the college was closed in 1978, it had failed in any way to fulfil the purposes of the foundation ; on the contrary, the evidence was that it had succeeded. In February 1975, Principal Buckmaster received this letter from Peter Guggenheim, then Headmaster of Sir Wilfred Martineau School in Tile Cross :

"I should simply like to place on record this School's acknowledgement of the enormous services in professional training rendered to it and to the education of children in East Birmingham by your College for so many decades in the past. I cannot help feeling that your College and this School, among others, have had a very special role to play in providing educational opportunities on this side of the City. I am sure that there is not a member of staff who would not join with me in commending your efforts to keep St. Peter's in Birmingham continuing and extending its role for the rest of this century. I am absolutely convinced that if you cease to offer the services you are currently offering, teacher recruitment, particularly in certain scarcity areas, throughout Birmingham, will suffer."

Six months later, the Bishop of Blackburn, chairman of the Church Board, whose post-bag must have contained many similar letters, received this letter from Peter Davies, Headmaster of a J.I. School in Hall Green, and one of the Teacher Representatives on the Birmingham Education Committee :

"The name of St. Peter's in our City is synonymous with all that is good in teacher education and many are the senior members of our profession who are proud to call themselves "Old Salts." We who have worked in partnership with the College in training its students over the years have noted with much satisfaction how its standards and expectations have remained high when others around us would seem to be in the less fortunate position of having to accept a second best from a much reduced intake.

"Saltley today is a very different place from the Saltley where I was born, a stone's throw from the College, in the mid 1920s, but the very nature of the change is proving of immense value to us in

209

Birmingham for here we have students living and training amongst a multi-racial population, the rewards of which are quite evident when these young colleagues begin their careers alongside us in our classrooms . . . we do urge you most sincerely to think deeply before you deprive Birmingham of the services and products of this esteemed and well-loved College."

St. Peter's is a Church college and received a modest portion (2·17%) of the £3,000,000 which the Church invested between 1945 and 1978 in its group of Church colleges. How far and in what sense may the College be said to have justified the Church benefaction upon it ? How far, indeed, may one justify at all the appropriation to teacher education of so much of the Church resources at a time when religious education is so rapidly losing its place in the curriculum of state schools ? Certainly if one looks at Church Colleges as centres for evangelism and counts the numbers of those attending the daily and weekly services, then, if the evidence of St. Peter's is anything to go by, the results may be disappointing. It would be idle to presume that all who worked in St. Peter's, Saltley, were conscious of the peculiar responsibility that they carried ; we must accept that they, staff and students, men and women, were professional people seeking to equip others or to be equipped with the tools of their profession. At the same time, most of them were prepared to listen to and receive with an open mind the idea that education was concerned with religious and moral values and became better men and women for so doing. That is not to say that there are not many sincere and dedicated Christian men and women working in and through the state system and the L.E.A. colleges, although it might be hard to agree with the Birmingham L.E.A. and its C.E.O. that there is nothing that St. Peter's could do that the Polytechnic could not do better.

But there are other functions for the Church besides evangelism and one of these is the service of caring for the community ; one of the functions of caring is education. When Canon Platten and his colleagues decided that Saltley Training College should be known as St. Peter's, it was not just that this was a spare saint, as yet unappropriated by one of the other colleges, or that the annual festival of St. Peter came on the convenient date of 29th June and could be made to coincide with end-of-the-year celebrations ; but also because of the three-fold charge made by Our Lord to St. Peter that he should "Feed My Sheep" and that staff and students might rededicate themselves to such service as they listened annually to the story being read, as was the custom, by the Vice Principal.

The last words may go appropriately to John Bradford, Priest, member of the R.E. department and chairman of the St. Peter's College Continuation Committee ; they appeared in an article written for a local publication entitled "Saltley Gas" in January 1977. "Saltley Gas" was printed by the "Saltley Action Centre" located at Saltley Gate, familiar to many generations of students. This paper, started by one of St. Peter's postgraduate students, Nick Wolfe, claimed to be non-political, and included, side by side, advertisements for the services at St. Saviour's Church, together with a welcome, in Urdu, to the Khyber Pass Restaurant, a microcosm of Saltley, 1977.

John Bradford wrote :

" . . . Saltley College is a community within a community — and the best way to produce teachers for urban schools is to prepare teachers who care for people. It is mad to break this up. Saltley College is set in an area where the birth rate is increasing rather than declining and where our understanding of the needs and our links with the work of the community in East Birmingham and its related areas were just beginning to become exciting and innovative . . .

"We at St. Peter's take education to be a community affair. We all share responsibility for improving our skills, appreciating our heritage, making good relationships and developing a really positive purpose in life. Then education is for liberation . . . "

ST. PETER'S COLLEGE LEAVERS

Year of Leaving	Two-Year Certificate		Three-Year Certificate		One-Year Postgraduate		Four-Year B.Ed.		F.T.C.	In-Service Courses
	Men	Women	Men	Women	Men	Women	Men	Women	Men	
1950	87									
1951	124									
1952	86									
1953	101									
1954	95				17					
1955	111				8					
1956	103				6					
1957	97				7					
1958	105				6					
1959	97				12					7
1960	142				13					9
1961	118				12	1				28
1962	38				9				15	17
1963	8		109		4				15	17
1964			106		10				15	25
1965			106		15				15	12
1966			118		11				16	21
1967			100	1	13				11	15
1968			158	2	14	7			13	21
1969			130	9	22	16	6		11	15
1970			143	56	45	31	8		13	17
1971			115	65	41	42	13	1	15	17
1972			105	76	47	48	9	7	15	34
1973			82	76	42	42	8	7	18	3
1974			86	95	36	37	7	3	14	14
1975			101	80	36	36	10	9	20	Nil
1976			81	66	33	32	9	11	21	9
1977			80	81	40	27	12	8	23	
1978			67	74	28	34	6	2	27	
TOTALS	**1,312**		**1,687**	**681**	**491**	**317**	**88**	**48**	**238**	**266**

212

APPENDIX A   DISTRIBUTION BY REGIONS OF ST. PETER'S STUDENTS

	2-Year Course Students (Men)	3-Year Course (Men)	3-Year Course (Women)	1-Year P.G. Course (Men)	1-Year P.G. Course (Women)
	%	%	%	%	%
BIRMINGHAM AND SUTTON COLDFIELD	18·86	18·20	32·78	22·56	29·43
WARWICKSHIRE, COVENTRY AND S. STAFFS	13·11	8·33	11·09	10·77	12·34
N. AND E. MIDLANDS	23·62	16·60	8·61	10·38	9·81
S AND W MIDLANDS	11·73	12·72	15·56	11·58	11·71
NORTHERN COUNTIES	21·70	22·22	13·74	15·45	12·34
EASTERN COUNTIES	2·08	2·84	2·48	2·64	1·27
S.W. COUNTIES	2·08	4·82	4·47	4·67	3·17
LONDON AND S. COUNTIES	3·29	8·70	7·45	16·26	15·82
WELSH COUNTIES	2·53	4·70	3·32	3·25	3·17
SCOTLAND, IRELAND AND OVERSEAS	1·00	0·87	0·50	2·44	0·94

REPRINTED FROM GENERAL SYNOD PAPER GS194
CHURCH COLLEGES OF EDUCATION
FINANCING COLLEGE EXPANSION IN POST-WAR PERIOD

College	Public Funds	Central Church Funds	College Governors' Funds	Total	1973/74 Total Student Numbers
Culham College Abingdon	560,054	88,468	69,607	718,129	591
St. Mary's College, Bangor (a)	356,915	32,198	102,199	491,312	321
St. Peter's College, Birmingham	414,750	68,131	76,228	559,109	643
Hockerill College, Bishop's Stortford	429,036	102,845	51,058	582,939	519
St. Matthias' College, Bristol	454,589	183,124	42,748	680,461	812
Christ Church College Canterbury	956,348	249,277	66,671	1,272,296	705
Trinity College, Carmarthen (a)	729,589	23,707	243,706	997,002	718
St. Mary's College, Cheltenham	455,589	124,848	50,283	630,720	688
St. Paul's College, Cheltenham	474,861	117,639	131,023	723,523	673
Chester College	673,116	204,033	81,086	958,235	925
Bishop Otter College, Chichester	541,838	160,149	45,173	747,160	739
Bishop Lonsdale College, Derby	1,130,064	156,540	63,743	1,350,347	791
Bede College, Durham (b)	552,526	109,064	86,878	748,468	557
St. Hild's College, Durham (b)	144,058	20,260	41,879	206,197	366
St. Luke's College, Exeter	531,456	85,391	166,755	783,602	1,249
St. Martin's College, Lancaster	945,416	166,302	140,031	1,251,749	750
Bishop Grosseteste College, Lincoln	499,327	123,606	82,076	705,009	676
St. Katherine's College, Liverpool	467,274	82,033	65,566	614,873	778
All Saints' College, London	481,924	Nil	360,512	842,436	665
St. Gabriel's College, London	581,001	156,500	32,087	769,588	301
Whitelands College, London	388,115	89,000	36,367	513,482	873
Keswick Hall College, Norwich	603,881	203,105	50,399	857,385	710
Ss. Mark & John College, Plymouth	271,074	87,214	18,590	376,878	666
Ripon College	419,810	150,792	32,366	602,968	608
Sarum St. Michael College Salisbury	317,380	91,100	74,116	482,596	510
King Alfred's College, Winchester	937,883	152,991	123,698	1,214,572	1,024
St. John's College, York	794,614	107,392	209,106	1,111,112	965
Totals £	15,112,488	3,135,709	2,543,951	20,792,148	18,862

NOTES :
(a) These colleges are in Wales.
(b) Joint buildings are shown under Bede's totals, but are shared with Hild's.
(i) Some figures are near approximations but indicate reasonably correct magnitudes
(ii) Figures have been supplied by the colleges and have been reconciled with C.B.F. records of grants issued from Central Church funds, which include money received from the Colleges.
(iii) Not shown in the table is a total contribution of approximately £200,000 by Colleges direct to Central Church Funds, to identify themselves with Diocesan contributions.
(iv) The amounts shown under College Governors' Funds includes bank and other loans still outstanding.
(v) Particular acknowledgement needs to be made in certain cases to the generosity of the National Society.

2 1981 PROPOSALS

SUMMARY OF THE SECRETARY OF STATE'S PROPOSED TEACHER TRAINING NUMBERS IN CHURCH COLLEGES, FOR 1981

A	*Independent Colleges.*	York and Ripon	790	
		Chester	575	
		Winchester	750	2,115
		Lancaster	575	
		Canterbury	500	
		Plymouth	460	1,535
B	*Colleges which have or are about to become part of a larger group of Colleges.*	Lincoln	500	
		Liverpool	330	
		Derby	450	
		Whitelands	300	
		Cheltenham St. Mary's and St. Paul's.	600	
		Bishop Otter	350	2,530
		Total		6,180
C	*Colleges which have or are about to become part of a University.*	St. Gabriel's (Goldsmiths)	120	
		St. Hild's and St. Bede (Durham)	400	
		St. Luke's (Exeter)	500	
		Keswick Hall (East Anglia)	400	1,420
		Total		7,600

D   Carmarthen College in Wales is to have 500 students.

E   Colleges closed or transferred to other instututions :—
Culham.
St. Peter's Saltley.
Hockerill.
Salisbury.
St. Mary's, Bangor. (Bangor Normal College).
St. Matthias, Bristol. (Bristol Polytechnic).
All Saints, Tottenham. (Middlesex Polytechnic).